ANCIENT
TURKEY

ANCIENT

TURKEY

A Traveller's
History of Anatolia

SETON LLOYD

UNIVERSITY OF CALIFORNIA PRESS

To Hydie,
my late wife and travelling companion

PHOTOGRAPHIC ACKNOWLEDGEMENTS

The author: Title page, Figs 4–7, 10, 17–18 (photos by T.
Koopman), 23, 30 (photo by T. Koopman), 32–3, 38–9, 43,
49–50, 58, 63–4, 66–7, 69–71, 72 (photo by Kim Philby),
76, 78–80, 82–3, 85–7. British Museum: Figs 13–16, 22,
26–8, 34, 36–7, 40, 42, 44–6, 51, 53–5, 59–60, 62, 65,
68. Dominique Collon: Fig. 25; Plates I–V, XI–XII. Kenan
Erim: Fig. 74 (photo by M. Ali Döğenci). J. D. Hawkins: Figs
29, 56; Plate IX. Marie–Christine Keith: Figs 35, 57, 61,
73, 75, 77, 84; Plates VI–VIII, X. Machteld Mellink: Fig. 47.
Thames and Hudson Ltd: Figs 8–9, 20–21, 24, 31.
Department of Medical Illustration, University of Manchester:
Fig. 52. The maps in Figs 1–3, 12 and 41 were drawn by
Christine Barratt.

©1989 Seton Lloyd
Published by the University of California Press
in the United States 1989

Library of Congress Cataloging-in-Publication Data

Lloyd, Seton.
    Ancient Turkey.
    Bibliography: p.
    Includes index.
    1. Turkey——Antiquities. I. Title.
DR431.L58 1989 939'.2   89-4785

ISBN 0-520-06787-8 (alk. paper)

Designed by Harry Green

Printed in Great Britain
by Butler & Tanner Ltd,
Frome, Somerset

TITLE PAGE Looking out across the Urartian heartland
from the citadel at Van.

Contents

Preface

If the nature and purpose of this book requires a preliminary definition, something should first be said about the circumstances under which it came to be written. It is not a conventional 'guide' to the antiquities of Anatolia, nor is it in any sense a textbook. Rather it is an attempt by the writer to share with others his own profound interest in the life-story of an antique land and its inhabitants, stimulated by long familiarity with the country itself and its surviving monuments.

The gulf between archaeology and history must seem to be exaggerated, if one remembers that the material remains with which the first is concerned provide much of the evidence on which the second is based. For my own part I am an archaeologist and have spent thirty-two years excavating in Near Eastern countries. The bulk of my published works has accordingly been devoted to the recording of my finds and theoretical conclusions. My main fields of research have been, first, Mesopotamia and, second, Anatolia; but it was during the early years of my long residence in Iraq that a new potential of my current occupation suddenly presented itself. The presence of British troops, for the time being idly occupying the country and anxious to know more about its past, tempted me to try my hand at historical writing. I published my first book on the subject and it was twice reprinted. Encouraged in this way, I then wrote a more ambitious history of Mesopotamian exploration, entitled *Foundations in the Dust*, which is still in print.

In Turkey, to which my activities were next transferred, much the same thing occurred. When I was not excavating, a very large proportion of my time was spent in travel and exploration. In a period when the idea of tourism as an industry was not yet conceived and the greater part of Anatolia was still unvisited by foreigners, I contrived, by primitive forms of transport, to reach almost every vilayet in the country where ancient sites were known to exist.

It was through these journeys and the use of good libraries that the history and prehistory of Anatolia came alive for me in their proper setting: a pageant of antiquity, now illuminated by detailed memory and nostalgia.

On my eventual return to this country, a task to which I found myself devoting much time was the purposeful reorganisation of my travel notes, bearing in mind a new temptation which had occurred to me. Not surprisingly, I found myself shaping my varied material around a skeleton of history which seemed spontaneously to have emerged. Belatedly I realised that such a thing had never before been attempted. Turkish historians, it seemed, had concentrated on the phenomenon of the Ottoman Empire; and indeed, up to that time very little could have been reconstructed from our still fragmentary knowledge of what had preceded its foundation.

Meanwhile in Turkey a prodigious change had taken place in the popularity and orientation of foreign travel beyond the Bosphorus. Then, as one had come to realise, the Magic Carpet of improved communications and a new understanding of tourist requirements had brought within reach of foreign holidaymakers the marvels of the Aegean coast and the inland countryside beyond, previously familiar only to a few privileged specialists. From Ephesus to Lake Van and the twin peaks of Ararat, tourists were now welcome. But for them, something was still missing: an informative introduction, both historical and topographical, to clothe the aridity of guide-book instruction – a more personal commentary on the goals which they should be seeking.

It seemed to me then possible that the private task I had set myself could be useful in this respect by meeting the lay visitor's requirements, and, having now found an enlightened publisher, I may perhaps hope that *Ancient Turkey* will prove acceptable to some 'purposeful' travellers.

At this point, an impending apology may become apparent. In the purely historical sections of this book there are points at which the intricacies of professional controversy have inevitably become involved. For this and other more practical reasons, I have at times found it necessary to rely largely upon direct citation or paraphrase. I have hoped that in such cases quotation from the most reliable authorities may be condoned, as contributing to the wider purpose for which the book was written.

Meanwhile, I must gratefully acknowledge the help and advice of a dozen friends, who have assisted during the prolonged period of gestation which the book has suffered. They must include, above all, my talented niece, Dr Dominique Collon, whose untiring collaboration has made light of my own disabilities. My special thanks are also due to three friendly scholars, David Hawkins, Charles Burney and Oliver Gurney, for checking my account of historical periods of which they have specialised knowledge.

Gazetteer

This Gazetteer lists only those ancient sites in Turkey which are most worth visiting, but the country is rich in sites of all periods. The following abbreviations have been used to indicate the main periods of a site: Pr = Prehistoric; B = Bronze Age; H = Hittite; H + = Neo-Hittite; P = Phrygian; U = Urartian; C = Carian; Lc = Lycian; Ld = Lydian; G = Greek; Cm = Commagenian; R = Roman. Further details concerning the chronology will be found opposite; for discussion of the sites marked with an asterisk, see the index. Ekrem Akurgal's *Ancient Civilisations and Ruins of Turkey*, first published in Istanbul in 1969 and frequently reprinted, is extremely useful and gives site-plans;

George Bean's *Lycian Turkey* (London 1978) and *Aegean Turkey, Turkey Beyond the Maeander* and *Turkey's Southern Shore* (all reprinted London 1979) provide detailed discussions of sites in south-western Turkey. There are also many foreign-language booklets dealing with specific sites or groups of sites, which can be purchased in Turkish museums and bookshops. The Archaeological Museum in Istanbul and, even more so, the Museum of Anatolian Civilisations in Ankara, are an essential introduction to any tour of ancient Turkey. Most large towns and major sites have their own local museums.

Aezani* R
Alaca Hüyük* BH
Anamur* R
Anavarza* R
Aphrodisias* B-R
Assus Ld-R
Aspendus* GR
Bodrum* C
Boğazköy* HP
Çatal Hüyük* Pr
Carchemish* B-R, esp. H +
Cnidus GR
Corycus* GR
Didyma* GR
Ephesus* GR

Gordium* P
Fethiye* Lc
Ivriz* H +
Karatepe* H +
Kaş* Lc
Kültepe* B-P
Magnesia-ad-Maeandrum* GR
Miletus* GR
Myra* Lc-R
Nemrut Dağ* Cm
Pamukkale (Hierapolis) R
Patara* Lc-R
Pergamum* GR
Perge* GR
Priene* GR

Phaselis* Lc-R
Sardis* Ld-R
Side* G-R
Termessus* Lc-R
Toprakkale* U
Troy* BR
Uzunçaburç* GR
Van* U
Xanthus Lc-R
Yazılıkaya nr Boğazköy* H
Yazılıkaya nr Eskişehir (Midas Şehri)* P
Zincirli* H +

Chronology

c. 8000–4500 BC
Neolithic
Early agriculture
Çatal Hüyük from *c.* 6000 BC

c. 4500–3000 BC
Chalcolithic
Mersin fortress *c.* 4500 BC

c. 3000–2000 BC
Early Bronze Age
Pre-Hittite Hattians
Alaca Hüyük tombs, Troy treasures
 c. 2300–2000 BC

c. 2000–1500 BC
Middle Bronze Age
Kültepe *karum* level II *c.* 1920–1850 BC
            level Ib *c.* 1810–1740 BC
 Beginning of written records
Hittite Old Kingdom *c.* 1700–1500 BC

c. 1500–1200 BC
Late Bronze Age
Hittite Empire *c.* 1400–1200
Battle of Kadesh against Ramesses II *c.* 1286 BC
Trojan War, and end of Hittite Empire
 c. 1200 BC

From *c.* 1200 BC
Iron Age
Dark Age *c.* 1200–1000 BC
First Greek colonies in Asia Minor *c.* 1000 BC
 Ionian League of 12 cities 8th century BC
 Artemisium at Ephesus founded *c.* 550 BC
Neo-Hittite or Luwian states. *c.* 1000–700 BC
Urartian Kingdom *c.* 900–600 BC
 Sargon of Assyria's 8th Campaign 714 BC
Phrygian Kingdom 8th century BC
 Ivriz relief *c.* 740 BC
 Midas' Tomb at Gordium *c.* 695 BC
 Midas Monument at Yazılıkaya/Eskişehir
 c. 560 BC
Lydian Kingdom
 Croesus *c.* 560–547 BC

546–330 BC
Achaemenid Persian Empire
Cyrus the Great (558–530 BC) captured Sardis 547
 BC
Darius I (521–486 BC)
 Ionian Revolt 499 BC
 Battle of Marathon 490 BC
Xerxes I (485–465 BC)
 Sack of Athens and Battle of Salamis 480 BC
 Battle of Plataea 479 BC
Xenophon's *Anabasis* 401 BC
Darius III captured by Alexander the Great 330 BC

334–323 BC
Empire of Alexander the Great (356–323 BC)
Alexander crosses the Hellespont 334 BC
Battle of the Granicus 334 BC
Battle of Issus 333 BC

323–64 BC
Greek city-states and Seleucid Dynasty

247 BC–AD 224
Iranian Parthian kings

c. 230–133 BC
Attalids of Pergamum
Attalus III leaves his kingdom to Rome 133 BC

From 133 BC
Roman period
Kingdom of Armenia (established *c.* 184 BC)
Mithridates of Pontus (123–63 BC)
 Wars against Rome 88–66 BC
Antiochus of Commagene builds Nemrut Dağ 69–
 34 BC
Pompey's settlement of the east 67–64 BC
Julius Caesar defeats Mithridates' son at Zela 47 BC
Roman Empire 30 BC
Birth of Christ *c.* 5 BC
Paul's missionary journeys AD 47–8, 49–51, 52–
 5
Paul's journey to Rome AD 57–8
Constantine the Great (AD 306–37)
 Adopts Christianity AD 312
 Moves capital to Byzantium AD 324
 Dedication of Constantinople AD 330

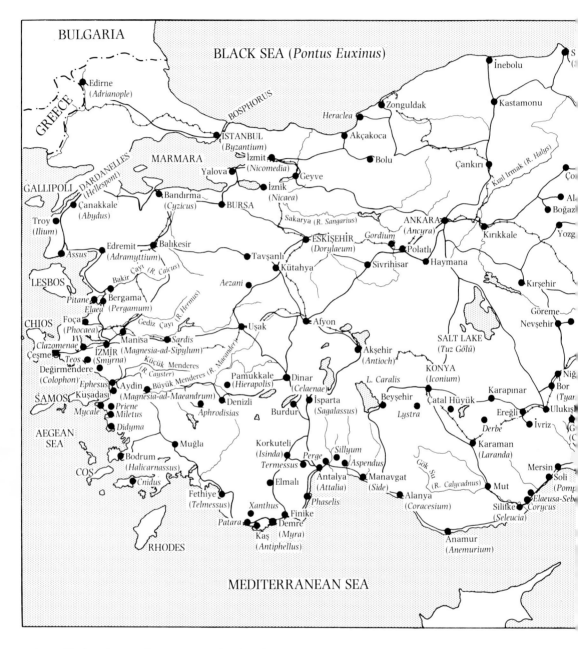

1. Map of Turkey. Ancient place-names are given in italics.

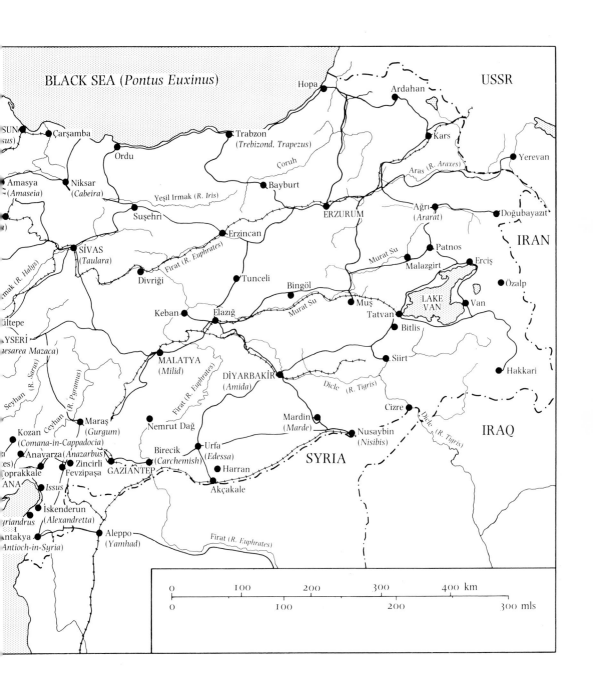

BLACK SEA (*Pontus Euxinus*)

USSR

Hopa

Ardahan

SUN
sus)

Çarşamba

Trabzon
(*Trebizond, Trapezus*)

Kars

Ordu

Yerevan

Çoruh

Amasya
(Amaseia)

Niksar
(*Cabeira*)

Bayburt

Aras (*R. Araxes*)

Yeşil Irmak (*R. Iris*)

ERZURUM

Ağrı
(*Ararat*)

Doğubayazıt

Suşehri

Erzincan

IRAN

SİVAS
(*Taulara*)

Fırat (*R. Euphrates*)

Patnos

Murat Su

Malazgirt

Erciş

mak (*R. Halys*)

Divriği

Tunceli

Bingöl

Muş

LAKE
VAN

Özalp

Van

Keban

Elazığ

Murat Su

Tatvan

iltepe

Bitlis

YSERİ
esarea Mazaca)

MALATYA
(*Milid*)

Siirt

Hakkari

Seyhan (*R. Sarus*)

Ceyhan (*R. Pyramus*)

DİYARBAKİR
(*Amida*)

Fırat (*R. Euphrates*)

Dicle (*R. Tigris*)

Cizre

Maraş
(*Gurgum*)

Nemrut Dağ

Mardin
(*Marde*)

Dicle (*R. Tigris*)

IRAQ

Kozan
(*Comana-in-Cappadocia*)

Birecik
(*Carchemish*)

Urfa
(*Edessa*)

Nusaybin
(*Nisibis*)

Anavarza (*Anazarbus*
es)

Zincirli
Fevzipaşa

GAZİANTEP

Harran

SYRIA

oprakkale

ANA

Issus

Akçakale

İskenderun
(*Alexandretta*)

riandrus

ntakya
Antioch-in-Syria)

Aleppo
(*Yamhad*)

Fırat (*R. Euphrates*)

| 0 | 100 | 200 | 300 | 400 km |

| 0 | 100 | 200 | 300 mls |

CHAPTER I

Anatolia: a Land-Bridge in History

It is a commonplace of modern political geography that, in recent times, the name Turkey has acquired a new meaning. Early in the present century it meant Istanbul of the Sultans and the Ottoman Empire; a loosely-knit assemblage of countries and provinces, from Albania to Mecca, where Turkish 'pashas' ruled over many races and creeds. It was a Muslim empire and its official language was Turkish; but it comprised Christian, Jewish and even pagan elements, and the religious language of Islam was Arabic. Today, in the minds of its inhabitants, Turkey is Anatolia: a well-defined geographical unit of manageable size; a lay state, in which Turkish nationality and the Turkish language are universally accepted. Yet 'Anadolu' (as the Turkish form of the name is spelt) had no meaning until the tenth century AD, before which the country had been loosely referred to by classical writers as 'Asia', or as 'Asia Minor' to distinguish it from the continent of that name. In pre-classical times it had no name at all, since it had never been sufficiently united politically for its frontiers to be defined.

Kemal Ataturk, the maker of modern Turkey, in his struggle to bring the present republic into being, found himself compelled either to assimilate or to exclude several well-established, non-Turkish minorities: Greeks in the west, Arabs and Kurds in the south and Armenians in the east. But the central plateau, which is the real Anatolia, was already almost exclusively Turkish. So it was there that he established first his military headquarters and then his centre of political administration. This fact alone should suffice to draw attention to the natural and historical division between the seaboard and the interior. Its significance will be further emphasised if we now discuss some geographical aspects of the country.

Much interesting variety will be found in the figures of speech used by modern writers to describe the physical structure of Asia Minor. The bare geological facts are naturally less picturesque but perhaps more capable of evoking a geographical reality.

> It consists of a block of older formation that has been overfolded at its edges with two converging ridges of the characteristic Mediterranean limestone. Its centre consists of a plateau ascending eastwards from 2,500 to 5,000 feet; its northern and southern rims, rising to 9,000 and 10,000 feet respectively, are made up of a series of overlapping ridges that admit of only a few narrow and tortuous passages between the coast and interior. On its frontier, where the southern coastal chain bends inwards and rises in Mt. Taurus to 13,000 feet, it is sharply separated from Syria and Mesopotamia.[1]

Such particulars as these may dispose one to understand more readily when Sir William Ramsay compares the peninsula to 'a bridge with lofty parapets'. Another figure which does perhaps convey a picture, at least of the mountain structure, is that of an open left hand, with the thumb curled inwards to represent the Taurus mountains. The palm would then suggest the hollow plateau; the heel of the hand the eastern massif, and the fingers the diminishing ranges which extend westward to find their echo in the islands of the Aegean.

Here then is the great central element of the country: the Anatolian plateau, separated by its mountain 'parapets' on the north and south sides from the climatically different coastal lands, and on the west side descending more gently to the river valleys which open on to the Aegean and the sea of Marmara. But the whole land-mass is also a peninsula, thrust out of Asia towards the south-eastern extremity of Europe. And it is this circumstance which has given it a predominant function in human history – the function of a land-link between two continents. For this reason, and because it is firmly attached to Asia, though not to Europe, it has appeared to another writer as a 'broad jetty' with good 'berthing-places' at the seaward end and wide approaches on the landward side. This comparison is however misleading, if it suggests that the historical migrations for which the peninsula has served as a 'land-bridge' were exclusively in one direction. Scanning the present horizon of our historical knowledge, we are indeed able to conclude that some of the earliest movements of Indo-European peoples converged upon the Thracian crossings before 2000 BC. These 'Luwian' peoples, among whom were the ancestors of the Hittites, would have crossed the Bosphorus from west to east, gradually populating the whole of western and southern Anatolia. Certainly a 'broad jetty' welcomed the Phrygians who swept eastward into Anatolia a thousand years later, and also the Greek colonists from Europe, who occupied its coastal areas. After that, westbound movements became more frequent, with three waves of Iranians crossing Asia Minor to break their strength against the bulwark of eastern Europe, Arabs nearing the limits of their expansion and Turks in transit from Central Asia to the Balkans. To Herodotus in the fifth century BC, the very concept of a 'land-bridge' would have been incomprehensible, since he imagined that the peninsula tapered to an almost impassable isthmus at its eastern end.

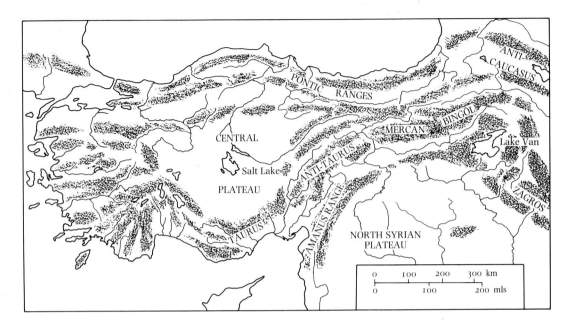

2. Topographical map of Anatolia.

Perhaps the passage of so many migrant peoples across its territory may help to explain the strange diversity of the country's inhabitants in pre-literate times. In studying the earliest peoples of the Anatolian Bronze Age, archaeologists have found themselves already able to recognise a number of 'cultural provinces': regional groupings of settlements, distinguished from each other by anthropological peculiarities. They have observed also how closely these provinces correspond to the natural divisions of the country into climatically different geographical areas. They find, for instance, sharp cultural variations between the interior and the coastlands; between the plateau and the piedmont country to the west, or between the climatic extremes of northern Mesopotamia and the Pontic Alps. By the time of the Hittites, these geographical divisions have acquired political significance, and can in many cases be equated with states and peoples whose names occur in contemporary written records. Anatolia by then seems to be composed of numerous political enclaves, where peoples of widely different racial affiliations, lacking a common heritage of cultural tradition, can be related to each other only by precarious alliances or ephemeral conquests. We shall presently see how the Hittites themselves, from their homeland east of modern Ankara, extended their influence over Cappadocia and across the Taurus to the plain of Adana. Yet the Homeric Greeks besieging Troy seem never to have heard of them, and when in the *Iliad* the Trojan allies are listed, it becomes clear that the writer's knowledge of Anatolian peoples is limited to the periphery of the peninsula. This may be explained by the fact that the Greek colonists of Homer's time had penetrated no further than the south and west coastal provinces, or clung to the narrow littoral of the Black Sea. Phrygians, Lydians and others had by then become heirs to the interior.

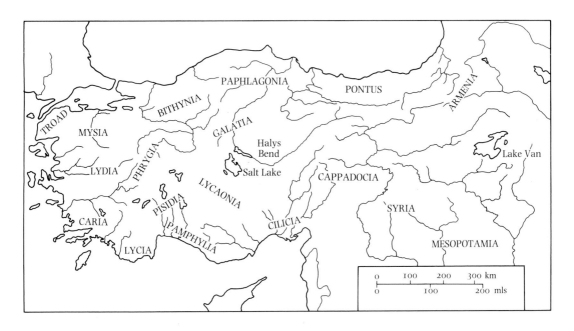

3. The Classical provinces of Anatolia.

In order to understand more clearly the complex effects of geography on the early history of Anatolia, let us first glance at the climate and conditions of living on the central plateau itself. To begin with, quite a large area around the Salt Lake (Tuz Gölü) is virtually desert, and much more of it is steppe land, producing little more than rough grazing for sheep and goats. In the moderate summer heat, water is scarce, save in the river valleys; bitter cold and heavy snowfalls in the winter months bring hardships to the peasants. True, in an age of improved communications and mechanised agriculture, its resources are today more effectively exploited and some of the austerity has been removed from the lives of cultivators and herdsmen. But, to remind oneself how comparatively recently such improvements have come about, one need look no further than the early years of the present century. Here is how Gertrude Bell recorded in 1909 the impressions of a European traveller approaching the plateau from the Aegean coast:

> Before him stretch wide plains, corn-growing where rainfall and springs permit, often enough barren save for a dry scrub of aromatic herbs, or flecked with shining miles of saline deposit; naked ranges of mountains stand sentinel over this featureless expanse; the sparse villages, unsheltered from wind or sun, lie along the skirts of the hills, catching thirstily at the snow-fed streams that are barely enough for the patch of cultivated ground below; the weary road, deep in dust or mud according to the season, drags its intolerable length to the horizon. It is Asia, with all its vastness, with all its brutal disregard for life and comfort and the amenities of existence; it is the Ancient East, returned after so many millenniums of human endeavour to its natural desolation.[2]

15

With this description in mind, it becomes less easy to understand why the only Bronze Age nation of whose imperial greatness and prosperity we have undisputed proof, should have chosen for its homeland and seat of government this unprepossessing region of Anatolia. One is even tempted to attribute certain aspects of the Hittite character, apparent in their history and art, to over-familiarity with the 'unupholstered' virility of the plateau landscape, or even to an ascetic appreciation of the austerities imposed on them by such an environment. Modern Ankara cannot reasonably be judged by the same standards, since its amenities have been artificially cultivated – and there is a well-worn escape route to Istanbul and the coast. Yet, no one forgets that in Ottoman times its name was most familiar as a place of political exile.

So now, for major contrast, let us turn to the 'jetty' end of the peninsula. Here, to the south-west, is the deeply indented coastline of the Aegean, with its four great river valleys – Caicus, Hermus, Cayster and Maeander (now the Bakir, the Gediz, the Küçük Menderes and the Büyük Menderes respectively) – 'a smiling country full of the sound of waters, with fertile valleys, hills clad in secular forests, coasts that the Greek made his own, setting them with cities, crowning them with temples, charging the very atmosphere with the restless activity of his temper'.[3] When Herodotus spoke of 'places more favoured by skies and seasons than any country known to us', it was scarcely an exaggeration; for the Aegean coast has milder winters than the mainland of Greece; the sea-breezes in the summer are more reliable and its more fertile soil responds easily to an average rainfall of some twenty inches. Fruit grows in abundance, especially figs, for which there is said to be no more favourable climate. It is a world of olive groves and vineyards, with wooded hillsides above rushing streams. It resembles the plains and prairies of the plateau as little as they resemble the alpine landscape of the far eastern provinces.

The plateau proper ends approximately on a north-south line drawn through Eskişehir, Afyon and Dinar. Between this line and the coast there is a rich hinterland of pastures and forests, which in their time provided the Greek cities with timber for shipbuilding and skins for all purposes, including the parchment which took its name from Pergamum (modern Bergama).

The south and north coasts of the peninsula differ from one another in character, and each has played its own minor role in Anatolian history. On the Mediterranean side, three separate provinces well illustrate the divisive effect of regional geography. At the eastern end, the Amanus and Taurus mountains withdraw from the sea, leaving a broad area of fertile alluvium traversed by the 'Rivers of Paradise', Sarus and Pyramus (Seyhan and Ceyhan). This is the plain of Adana (Cilicia), noted for the humidity of its summer heat and the prodigality of its winter rains. It was inhabited at an early stage in prehistory by Neolithic farmers, whose settlements formed a link between parallel developments in Syria and on the Anatolian plateau. Culturally associated with both, throughout the Bronze Age, it acquired a Hurrian aristocracy and, under the name Kizzuwadna, became an integral part of the Hittite Empire. Separated from Cilicia by an 'elbow' of the Taurus range, where the mountains rise steeply out of the sea, is a smaller coastal plain, called in classical times Pamphylia (Antalya). From its appearance on the map one would expect it too to be flatly composed of river-borne alluvium. On the contrary, it is undulating country, criss-crossed with sand-dunes and partly covered with scrub. Even the climate differs from that of the Adana plain. The vanguard of human occupation seems to have by-passed this particular corner of the Mediterranean, and the small province has little known history until it became densely populated by colonial Greeks. West of Antalya (on whose site no city existed until Hellenistic times), there is one more distinctive province, Lycia, which may have been what the Hittites called the Lukka Lands. By contrast to the plains, here is a knotted formation of high mountains, with surrounding cliffs falling almost vertically to the shoreline. In the confines of this strange highland with its narrow approaches and elevated interior, an indigenous people, speaking a language of their own, are already to be found in the Bronze Age and surviving until the Christian era, maintaining their cultural traditions with obstinate tenacity.

The Black Sea littoral bears little resemblance to the west and south coasts. Long mountain ranges run parallel to the shore, leaving a narrow coastal strip, furrowed across by the torrents which spill from their flanks. In two places deltas are formed by major rivers, the Yeşil Irmak (Iris) and Kızıl Irmak

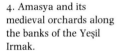

4. Amasya and its medieval orchards along the banks of the Yeşil Irmak.

(Halys), which have forced their way down from the plateau through deep gorges. Most of this coast is subject to continual northerly winds, which produce a moderate climate, cool and frequently rainy, even during the summer months; a climate favourable to the cultivation of maize (since its introduction from the Americas) rather than wheat, and above all to the hazelnut plantations which today supply the world market. Only the zone around Trabzon (Trebizond) at the extreme eastern end enjoys more Mediterranean temperatures, for it is protected by the Caucasus from the prevailing northerlies. The seaward-facing flanks of the mountains above it are covered with rhododendron forests or semi-tropical vegetation. Little was known about the natives of Pontus and Paphlagonia until their shores were belatedly and rather half-heartedly colonised by the Greeks.

To the east of the Halys river, where altitudes increase towards the uplands of Erzincan and Malatya, Cappadocia forms a well-populated province between the plateau and the highlands. Here lies Kayseri (Caesarea Mazaca) beneath the magnificent silhouette of Mount Argaeus (Erciyes Dağ), an extinct volcano, whose legacy of igneous soil is most favourable to vine growing and affords broad pastures associated historically with the breeding of horses. Moving eastward again, beyond the upper reaches of the Euphrates, there is an alpine world, sharply differentiated from the plateau and the peninsula. These high eastern provinces of Anatolia were the first to be occupied by the Seljuk Turks after their defeat of the Byzantine army in AD 1071. They include the great strategic centre of Erzurum, the remotely elevated waters of Lake Van and, where the frontiers of Turkey march with those of Persian Azerbaijan and Soviet Russia, the twin peaks of Ararat rising 5195 metres above sea level.

Linking together these component regions of Anatolia are the great caravan routes of ancient times which traversed the length and breadth of the country and acted as arteries of migration and trade and channels of imperial communication. Their western termini were various: the Bosphorus or Hellespont crossings from Europe, the harbour town of Nicomedia (Izmit), at the head of its deeply recessed inlet, or the port of Cyzicus (Bandırma), used by shipping in transit through the Marmara. From all these directions there was a conventional approach to the plateau by way of Dorylaeum (Eskişehir), where the modern railway follows in the track of the First Crusade. Alternatively, one might start from the great maritime cities of the Aegean coast, Smyrna (Izmir), Ephesus or Miletus, or set out like Cyrus the Younger and his Greek mercenaries from the old Lydian capital at Sardis in the Hermus valley. Roads from these places converged on a second and equally famous entry to the plateau at Celaenae (later Apameia, modern Dinar). Coming from Sardis the great highway which became the Royal Road of the Persian kings swung northeastward to cross the Sangarius (Sakarya) river at Gordium, the Phrygian capital. Passing modern Ankara, it crossed the Halys into Hittite country and continued eastward by Kayseri, over the passes of Anti-Taurus to Malatya and the Euphrates. From Kayseri a branch ran southward by Bor (Tyana), where it met a lower road coming east from Dinar along the southern lip of the

plateau. The two then united to negotiate a famous passage through the Taurus, the Cilician Gates. From Adana more devious ways led along the coast into Syria or across the Amanus range to the crossings of the middle Euphrates, From Kayseri too, an ancient highway, still rutted by the wheels of primitive transport, set a line for the modern motorway north-eastward to Sivas and ultimately Erzurum. Here it connected with the famous 'Transit Route', which in earlier times brought Persian traders from Tabriz over stupendous passes to the Black Sea. But there were minor highways also, like the arduous coastal road leading westward from Trebizond (Trabzon), and others connecting the

6. Countryside near Sivas, on the main east-west route through Turkey.

northern seaports with the interior. All these will attract our attention in later chapters, as their commercial or military significance becomes apparent.

Today, half a century of road-building has vastly changed the aspect of Anatolia, both for the Turks themselves and for their summer visitors from abroad. Travellers seeking the legacy of ancient peoples and the setting of historical events now benefit from the virtue of commercial and military necessity. For an initial journey from Istanbul to Ankara, the Bosphorus Bridge and the wide motorway beyond offer an inviting alternative to the restrictions of travel by rail or air. The modern road follows the Marmara coast as far as the naval base at Izmit, after passing a place called Gebze, where the Crusaders first set foot in Asia. From Izmit, however, it turns northward in search of an easier ascent to the plateau, leaving the old German railway to follow the traditional southern route. Winding more leisurely through river valleys, this southern route emerges near Eskişehir – a scene of many battles – and then runs out across the level uplands of central Phrygia. The tedium of an unvaried landscape is thereafter only broken when the road descends suddenly into the rift of the Sakarya river and finds a bridge within sight of the mounds and burial tumuli at Gordium. Between here and nearby Polath, another battle, in our own time, settled the fate of the Greeks whose presence in Asia Minor had so long been sanctioned by historical tradition.

Having reached Ankara, all parts of the country become accessible by a network of road and rail communications, today impressively presented on the most up-to-date maps. There is no intention here of discussing tourist itineraries or the relative attractions of ancient sites. Rather, as a preface to the review we are about to make of the country's early history, we may perhaps be permitted a reference to the most recent of all phases in its development.

Any foreigner with memories of a long residence in Turkey must above all be urgently reminded once more of the startling change which has taken place within the accepted span of a single generation: change, that is, in the tempo and conditions of travel. Casting one's mind back, even to the middle years of the present century, one remembers a country whose provinces, outside the main centres of administration, were almost unknown to foreigners, save for a few privileged adventurers; and even for those whose purpose in travelling was no more sinister than that of enlightened enquiry, security regulations created intimidating complications. As for the actual logistics of travel, the pattern of motor roads on the map we have mentioned were then still a dream of the future. In the 1940s, transit between cities was normally accomplished by rail or by the few hundred miles of metalled roads which then existed. Even the most celebrated ancient cities or archaeological sites, of the sort which have today become the focal points of tourism, could be reached only by those with unusual tenacity of purpose. From Ankara for instance, a visit to the Hittite country in the Halys bend and to the old capital city of Hattusas (Boğazköy) meant the careful planning of a journey to last several days and the hire of a farm waggon for one stage of some hours. Kayseri, with its Seljuk fortress, and the famous rock-cut churches of Göreme could best be reached by breaking the Taurus express journey to Adana, trusting thereafter to various primitive forms of hired transport. All such places are now served by fast motor-roads. From Ankara a motorway across the lonelier part of the plateau brings one in a few hours to the Cilician Gates and Adana; another, running west of the Salt Lake, leads to the old Seljuk capital at Konya (Iconium), to Karaman (Laranda) and the spectacular gorge of the Gök Su (Calycadnus) river, where Barbarossa was drowned. At Silifke (Seleucia) it joins the coastal road coming from the port of Mersin, through 'Stony' Cilicia.

This road is now prolonged, to follow the entire length of the southern littoral. Its scenic effects are much in favour with summer visitors and amply

7. The Pamphylian coast, with the headland and citadel of Alanya in the background.

reward those prepared to cover the distance in leisurely stages. West of Silifke, the 'corniche' winds high above a rocky foreshore, haunted in Roman times by a race of Mediterranean pirates, until the cliffs recede, and a tiny coastal plain, with level cultivation, is dominated by the Windsor-like silhouette of Anamur Castle. After a further spell of even more hazardous 'corniche', the road at last descends into a world of palm-trees and fruit orchards where the Seljuk fortress of Alanya, thrust out into the sea on its rocky promontory, signals the approach to softer perspectives in Pamphylia.

Before completing the journey to Antalya, all the Greek cities of the plain are now in reach – Perge, Sillyum, Aspendus or Side – and, if these are not enough, a new road makes the circuit of Lycia, carrying one coastwise to the Myra of St Nicholas and Fethiye, or inland in search of Termessus and other cities of the Lycian federation among their mountains. Also to be reached from this direction is the Cnidian peninsula, facing the island of Rhodes, and finally the Crusader castle at Halicarnassus (Bodrum). Some visitors, meanwhile, give priority to the more famous Ionian cities of the Aegean coast: Pergamum, Ephesus, Priene, Miletus and Didyma – names that occur so frequently in this book that an attempt has been made elsewhere to invoke the atmosphere of their ruins, as they are to be seen today. But the centre for visiting these is Izmir (Smyrna), a great seaport town, haunted by the memories of past violence, to which industry and the United Nations have lent the recompense of increasing prosperity. In the 1940s, this city too was still best reached by train through Eskişehir and Afyon. Today a fine motorway swings due eastward through the ruins of Sardis, eventually to join the old Istanbul-Ankara highway at Sivrihisar.

But there are other roads from Ankara, leading north through the Tyrolean world of the Paphlagonian forests, to harbour towns on the Black Sea. Nor need an eastward journey end at Kayseri. Beyond the old Seljuk university town of Sivas, there is the mountain road to Erzurum, with Kars and Ani on the Soviet frontier beyond; or one can make the circuit of Lake Van and turn homewards by way of Diyarbakır and the fortress-cities of Diocletian's *limes*. A thousand miles from Van, on the last stage of his return journey, the traveller may find himself among the mosques and lime trees of Bursa, and, savouring his impressions of the modern republic, remember the first Ottoman Turks, who made this city their capital when Byzantium was still beyond their reach.

Preludes
to Civilisation:
Prehistoric Anatolia

In dealing with the earliest development of civilisation among the various peoples of the ancient Near East, one recognises in every case a fixed point in the chronology of their existence, when the first appearance of actual written records marks the beginning of their history in the strictest sense of the word. Depending as it does on the date at which the art of writing was discovered or adopted, this varies widely in time from country to country. The Sumerians, for instance, in Mesopotamia, and the early inhabitants of the Nile valley, were ahead in this respect; and neighbouring peoples began to profit from their initiative only after a considerable delay. In the case of Anatolia, this time-lag is particularly in evidence. No writing of any sort appears earlier than the beginning of the second millennium BC, and even then it is not an indigenous development but a remote extension of Mesopotamian culture. For the earliest inscriptions yet found in Turkey are the records of a commercial colony, maintained by the Assyrians during the twentieth to eighteenth centuries BC, at a city called Kanesh (modern Kültepe) in Cappadocia. They were of course written on clay tablets in the cuneiform script of Assyria; and it is interesting to note that documents found at the same site, belonging to the palace of a local Anatolian ruler, show him, for lack of any alternative method of expressing himself, adopting both the script and the language of these foreign merchants.

From the very nature of the records discovered at Kanesh – business letters, accounts, bills of lading etc. – it will be realised that little can be expected of them in the way of precise historical information. Something can, of course, be learnt from their occasional mention of proper names; the names of contemporary Assyrian kings, whose dates are known, or those of neighbouring Anatolian cities and their native rulers. But the kind of inscriptions which provide the raw material of history, in the form of references to political and military events, do not become available until the founding of the Hittite kingdom in about 1700 BC.

Our knowledge of all that happened in Anatolia before that date must depend exclusively on the results of archaeological research. Although work of this sort has been in progress for hardly more than a century, the contribution it has made is undeniably impressive. In theory, it has carried the story of human development in this area back another five thousand years. It has introduced us to peoples who were, and would otherwise have remained, completely unknown to us; to manners of life and idiosyncrasies of technology which have no exact parallel elsewhere. It has even made it possible for us to apprehend some moral and intellectual reactions of the earliest settlers to the environment which the Anatolian peninsula provided for them. Yet these and other accomplishments must be judged strictly on their own merits. One must not be misled by approbation of the initiative which made them possible, into exaggerating their significance, nor must one for a moment lose sight of the fact that they still remain incomplete and inadequate.

In the absence of historical events or of kings whose reigns may be conveniently grouped into dynasties, some other system has had to be devised for the division of time in the prehistoric period. In Anatolia, as in many neighbouring countries, chronology has come to be reckoned rather arbitrarily in epochs corresponding to successive stages in the evolution of man's knowledge of metallurgy. Here, as elsewhere, there is first a Stone Age, divided into Old (Palaeolithic) and New (Neolithic) phases and distinguished rather by his ignorance of that subject. This is followed by a Chalcolithic period, during which simple copper implements were for the first time in use, side by side with the stone or chipped flint tools of the previous Neolithic phase. Next comes a Bronze Age, when copper was mixed with tin to produce a metal of more durable quality, and great advances were made in the metal-smith's craft generally. This period too is divided into Early, Middle and Late phases, the Early Bronze occupying the greater part of the third millennium BC; the Middle Bronze covering the period of the Assyrian colonies in the first half of the second millennium BC; and the Late Bronze corresponding to the centuries illuminated by the Hittite records, ending with the destruction of the Hittite Empire in about 1200 BC.

The clear historical imagery of this latest period, the evidence of political development and religious thought, the sequence of royal names and the battles or treaties associated with them, were all subjects which urgently invited further study and understandably monopolised the attention of the first travelling scholars. When excavations began, therefore, priority was given to the sites of historical cities. By contrast, the drab impersonality of undocumented events in remoter ages had little appeal, and when a younger generation, trained in prehistoric research, started to investigate the earlier occupations of Anatolian sites, their finds at first attracted little attention. Happenings of an antiquity so remote that the biography of a nation could be reconstructed only in terms of broken pottery and the discarded remains of its most humble artisans, could hardly be of interest except to specialists, who would themselves need time to determine their significance.

These attitudes greatly changed during the early years of the Turkish republic, when foreign excavators returned to work side by side with newly qualified Turkish prehistorians. A number of major sites on the central plateau and elsewhere were patiently examined stratigraphically, and the developments of which they provided evidence were allotted their appropriate places in a newly devised system of chronology. Criteria of successive periods emerged from the typology of pottery and small objects, and the periods themselves were tentatively named. The process of routine investigation was next extended, by means of archaeological surveys, to unexcavated sites whose occupation could now be dated by surface finds. A new stage was reached when, among these finds, regional variations began to be detected, and a close study of their distribution revealed the existence of 'cultural provinces', of a sort which could be approximately delimited on a map. In a country populated from the earliest times by diverse ethnic elements, this was of course an important discovery.

All such operations, then, must be regarded as contributory to the creation of a framework around which the prehistory of Anatolia could be reconstructed. they required, as we have said, much patience and ingenuity, both of which have in the course of time been amply rewarded. During the 1930s a series of discoveries were made in Turkey whose imaginative appeal at once translated them beyond the confines of mere professional interest. It was as though, in diverse archaeological settings, a veil had momentarily parted, bringing suddenly into focus episodes in the drama of cultural evolution. At points in time which could be reliably computed, the lives of ancient peoples were clearly disclosed in the authentic setting of domestic routine, ritual performance or communal emergency.

A revelation of this sort had in fact come near to being made half a century earlier at Troy. Heinrich Schliemann, the German visionary, seeking the remains of Homer's legendary city, had come upon treasures of gold and silver dating, as we now know, from the second phase of the Early Bronze Age. Unfortunately, the time was not yet ripe for their significance to be understood, and primitive methods of extraction defaced the evidence of their archaeological setting. By contrast, the later discoveries to which we have referred were made at a time when archaeology had already become a recognised discipline, with a precisely defined 'procedural liturgy' regulating the processes of excavation and recording. Their results, therefore, are no longer confined to the spectacle of fine objects in a museum. Anthropological implications have also been studied, and their message articulated by reasoned interpretation and pictorial reconstruction.

Moving backwards in time from the foundation of the Hittite Kingdom, the first important discovery was that of the Assyrian colony at Kanesh (Kültepe), as revealed by Turkish excavations over a period of many years.[1] A reconstruction of the settlement is shown in Fig. 8. In the foreground are the merchant's houses; modest but adequate dwellings, built of brick in a frame-

8. Assyrian merchants keeping accounts in their colony (*karum*) beneath the walled city of Kanesh in the twentieth century BC. A reconstruction by Gaynor Chapman and the author.

work of timber, often with two storeys. Everywhere the importance of business documents is emphasised. Much space on the ground floor is occupied by small kilns for the hardening of clay tablets (Fig. 14), which themselves are stacked on shelves or stored in earthenware jars. The suburb has its own enclosure wall, through whose gateway caravans of 'black' donkeys with their loads of trade goods arrive or leave for the arduous journey to Mesopotamia. Behind, the track winds upwards to a more formidable gateway in the towered walls of the city itself; for all merchandise must be checked in 'the palace', where tithes are paid to the native ruler. On its ancient mound, covering the remains of earlier settlements, Kanesh creates an impressive silhouette with the snow-covered peak of Mount Argaeus rising behind it. The seat of local government is housed in dignified buildings (the Early Bronze Age palace of *c.* 2300 BC included a residence planned around a *megaron* hall with four stout wooden columns and a gigantic circular hearth, like the Mycenaean palaces of a thousand years later). To judge by their surviving belongings – graceful pottery vessels and modelled or carved ornaments – these Kaneshites of the Middle Bronze Age, like their foreign guests in the compound below the city, were men of cultivated taste which must have contrasted strangely with their illiteracy. More will be said about them in a later chapter.

The second picture we again owe to the work of Turkish excavators, this time in the mound called Alaca Hüyük, near Boğazköy. The sounding made here, beneath the foundations of the Hittite city, was at first a routine affair; but fortune had attended the choice of a site for, in the season of 1935, a

cemetery of the Early Bronze Age came to light. Thirteen tombs were opened, containing apparently the bodies of local rulers and their families. The graves themselves were rectangular pits, enclosed by rough stone walling and roofed with timber, allowing space for wooden furniture of which only the metal trappings and ornament had survived; but the bodies were accompanied by a wealth of personal belongings. Men were provided with weapons, women with ornaments and toilet articles, as well as domestic vessels and utensils, many of them in precious metals. Other objects seemed to be associated with a funeral ritual, which could in part be reconstructed. The cemetery had evidently been in use for several generations.[2] Here, the so-called 'standards' – curious metal grilles and animal figures, which appear frequently among the tomb furniture – are taken to have been finial ornaments, decorating the catafalque or a temporary baldachin over the open tomb. A ritual funerary feast is suggested by the heads and hooves of slaughtered cattle laid over the tomb.

At the time that this discovery was made, little was as yet known about life in Anatolia during this early period. Excavations elsewhere had indeed presented a picture of an agricultural people, peacefully cultivating the upland soil of the plateau throughout most of the third millennium BC. But we had till then been hardly more than apprised of their existence and our knowledge of their character or racial identity still depended on the limited testimony of small domestic relics, mostly associated with village communities. The Alaca Hüyük discovery changed all this. The contents of the tombs could be approximately dated to the twenty-third century BC and this showed them to be

9. Preparations for a burial in the 'royal cemetery' at Alaca Hüyük, about 2300 BC. A reconstruction by Gaynor Chapman and the author.

contemporary with the 'second settlement' at Troy, in which Schliemann's famous 'treasures' had been found. When comparable finds of the same period were presently made in other regions of Anatolia, a substantial volume of material evidence began to accumulate, showing the wealth and sophistication of the ruling classes in Anatolia at this time. The combined inventory of artefacts from all these sources seemed in particular to emphasise a high degree of efficiency in metallurgy and craftsmanship. The skills, for instance, of metal-smiths in this second phase of the Early Bronze Age included casting by the *cire-perdue* method, metal inlay, sweating and soldering, hammering and repoussé, granulation, filigree and even cloisonné. No less surprising was the repertory of semi-precious stones and other luxury materials apparently available to their craftsmen. Among those obtainable in their own country were rock-crystal, carnelian, jasper, nephrite, obsidian and meerschaum. Added to these through foreign trade were ivory, amber, lapis lazuli and turquoise.

Three years after the discoveries of Alaca Hüyük, a team of British archae-ologists had begun excavations in a comparatively small mound on the out-skirts of Mersin, four hundred miles to the south in the westernmost corner of the plain of Adana.[3] Here they found themselves dealing with village occupa-tions of the Chalcolithic period, which preceded the Bronze Age, and, at a level dating from approximately 4500 BC, a most striking discovery was made. At this time the summit of the mound had been levelled and the whole settlement systematically rebuilt in the form of an easily recognisable military fortress, the earliest of its sort in the history of architecture. Within the heavily built enclosure wall, with its towered gateway and 'slit' windows, accommodation for the garrison was arranged in standard units, each with its own well-equipped living room and a tiny courtyard containing piles of 'sling-pellets', which were the ammunition of the defenders. By contrast, the more roomy quarters of the 'commander' boasted some finely painted pottery vessels.

Beneath the little fortress at Mersin, as the excavation descended level by level, the shapes and decoration of the pottery became increasingly crude. No

10. Part of the prehistoric fortress at Mersin, dating from about 4500 BC, showing the garrison quarters with slit windows.

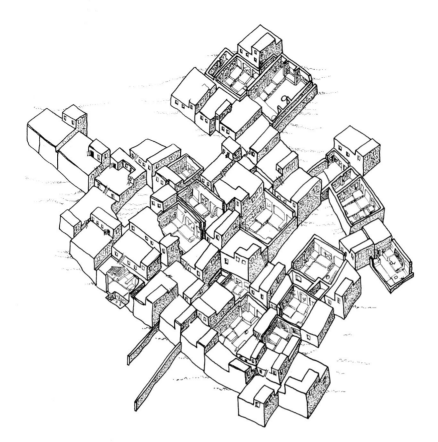

traces of metal were now to be seen, though chipped flint or obsidian implements proliferated. The sounding was clearly reaching the upper levels of the Neolithic occupation, but its area had become so much reduced that no clear picture could be obtained of the contemporary settlement. Twenty years were to elapse before this disappointment could be remedied by the discovery of a Neolithic habitation in an archaeologically accessible situation; and when this did occur, it was not on the periphery of the so-called Fertile Crescent but on the Konya plain in central Anatolia.

We have now reached the fourth and last scene, chosen here to represent successive stages in the progress of Anatolian peoples towards what is still referred to as civilisation. The horizon of our knowledge has now receded in time to perhaps 6000 BC, yet anyone expecting to be shown a life-pattern of primitive immaturity would indeed be mistaken. In 1961, British archaeologists tackled the mound called Çatal Hüyük, which they had chosen because its entire fifteen metres of height seemed to represent a long sequence of occupations in the Neolithic period.[4] This proved to be so, but another implication which they had not fully appieciated was the area which it covered. This was no mere village, but a township covering almost 32 acres of ground. In the town, houses were built of sun-dried brick, closely contiguous, like the cells of a honeycomb, but each had several rectangular rooms similarly planned, and was accessible only by a wooden ladder from its flat roof. The roofs were, of course, intercommunicating and provided space for the communal life of the inhabitants. There were many strange features in the

11. A reconstruction of the excavated area in Level VII at Çatal Hüyük in about 6000 BC. After J. Mellaart, *The Archaeology of Ancient Turkey*, London 1978, p. 13.

buildings. Some of them appear to have been religious shrines, and these were elaborately ornamented with heads or horns of animals, either real or imitated in plaster. The walls were decorated with coloured murals, repeatedly repainted after plastering, and the designs closely resembled the cave paintings of the Palaeolithic era. As a source of information about early man's activities, his appearance and dress and even about his religion, these paintings are naturally of great significance, but other arts and crafts were also well attested. Human or animal figures were carved in stone and modelled in clay. Bone was used for tools and implements, sometimes with finely carved ornament. Weapons included polished maces, arrows and lances with tanged obsidian heads. Impressions of mats and baskets were found. Implements used for spinning and weaving were common and – miraculously – fragments were recovered and preserved of actual textiles. Extensive trade was suggested by the presence of Mediterranean shells, metal ores and pigments not locally available. Undecorated pottery was in use throughout the life of the settlement, its shapes often imitating those of wooden vessels of which examples were found intact.

In the Çatal Hüyük settlement, agriculture evidently formed the main basis of the economy, since deposits of food grains were actually found. The position of the site on a river subject to regular flooding suggested that artificial irrigation would already have been possible. No actual proof was found that animals had been domesticated, but the bones of wild cattle, deer and boar confirmed the implications of the wall paintings that hunting was also still a primary preoccupation. Generally speaking, there was nothing to suggest that this precociously advanced culture had its origin elsewhere than in Turkey.

The special interest of this monumentally important excavation at Çatal Hüyük is self-evident. It illustrates man's apparently recent transition from the economy of food-gathering cave-dwellers in the Palaeolithic age to that of a settled and part-agricultural community. Here is a people who still decorate their walls with murals, reminiscent of those which their ancestors painted in caves. Yet in other respects their way of life has rapidly attained an astonishing degree of cultural sophistication. Perhaps their precocious development in the end proved also to have been premature; for in our present view of prehistory, it appears to have had no immediate sequel. After the abandonment of the settlement at Çatal Hüyük, Neolithic culture relapses into temporary stagnation.

This then is the last of the four representative discoveries that we have chosen to typify the accomplishments of prehistoric archaeology in Anatolia. The conclusions drawn from them have of course been supported and diversified by the less obviously spectacular results of other excavations, by many forms of environmental research and through lively debate in innumerable archaeological publications. Yet the areas of our knowledge are still too widely spaced and elusively connected. There are times, even, when they seem to resemble unexpected scraps of finished painting, spaced at infrequent intervals in the rough cartoon for some great mural whose composition is only now beginning to make itself clear.

CHAPTER 3

The Quest
for the Hittites

It would seem wrong to embark on a summary of Hittite history without first explaining to what people and what language the term 'Hittite' is today specifically applied. In doing so, one is confronted by the initial difficulty that it is not a name at any time claimed for themselves by an Anatolian people. It is a Biblical name, and it was at first loosely associated by historians of the nineteenth century with a pre-Christian people in Syria and Asia Minor, of whose existence they were beginning to find evidence other than the mere mention of its name in the Bible. The earliest references in the Old Testament make it clear that the Hebrew writers regarded the Hittites merely as one of several tribes inhabiting the Levant in the time of the Patriarchs.[1] Later, however, during the monarchy, mention is made of King Solomon's Hittite wives, and there are two references to 'Kings of the Hittites' with their chariots and horses.[2] When, therefore, in the 1860s, basalt slabs carved with pictographic inscriptions unrelated to the Egyptian hieroglyphs were discovered at places like Hama and Aleppo in Syria, scholars felt justified in identifying them as the work of 'Hittites', and when other comparable inscriptions were reported, carved on rock-faces as far afield as Ivriz, north of the Taurus, the quest for 'Hittite' remains was extended to the Anatolian plateau.

Meanwhile, two new sources of historical information about this enigmatic people had become available: first, through the decipherment of the Egyptian hieroglyphic records and, secondly, through that of the Mesopotamian cuneiform writing. Though the Hebrew name would hardly have been expected to take an identical form in another language, the Hittites were unmistakably recognisable both in the Kheta of the Egyptian texts and in the Hatti of the Assyrian. The historical context of these names in either language suggested that they referred to a country or nation whose political status in the Near East had been accepted at a very early period. The Egyptian records showed

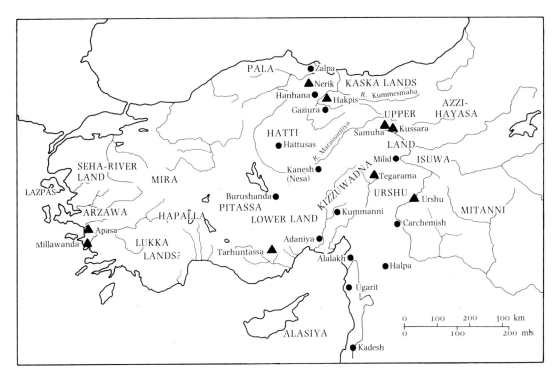

12. Anatolia in Hittite times. The locations of those places marked with a triangle are conjectural.

that the armies of Kheta had opposed those of Egypt as early as the reign of Tuthmosis III (1504–1450 BC), and 200 years later, in the thirteenth century, a king of Kheta had made a treaty with Ramesses II. The famous 'Amarna letters', written in cuneiform during the reigns of Akhenaten (1379–1362 BC) and of his father Amenophis III (1417–1379) included one addressed to the Pharaoh by Suppiluliumas, a 'King of Hatti' whose seat of power seems to have been somewhere in Asia Minor. Yet it became equally clear that in Assyrian records of the eleventh century and later, the 'Land of Hatti' meant Syria. Geographically, this must all have been somewhat confusing. But, at the beginning of the present century, the whole problem was to be solved by new archaeological discoveries.

The search for 'Hittite' inscriptions and for relief carvings of the sort which often accompanied them, had long ago led to the discovery of the huge ruined city of Boğazköy in the bend of the Halys river, and the rich array of sculptured reliefs in its neighbouring rock sanctuary at Yazılıkaya. In 1906, German excavations began in the high citadel known as Büyükkale and a vast archive of cuneiform tablets was immediately brought to light. Their contents made it possible to identify the city as Hattusas, capital of the 'Land of Hatti' mentioned in the Amarna letters, and, as though further confirmation were needed, among the first tablets found was a text which proved to be the 'Hatti' version of the treaty, already mentioned, between Ramesses II and 'Great Kheta'. When the whole archive had eventually been deciphered and studied, the historical pattern at last became clear.

For five centuries, then, beginning in about 1700 BC, a great nation whose rulers were of Indo-European origin occupied an increasingly large proportion of central Anatolia, contesting its more southerly territories with Egypt and Assyria. In Mesopotamian languages it was called Hatti, simply because this had been the name applied by them to the indigenous inhabitants of Anatolia, ever since the third millennium BC. In an Assyrian text of about 1400 BC recounting the exploits of the old Akkadian kings of almost a thousand years earlier, Naram-Sin is said to have encountered a king of 'Hatti' somewhere in southern Anatolia.[3] For convenience, its people are today referred to by the old Biblical term Hittites, to distinguish them from the native 'Hattians' whose country they occupied. The mainstream of Hittite history ended abruptly in about 1200 BC, when they were driven from their home on the plateau by an ethnic upheaval in west Anatolia which is still only partially understood. But there is an aftermath in the tenth to seventh centuries, during which they re-appear as part-occupants of small city-states among the Taurus mountains and in north Syria (see Chapter 7). This period is variously referred to as Neo- or Syro-Hittite and in Palestine it corresponds to the time of the Hebrew monarchy.

Next, the question of languages should be clarified. Before the arrival of Indo-Europeans late in the third millennium BC, the indigenous people of

13. The rock-cut shrine at Yazılıkaya near Boğazköy has not changed since it was depicted by William J. Hamilton in *Researches in Asia Minor, Pontus and Armenia*, London 1842 (facing p. 394).

central Anatolia spoke various dialects of a language which may be called Hattian, but they were entirely illiterate. Elsewhere in the Near East at that time, the most common form of writing was that which used cuneiform characters impressed on clay, and this provided a vehicle for the Akkadian language of Mesopotamia, which had become the *lingua franca* of trade and diplomacy. It was first introduced into Anatolia, as we have seen, by Assyrian merchants, who founded trading colonies at Kanesh and elsewhere. The successive waves of Indo-European immigrants, when they came, spoke languages of a totally different character. Luwian was spoken by the earliest immigrants into south-west Anatolia, and Palaic in the northern district afterwards called Paphlagonia. But there was a third, more important language spoken by settlers in the Halys country and Cappadocia. This, for reasons which are not entirely clear, they themselves referred to as Neshite. Today it is known to us as Hittite, and at an early stage it replaced Akkadian in the cuneiform archives of the Hittite capital at Hattusas. It should be added that the pictographic inscriptions referred to by early travellers as 'Hittite' hieroglyphs (Fig. 27) in fact represent a Luwian form of writing, adopted much later by the Neo-Hittites of the Iron Age.

After this preliminary identification of the Hittite people and their language, we may more confidently approach the story of their rise to fame.

The movement of peoples, some time before 2000 BC, which brought the Hittites into central Anatolia, has been the subject of much speculation and controversy. But little doubt now remains that they had moved southward around the western end of the Black Sea and entered Anatolia from the

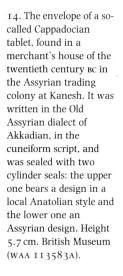

14. The envelope of a so-called Cappadocian tablet, found in a merchant's house of the twentieth century BC in the Assyrian trading colony at Kanesh. It was written in the Old Assyrian dialect of Akkadian, in the cuneiform script, and was sealed with two cylinder seals: the upper one bears a design in a local Anatolian style and the lower one an Assyrian design. Height 5.7 cm. British Museum (WAA 113583A).

Bosphorus crossings. The picture is not one of a conquering army, leaving a trail of damaged settlements behind it, but a gradual infiltration of Anatolian society by a people of superior military skill and political sagacity. To obtain a clearer idea of this development, one would need to know more about the Hattian people and their rulers, with whom the Hittites found themselves in contact. Unfortunately the earliest cuneiform inscriptions do not throw much light on this subject. Among the archives, for instance, of the Assyrian merchants at Kanesh references to subjects of general interest, other than the immediate business of trade and exchange, are extremely scanty. From about 1870 BC onwards, however, we begin to find the names of cities other than Kanesh which have kings, or at least boast of palaces, suggesting the dignity of local rulers. Among them is one to which a queen is attributed and another called Burushattum (Burushanda) is singled out for special distinction in that its ruler is dignified with the title of 'Great King'. It has been almost certainly identified with the site called Acemhöyük, south of the Salt Lake, which has been partially excavated, and the ruins of its palaces exposed.[4]

Rather more helpful are the names of private individuals mentioned in the Kanesh tablets. The Mesopotamian merchants were not only closely associated in business with the native population, but had evidently freely intermarried

15. Head of a lion-*rhyton* (a libation vessel) of red burnished clay similar to many found in the *karum* at Kültepe. It dates from about 1800 BC and is 11.2 cm high. British Museum (WAA 132963).

with them, so that their names are frequently mentioned and something is to be learnt from them linguistically. The majority belong to the indigenous Anatolian families; but there is also a plentiful admixture of Indo-European names, and these have a special significance in the present context. In them, the characteristics of both the Luwian and the Neshite languages are recognisable, and since the second of these may positively be called Hittite, it is possible to conclude that there was already an admixture (or, as some now think, a predominance) in the population of the racial material from which the Hittite nation was later to consolidate itself. Clearly this intrusion of foreigners must eventually have created some sort of political upheaval, for the colony of Kanesh was twice destroyed by fire. After the second disaster, in about 1740 BC, its function as a trading station was never revived.

During the final phase of the colony's occupation, the evidence of the Assyrian records is supplemented by inscribed material from new sources. There are tablets from sites other than Kültepe, including Boğazköy and Alişar, where similar colonies were in existence, and inscriptions from Acemhöyük, naming the Assyrian king Shamshi-Adad I.[5] But of equal importance are texts from the mound itself at Kanesh, which represents the remains of the Hattian city and covers the ruined palaces of its native rulers. One purpose which these writings have served is to throw new light on a famous text, recopied and preserved in the Hittite archives of much later times. It concerns two Hattian kings, Pithanas and his son Anittas, and clearly refers to events preceding the foundation of the Hittite kingdom.

Anittas, to whose hand the record is attributed, was ruler of a city called Kussara and he gives a list of neighbouring cities which he had conquered. One interesting point about this list is that it includes the name of Nesha, which is now known to be identical with Kanesh, and there are indications that in Anittas' time, the Hittites had begun to concentrate their forces at Kanesh. In any case, he seems to have treated the conquered city with notable leniency, having perhaps understood the advantages to be gained from an alliance with this new and virile element in the population. He even transferred his capital from Kussara to Kanesh, which he refortified; and it may well have been with the help of Hittite chariots and horses that he afterwards sacked and destroyed Hattusas. He completed his conquests by gaining control of Burushanda and thereby acquired the title of 'Great King'.

An important document was found in 1955 among the palace ruins in the Kanesh mound. This took the form of a letter addressed to Warsama, King of Kanesh, by a neighbouring ruler, Anum-Hirbi of the city of Mama. In it he complains of being exposed to the hostility of surrounding princes, and seems to suggest an alliance with Warsama. This letter dates from the very last years before the destruction of Kanesh and the disappearance of the Assyrian colony. It seems to reflect a state of political instability and the threat of military violence, which foreshadows the imminent establishment of Hittite rule.

Politically, little more is known about the Hattians. Yet, from the archaeological evidence, it has been possible to conclude that their way of life provided a basic component of Hittite civilisation. Certainly their thought, expressed in religious symbolism, exerted a strong influence on Hittite art.

We shall now find that, for a period of five centuries starting in about 1650 BC, the known history of Anatolia is predominantly that of the Hittite state. In the records from which it has been reconstructed, there are frequent references to neighbouring states with whom its kings were, for one reason or another, periodically in contact; but their topography is so imprecise and place-names so difficult to identify that their frontiers cannot be defined, nor even their relative locations generally agreed upon. Other parts of the country, of whose existence the Hittites were ignorant, have no history until the arrival of the Greeks.

Hittite history, as it is known today, has come to be conventionally divided into two periods: the Old Kingdom (c. 1700–1500 BC) and the Empire (c. 1400–1200 BC). The 1973 edition of the *Cambridge Ancient History* adds a Middle Kingdom to account for the less well documented century between.[6] It would be too much to expect that the inscriptions from the archives would resolve themselves into a tidy and explicit historical narrative. And this applies in particular to the Old Kingdom from which hardly more than two major historical inscriptions have survived. These are also the only source from which we can expect to obtain any information about the actual foundation of the Hittite monarchy. The longest of the two does give some help in this respect. It is in fact the constitutional decree of a king called Telipinus – perhaps the last of the Old Kingdom – in which he contrasts the prosperity of the nation under his earliest predecessors with its decadence at the time of his own accession. The translation of the text most often quoted is as follows:

> Formerly Labarnas was Great King; and then his sons, his brothers, his connections by marriage, his blood relations and his soldiers were united. And the country was small; but wherever he marched to battle, he subdued the countries of his enemies by night. He destroyed the countries and made them powerless [?] and he made the sea their frontier. And when he returned from battle, his sons went each to every part of the country, to Hupisna, to Tuwanuwa, to Ninassa, to Landa, to Zallara, to Parsuhanda and to Lusna, and governed the country, and the great cities were firmly in his possession [?]. Afterwards Hattusilis became King ...[7]

If we infer from this that Labarnas was first in the line of Hittite kings, it is confirmed by the more recent discovery that his name and that of his wife, Tawannannas, came to be used as eponymous titles by subsequent kings and queens. Evidence to this effect is to be found in the second of the two texts mentioned above. This time it is a bilingual Hittite-Akkadian inscription recording the testament of Hattusilis, who succeeded the first Labarnas. He refers to himself as 'Labarnas Hattusilis, Great King of Hattusas, the man from Kussara'.[8] This has been taken to imply that it was he who first transferred the Hittite capital to Hattusas, the old Hattian city long ago destroyed by Anittas, who had himself abandoned Kussara in favour of Kanesh. In these circumstances, the term 'Neshite', applied by the Hittites to their own language, is difficult to explain.

Some of the names of conquered cities mentioned by Telipinus can now be reliably identified. Hupisna is classical Kybistra, and Tuwanuwa is Tyana near modern Bor; Landa or Laranda is modern Karaman, and Lusna the Lystra of St Paul's journeys. Geographically, it can be seen how these places group themselves in an area south of the Halys river, extending from the Konya plain eastwards to the Taurus. It is a province which, in later times, became known to the Hittites as the Lower Land; the 'home counties' of their realm. But Telipinus' claim that the early kings had 'made the sea their frontier' is borne out in Hattusilis' own annals, in which he lists the events of six successive years in his reign.

In the second of these, one finds that he has already reached North Syria, and the name is mentioned of Alalakh (Tell Atchana, on the Orontes). To get there he must have passed through Cilicia and crossed the Amanus mountains. The city of Urshu, which he destroyed and looted on his return journey, is thought to have been on the middle Euphrates above Carchemish; so he returned by a more easterly route, for the time being avoiding Yamhad (modern Aleppo) of which Alalakh was a dependency. In his third year, Hattusilis led his army south-westward, against a powerful state called Arzawa in western Anatolia. But while so engaged, much of the territory which he had gained in the previous year was overrun by the Hurrians, a people who are now mentioned for the first time. The Hurrians, like the Hittites themselves, had infiltrated into eastern Anatolia early in the second millennium, moving on into northern Mesopotamia, where the Assyrian kings were able to profit from their knowledge of horse-breeding. Having abandoned his attack on Arzawa, Hattusilis contrived to restrain their advance, but two further years passed before his frontiers were re-established. After that, his sixth and final year was spent in fighting an inconclusive war against the ruler of Aleppo, who had enlisted the Hurrians as allies. At the end of it he returned, badly wounded, to his old residence at Kussara.

Understandably, therefore, Hattusilis' testament is much concerned with the choice of a successor. The nephew who was initially appointed as his heir has proved an unsatisfactory character, and for this he blames his sister, to whom her son's upbringing had been entrusted. He therefore decrees that the boy's claim to the throne shall be rejected in favour of his own grandson, Mursilis. In the bilingual inscription, the king's attempt to justify this decision occupies considerable space on the tablet. It would be of some human interest, were it not for the banality which such texts acquire when literally translated into a modern language. A passage from an English version will illustrate this:

> I, the king, summoned him to my couch and said: 'Well. No one will in future bring up the child of his sister as his foster-son. The word of the king he has not laid to heart, but the word of his mother, the serpent, he has laid to heart.... Enough! He is my son no more.' Then his mother

bellowed like an ox: 'They have torn asunder the womb in my living body! They have ruined him, and you will kill him.' But have I, the king, done any evil?

Dismissing this subject, the king continues with a valedictory exhortation to his subjects, which includes the words:

> ... you shall serve the gods humbly. Attend to their offerings of bread and wine, their broth and groats. . . .[9]

Mursilis seems to have been a good choice. His first concern, out of fidelity to his grandfather, was to settle accounts with Aleppo, and this he did after effectively defeating a Hurrian army. Encouraged by this success, he directed his march eastward towards the Euphrates and the rich country that lay beyond. Mesopotamia had at this time been united under the great Amorite kings of the First Dynasty of Babylon. Yet its armies now seemed powerless to resist the onslaught of these virile invaders from the north, with their horses and chariots. Babylon fell: and the death of Samsu-ditana (1595 BC) brought the Amorite dynasty to an end. But now indeed the Hittite lines of communication and the political resources of so young a nation had been tested beyond their capacity. Suddenly to find themselves masters in the Babylon of Hammurabi, surrounded by the pomp and luxury which distinguished so great a centre of world civilisation, must have surprised these simple highlanders. Nor were they in a position to reap the fruits of their extraordinary victory. Rumours of political disturbances in Anatolia, arising from Mursilis' long absence, brought him back in haste to the capital, where he was assassinated by a pretender to the throne, called Hantilis.

For the Hittites, the accession of Hantilis initiated half a century of political and military disasters, which not only robbed them of their major conquests in the south, but impaired the stability of the monarchy itself. The Hurrians stripped them of their southern possessions, including Cilicia, which was from then onwards referred to as Kizzuwadna. Arzawa remained aggressively independent and tribal enemies in the north pressed forward into the Halys bend itself. They were rescued from this threatening situation by Telipinus, a king of ability and determination, who seems to have been successful both in establishing his own authority and in stabilising the now constricted frontiers of his kingdom. Among other accomplishments he even concluded a treaty of alliance with Kizzuwadna, which once more assured the Hittites access to the Mediterranean.

In his 'Decree', Telipinus also redefines the laws governing accession to the throne and the replacement of one king by another. A relevant passage (in this case more freely translated) reads:

> ... the nobles must again stand united in loyalty to the throne, and if they are dissatisfied with the conduct of the king or of one of his sons, they must have recourse to legal means of redress and refrain from taking the law into their own hands by murder. The supreme court for the punishment of wrong-doers must be the *pankus* or whole body of citizens.

Commenting further on this word *pankus*, O. R. Gurney says:

> It is clear that the king's kinsmen, called the 'Great Family', enjoyed special privileges, which they constantly abused. The highest offices of state were generally reserved for them. . . . The names of most of these functionaries show them to belong in origin to the staff of the palace, and if we find (as we do) that the holding of these appointments often carried with it a high military command, it is evident that the Hittites had a long tradition of settled Court life. . . . The departments of the palace over which these 'dignitaries' presided apparently had their own personnel, though we cannot always identify each class of person mentioned in the text with its respective officer. . . . Thus, when we find the assembly convened by Hattusilis described as the 'fighting men of the *pankus* and the dignitaries', and later as 'fighting men, servants, and grandees', it is evident that the same classes are there intended and that these classes constitute the entire community in so far as it is concerned in affairs of state.[10]

This seems to confirm the impression that the Hittites were an exclusive caste imposed on the indigenous population of the country, and we must assume that, as Gurney says, 'the isolated city communities of Anatolia had been . . . gradually welded into a semblance of unity by the genius of the kings of Hattusas, but yet preserved to the end their local councils and many of their local rights'.

CHAPTER 4

Suppiluliumas
and the
Hittite Empire

The so-called Middle Kingdom covers the reigns of perhaps eight kings; the dates of their accession and even the orthography of their names are in some cases uncertain.[1] It is, however, in this period that the affairs of the Hittites begin to be freely mentioned in the Egyptian records, and it accordingly becomes possible to follow the main sequence of events. The Syrian provinces, which Telipinus had temporarily abandoned after his settlement with Kizzuwadna, were now referred to as Hanigalbat, apparently one of the political divisions into which the Hurrians had been organised. But they found themselves in conflict with Egypt and were defeated by Tuthmosis III during one of his most successful campaigns. This was the first occasion on which the Hittites formed an alliance with the Egyptians and, in 1471 BC, an equitable settlement was agreed upon between them. Meanwhile, the Hurrians seem to have been revitalised by the acquisition of a new aristocracy, and a formidable nation called Mitanni makes its first appearance in the northern confines of Mesopotamia.

Little is known about the Mitannian kings, save for the references made by other states to their relations with them. Even the remains of their capital, Wassukkanni, have not yet been identified, though it is known to have been located near the head waters of the western Khabur river, between Harran and Nineveh. Yet, from the Egyptian texts it is possible to understand that, whereas Tuthmosis III had found little difficulty in defeating Hanigalbat, Amenophis II (1450–1425 BC) met with a powerful enemy in Mitanni and was compelled once more to abandon control over Syria (1440 BC). For the Hittites also this was a serious matter, since their part-Hurrian dependencies were encouraged to revolt. There follows a period of about fifty years (c. 1440–1390 BC) during which the sources of history cease to flow. The reigns of six or seven obscure rulers are attested, two of whom have the same name

(Tudhaliyas II and III). For the rest, it appears to be a time when the fortunes of the Hittite state sink to their lowest ebb. All its most formidable enemies are seen to be in league against it. Egypt and Mitanni have come to an agreement and formed an alliance, sealed by a royal marriage. Arzawa, too, appears to be in the ascendancy, for in the Amarna letters Amenophis III is found to be in correspondence, not with the Hittite king but with an Arzawan ruler, and there is trouble with the Kaska tribes in the mountains to the north. A later inscription, recounting the history of these times, lists the enemies who are closing in from all sides on the Hittite homeland, and ends by recording a raid on Hattusas itself in which the city was destroyed by fire.[2] This was the situation when Suppiluliumas, probably the greatest of all Hittite kings, came to the throne.

For four decades, from about 1375 onwards, the name of Suppiluliumas dominates the history of the Near East. When he became king, he was already an experienced soldier, having commanded the army of his father, Tudhaliyas III, in previous campaigns. His first years were spent in rehabilitating his people in their homeland, while he enlarged and refortified Hattusas on a very ambitious scale. It is in fact safe to assume that the huge circuit of walls around the outer city at Boğazköy was rebuilt in his time. His next task was again to confront the military power of Mitanni, which, in his father's time, had encroached almost to within striking distance of the capital. His approach to this enterprise is well described in an official record of later times.[3] At the outset, there is an authentic ring of truth in his confession to the failure of his initial attack, through the Taurus passes, on the military establishment of the Mitannian king, Tushratta, in Kizzuwadna. One sees also the more prudent planning and preparation of his second attempt, which took the form of an outflanking movement to the east, across the Euphrates, and a direct attack on the Mitannian capital from a direction which would be least expected. This time he was successful. His armies met with little resistance, and, after taking Wassukkanni, they swept westward into Syria, easily subduing the minor states and cities, which now found themselves deprived of Mitannian support. It must also have surprised Suppiluliumas to encounter so little Egyptian opposition in Syria. For Egypt, under the apostate Pharaoh Akhenaten, had temporarily lost interest in imperial defence and none but the vassal state of Kadesh dared to resist his armies. When this city too fell, no further obstacle remained. Suppiluliumas penetrated into Syria up to the district of Damascus and, in the words of the chronicle, 'made the Lebanon his frontier'.

This had been a brilliant campaign (c. 1365 BC) but it did not yet amount to a total conquest of Syria. The Mitannian army had not been effectively defeated, though Tushratta had been driven to take refuge in Carchemish, leaving Wassukkanni untenanted. Treaties of various sorts had been made with the cities of inland Syria and Lebanon, but Ugarit and the Mediterranean seaports remained under Egyptian control. Understandably, however, the king's presence was by now urgently required in the capital. He accordingly returned to Hattusas, after installing his son, Telipinus, in the temple-city of

Kummanni (classical Comana-in-Cappadocia) to protect his communications with the south. During his absence, a new development took place in Mitanni. A dissident faction among the nobility had contrived the assassination of Tushratta, and his successor, Artatama, unwilling to place any further reliance on Egypt, allied himself instead with Assyria. On the part of the Hittites, this situation clearly called for drastic action, and in 1340 BC Suppiluliumas returned to the Euphrates at the head of his army. Carchemish fell after an eight-day siege, and was provided with a Hittite king in the person of the young prince Piyassilis. Telipinus became king of Aleppo. From the remnants of the Mitannian state Suppiluliumas created a client kingdom, with the disinherited son of Tushratta acting as puppet ruler in Wassukkanni. The Great King then brought his Syrian war to a conclusion by signing a treaty with Kizzuwadna.

While Suppiluliumas was encamped with his army before the walls of Carchemish, one of those episodes took place which clearly confirm the status and reputation that he had acquired among the courts of the Near Eastern nations. News may already have reached him that, in Egypt, a Pharaoh – whom we may now confidently identify as Tutankhamun – had recently died. But this can hardly have prepared him for the deputation which he now received, bearing a letter from the Pharaoh's widow, Ankhesen-Amun. The following translation of it is quoted from A. Goetze.[4]

> My husband has died, and I have no son. They say about you that you
> have many sons. You might give me one of your sons, and he might
> become my husband. I would not want to take one of my servants. I am
> loath to make him my husband.

Suppiluliumas was so astonished at this invitation that, after calling a council of his noblemen, he decided first to investigate whether the request was sincere and sent an envoy to Egypt for this purpose. The envoy returned with a second message bitterly complaining of the king's distrust and hesitation. In O. R. Gurney's translation,[5] it runs as follows:

> Why do you say, 'They wish to deceive me?'. If I had a son, would I write
> to a foreigner to publish my distress and that of my country? You have
> insulted me in speaking thus. He who was my husband is dead and I have
> no son. Must I then take one of my subjects and marry him? I have written
> to no-one but you. Everyone says you have many sons; give me one of
> them that he may become my husband.

This time the king complied with her wish; but unhappily the son whom he sent was murdered on the way to Egypt. Poor Ankhesen-Amun was, as is known, compelled to marry an ambitious courtier-priest, called Ay.[5]

Syria and the south-eastern provinces were of course not the only concern of Suppiluliumas during his long reign. We know for instance that the Kaska people, who since the days of the Old Kingdom had incessantly harassed the Hittites' northern border, were a great trial to him, and it is recorded that it took him twenty years to restore the northern frontier as it had existed at the time of his accession. At the opposite extreme, he had to keep a close watch on the country described as the 'Arzawa Lands'. Since these included the 'Seha-River Land' (perhaps to be equated with the modern Bakir Çayı which flows past Pergamum), Mira and Hapalla (both beyond the western edge of the plateau), this country must have accounted for a large part of southwest Anatolia. This makes more credible the record, which we have already mentioned, of an earlier correspondence between an Arzawan king and the Pharaoh Amenophis III. But mention is also first made at this time of other peoples near the Aegean coast with whom Suppiluliumas was in contact. These will be discussed in Chapter 5.

Goetze[6] thinks that Suppiluliumas died in 1346 BC, a victim of the plague which his soldiers had brought back from North Syria. His accomplishments had been tremendous and at the close of his reign he wielded more power than any contemporary monarch. But, as so often happens when responsibility for affairs of state is invested in a single individual, his death loosened the ties by which the empire was bound together and was followed by a succession of political disasters.

Arnuwandas, the elder son of Suppiluliumas, only survived his father for one year, but of his brother Mursilis II, who succeeded him, the records have a good deal to say. Among his earliest misfortunes was the loss of the small Mitannian kingdom, intentionally preserved by his father as a buffer-state between himself and the Assyrians. This was now annexed by the Assyrian king Ashur-uballit I. Elsewhere, the old pattern of punitive expeditions and the reconquest of rebellious dependencies once more repeated itself. Apart from his 'ten campaigns' against the turbulent Kaska mountaineers in the north, Mursilis found himself in almost continual conflict with Arzawa, and this was complicated by the unpredictable behaviour of Millawanda (Miletus?), a city controlling part of classical Caria, which now appears in the Hittite records for the first time. On his Syrian frontier, another problem for Mursilis was created by the temporary loss of Carchemish. Its Hittite king, who was his brother, had unfortunately died while attending a religious ceremony at Kummanni and, on receiving the news, the city had made a bid for independence. It is of some interest that, on this occasion, the very appearance of the Hittite army under its royal commander on the banks of the Euphrates was sufficient to ensure the rebels' immediate submission.

Nevertheless, in 1310 BC, after a reign of twenty-eight years Mursilis bequeathed to his successor, Muwatallis, an empire hardly less extensive and secure than it had been in his father's time. Muwatallis was almost at once faced with a formidable threat from the direction of Egypt. The early Pharaohs of the Nineteenth Dynasty seemed intent upon re-establishing their authority in the Levantine states relinquished during the time of Akhenaten, and this led inevitably to a confrontation with the Hittites. It took place in 1286 BC, the fifth year after the accession of Ramesses II, when the two armies met at Kadesh on the Orontes.

The battle of Kadesh is one which has captured the imagination of historians, because it is the earliest of which a written account survives, complete with tactical details. Ramesses himself has bequeathed to posterity a wordy description of it and pictured it on the walls of his temples at Thebes. Based upon these, a long and well-reasoned reconstruction of the battle (with plans) is to be found in an early edition of the *Cambridge Ancient History*.[7] But perhaps one may here be content to quote a much briefer account of what happened, in the words of O. R. Gurney:

16. The Battle of Kadesh (about 1286 BC) as depicted on a pylon of the palace of Ramesses II at Luxor in Egypt. From I. Rossellini, *I monumenti dell'Egitto e della Nubia*, I, *Monumenti Storici*, Pisa 1832, pl. 104.

> The Hittite army based on Kadesh succeeded in completely concealing its position from the Egyptian scouts; and as the unsuspecting Egyptians advanced in marching order towards the city and started to pitch their camp, a strong detachment of Hittite chariotry passed round unnoticed behind the city, crossed the river Orontes and fell upon the Egyptian column with shattering force. The Egyptian army would have been annihilated, had not a detached Egyptian regiment arrived most opportunely from another direction and caught the Hittites unaware as they were pillaging the camp. This lucky chance enabled the Egyptian king to save the remainder of his forces and to represent the battle as a great victory.[8]

Unfortunately, no Hittite text has survived which refers specifically to the battle of Kadesh and its results. There can, however, be little doubt that its outcome was grossly misrepresented by Ramesses, since after its so-called 'defeat' the army of Muwatallis was able to continue its progress through Syria as far as Damascus. It is also known that Amurru (central Syria) continued to be regarded as part of the Hittite Empire until, sixteen years later, a political settlement with Egypt finally became practicable.

During his Syrian campaign, Muwatallis had moved his official residence to a city called Tarhuntassa, somewhere in the Taurus area. The north-eastern provinces remained in charge of his brother, Hattusilis, and it was he whom one would have expected to be considered heir to the throne when Muwatallis died in 1294 BC. What in fact happened is explained by Goetze as follows: 'Muwatallis died without leaving a legitimate son to succeed him. Hence it was necessary to invoke the "constitution" of Telipinus, which provided that in such a case the oldest son of a royal concubine should be made king. In this manner Urhi-Teshub was proclaimed king.'[9] This young man's reign of seven years was, as might have been expected, largely occupied by an interminable quarrel with his uncle, Hattusilis, who eventually replaced his nephew on the throne after a popular uprising. Among the inscriptions of this time there is a long 'apologia', in which Hattusilis attempts to justify himself for having taken the law into his own hands.

The reign of Hattusilis III seems to be one of the first in which skilful diplomacy contributed towards the attainment of political tranquillity. It was he who, in 1284 BC, negotiated with Ramesses II the famous treaty of which, as has already been mentioned, both the Egyptian and the Hittite texts are preserved. Its ratification was followed by a cordial exchange of letters, not only between the two kings but also from one queen to another. Thirteen years later a daughter of Hattusilis was married to the Egyptian Pharaoh. It was a détente which assured the mutual support of the two powers against any threat from Assyria, and must at the time have seemed to inaugurate a new and more peaceful era. Hattusilis himself, ten years before his accession to the throne, had married Puduhepa, the daughter of a Kizzuwadnan priest, and evidence of the couple's combined interest in administration and religion is provided by the numerous edicts which they issued in both connections. During Muwatallis' absence in Syria, the old capital at Hattusas had apparently been sacked by the Kaska, so that one of the major tasks with which they were faced was that of rebuilding the city. They also appear to have busied themselves with recopying the Hittite state archives. Puduhepa was of Hurrian birth, and it is now understood that her influence is to be detected in the rock-sculptures of the famous shrine at Yazılıkaya, outside the walls of Hattusas. The figure of a king which appears prominently among these reliefs is that of her son, Tudhaliyas IV, who became king after the death of his father. Though the sculptures would seem to have been carved in his reign, it is known that for a time he accepted his mother as co-regent, and this has been taken to account for the fact that some of the mythological figures by which he is

17. A procession of Hittite soldier gods carved in the thirteenth century BC at the rock-cut sanctuary of Yazılıkaya near Boğazköy.

surrounded are recognisable not as Hittite deities but as those of the Hurrian pantheon.

Despite all this, it would be wrong to suppose that Tudhaliyas was spared the usual sequence of military involvements. In the west, he was almost continually at war with kings of the Arzawan states and to the east with the armies of Assyria. One other country about which the Hittites seem hitherto to have shown little concern is Alasiya (Cyprus). Its importance as a major source of copper must by now have been recognised, for the island was invaded and occupied by Tudhaliyas. For the rest, towards the end of his reign, this king's preoccupation with his western defences tends to suggest some undefined yet ominous menace to the empire from the direction of the Aegean and the European countries beyond. We now know that, at the time of his death in about 1220 BC, its fate was already in the balance.

Two more kings, Arnuwandas III and Suppiluliumas II, were to rule in Hattusas before the final collapse of the Hittite Empire, but there is little coherence in the surviving records of their reigns. The Phrygian migration into western Asia Minor had already begun and it was accompanied by a massive southward movement of Aegean and other displaced peoples, which eventually reached the Egyptian frontier. The historical background to these events will presently have to be considered.

In this chapter, our reconstruction of Hittite history has necessarily been concerned largely with the reigns and varying fortunes of successive kings; with their conquests or reconquests of neighbouring countries and, to a lesser extent, with their failures and frustrations. For anyone wishing to obtain a more detailed picture of the state and empire over which they ruled, there are, as usual, two main sources of evidence to be explored; namely, the archaeological record and the written texts. And in this last respect one must emphasise that the inscriptions are by no means confined to the purely historical documents with which we have hitherto been primarily concerned. For there is a wealth of other information available. By a systematic study of all this material, scholars have familiarised themselves with many aspects of contemporary life under the Hittite Empire. It has in fact proved possible, as Gurney has shown in his admirable summary of Hittite achievements,[10] to bring into clearer focus the people and events with which this chapter has been concerned; to understand how, in a few centuries, a wave of adventurous immigrants succeeded in imposing on the native states of Anatolia and Syria a unified civilisation, which today we call Hittite.

We have seen how, in the early stages, the aggressive proclivities of the old 'warring states' were canalised in the service of a single power with a sense of national purpose, and how they adapted themselves to its feudal organisation. Warfare was still the overall preoccupation of the state, but it was a new kind of warfare in which the use of horse-drawn chariots had already proved a primary factor. The breeding and training of horses was a specialised occupation, and from those to whom it was entrusted a new élite came to be created. Goetze describes them as 'a veritable class of knights, which had to be made economically independent, so that it would devote itself to its vocation'.[11] For this purpose, fiefs of land and peasantry were allotted to this class, raising their status to that of the high court officials whom we have mentioned in another context. At the apex of this feudal pyramid there was still always the supreme ruler, but here, too, there was a change, for he had acquired semi-divine attributes. The simple title of 'king' used in Hattian times had now been discarded. As a deputy of the Storm-god, Tarhunda, and his queen, the Sun-goddess of Arinna, he was now addressed as 'My Sun', and through his cultic observances it was his duty to keep these and other deities favourably disposed.

There is much to admire in the ethical disposition and deportment of these Hittite priest-kings, as reflected in their recorded edicts and pronouncements. When their consciences are troubled, they go to surprising lengths in their attempts to justify their actions. Their approach to warfare is pragmatic and their accounts of conquest factual. The bombast and magniloquence of the Egyptian Pharaohs is not emulated, nor the vindictive brutality of the Assyrian kings. During the fourteenth and thirteenth centuries, when communication between the powers was improved by a common knowledge of the Akkadian language, one sees in the Hittite rulers a new sense of international consciousness. The potential value of diplomacy as an alternative to perpetual hostilities is increasingly appreciated, and resulting agreements may be strengthened by royal marriages. This last expedient may well have seemed especially congenial to the Hittites, amongst whom the status of women was highly respected and a king's wife could be a queen in her own right.

If further psychological characteristics of the Hittites are to be sought in evidence other than that of their writings, it is in their art and architecture that one would expect to find some expression of their thinking. Unfortunately this is less revealing than one could wish; for here in Anatolia, to a greater extent than in Egypt or Mesopotamia, time has deprived us of the most revealing monuments. Architecture is restricted to the ground-plans of stone temples, and of sculpture in the round hardly a single example has survived. Only the relief carvings are left, on rock-faces and wall-slabs, with here and there much-weathered portal figures, of the sort which set a fashion in Assyria some centuries later. For the rest, our knowledge of Hittite plastic art depends upon carvings in miniature, clay modelling and the craft of metal-smiths.

Despite all this, it remains indisputably true that the most effective testimony of all to the stature and ability of this Anatolian nation, at the height of its political ascendancy and aggrandisement, is to be found in the ruins of the Hittite capital itself at Boğazköy.[12] The remnants of its temples and palaces, its high citadel and the four-mile circuit of its ponderously constructed fortifications cannot fail to convince one that this city has been the cradle and home of a great imperial people. If further evidence is needed of the religious convictions which bound the Hittites to their rulers and the rulers themselves to their gods, it is to be found in the splendid conclave of sculptured figures in the rock sanctuary at Yazılıkaya, outside the city. High above the modern

village, an outcrop of rock embraces a system of natural galleries, isolated
from the surrounding countryside but open to the sky. Their vertical sides are
ornamented in relief with processions of mythical beings, converging on scenes
of symbolic confrontation or ritual performance. More than sixty such figures
are represented – some identified by inscriptions – and their composition is
skilfully contrived. To this day the place retains an atmosphere of sanctity
which seldom fails to impress modern visitors.

Since much has now been said about the aggrandisement of the Hittite
nation during its periods of military ascendancy, it would be unfair to ignore
the reservations expressed by some recent writers in assessing its historical
status. J. Mellaart, for instance, hesitates to adopt the word 'empire', pointing
to the inherent weakness in the Hittite political system, by which wealth was
concentrated in a few great cities, leaving the rural districts impoverished; to
the failure of its victorious rulers to provide for the administration of conquered
territories and their consequent inability to maintain suzerainty over unwilling
vassal states. In his opinion, 'One can hardly escape the conclusion that
the Hittites effectively managed to ruin central Anatolia, and many of their
neighbours as well.'[13]

CHAPTER 5

The Trojan Enigma

In the last year of the thirteenth century BC, this first well-defined instalment of Anatolian history is considered to have reached an abrupt end. As it happens, no actual event of any significance is satisfactorily proved to have taken place in that particular year, and indeed, its almost arbitrary selection by historians brings to mind the hands of a clock whose position has been imperfectly memorised in the failing light of a darkened stage. The 'intermission' which followed lasted four hundred years, and the historical changes which took place in the peninsula during that time are illuminated by hardly any kind of documentation.

The far-reaching upheaval which initiated these revolutionary changes is still imperfectly understood. Any attempt to explain it must therefore begin with a search for evidence of significant events known to have occurred around the turn of the thirteenth century. Since our concern is primarily with Anatolia, it is there that our enquiry should begin, and it will first be necessary to take a closer look at the geographical background against which the political and military developments described in the last chapter took place. Here, unfortunately, we shall find that the picture is a great deal less well-defined than might have been expected, in view of the plentiful sources from which attempts have recently been made to reconstruct it.

First among these sources are of course the written texts, especially those of the Hittites themselves, which constitute the bulk of the Boğazköy archives. These documents, treaties with other states, diplomatic correspondence and records of military campaigns, together provide an almost bewildering index of place-names and of countries with which the Hittites were at various times in contact. These of course include other major powers such as Egypt and Assyria in whose own surviving records significant references are often made to cities or peoples in Anatolia. Nor is it possible to ignore the few but well-attested contacts between the proto-Greeks of the Aegean and the coastal provinces of Asia Minor.

Let us, then, first look at the basic facts of Hittite geography which have long been beyond dispute: the 'Homeland' in the curve of the Halys river and the 'Lower Land' annexed to it in the south; Kizzuwadna, occupying the whole of classical Cilicia and ruled latterly by relatives of the Hittite kings; Mukish, Kadesh, Amurru and other small states south of the Amanus mountains, with inland cities such as Alalakh and Aleppo, containing the northward thrust of Egyptian armies into Syria; Carchemish, guarding the crossings of the Euphrates; and Mitanni, on the frontiers of Mesopotamia, at times creating a buffer-state between Hatti and Assyria. Barring the Hittites from access to the Black Sea are, as we have seen, the Kaska tribes, a formidable people living among the Pontic Alps on either side of the Halys Gorge. Another habitual rival of the Hittites, the kingdom of Arzawa, can confidently be assigned to the south-west of the peninsula, covering the river valleys which run westward to the Aegean.

So far we are on safe ground; for all these countries seem on at least one occasion to have made common cause with the Hittites against Egypt, and their names are listed as allies of the former at the battle of Kadesh in 1286 BC.[1] Complications do not arise until we turn to the coastal provinces beyond Arzawa, and especially to their relations with an intrusive people from an unknown provenance: the enigmatic 'Land of Ahhiyawa'.

Ahhiyawa was a state ruled by kings or princes, who corresponded with the Hittite rulers from the city of Millawanda, and they often referred to their nearest neighbours as people of the Lukka Lands. The Ahhiyawans appear to have been a powerful, sea-going nation, and seemed at first to historians to be easily equatable with Homer's *Akhaiwoi* (the Achaeans).[2] This fitted well with the identification of Millawanda as classical Miletus (beneath which archaeologists had already located a Mycenaean colony), and with that of Lycia as the Lukka Lands. Beyond this, much of what was known about the Ahhiyawans was derived from an important group of texts which included the actual annals of a Hittite king named Tudhaliyas. From the evidence then available there seemed every reason to conclude that this ruler must be the fourth of that name, who, as we have seen, reigned during the penultimate years before the collapse of the empire (c. 1250–1220 BC).[3] Other texts in the same group included not only a vital exchange of letters between the king and a prince of Ahhiyawa, but the account of an insurrection by a confederation of west Anatolian states, described as the Assuwan League, which seemed to extend from Lycia northward as far as the Troad. With the help of the Ahhiyawans, they were said to have attacked Arzawa before being suppressed by Tudhaliyas.

All this provides historical 'in-filling' for the reign of Tudhaliyas IV in our last chapter. However, the whole of this very plausible reconstruction was on the point of being discarded, owing to the growing conviction among scholars that the texts on which it was based must be attributed to a much earlier

Tudhaliyas, who reigned in the late fifteenth century BC.[4] At the same time, and once more on linguistic grounds, objections increased to the equation between the Ahhiyawans and the Achaeans. However, new evidence has led to the two crucial texts being once more dated to the end of the fifteenth century BC.[5]

There remains also the problem of locating the actual land of Ahhiyawa on the map, a question to which a wide variety of answers has been proposed. Indeed, the whole subject of west Anatolian states and their geographical situation as implied by the Hittite texts has provoked a debate among historians which until recently showed few signs of reaching a conclusion.[6] However, the recent reappraisal of the texts[5] shows that the Hittite king treated on terms of equality with the ruler of Ahhiyawa, who was also a Great King and whose brother was stationed in Millawanda as his representative on Anatolian soil. It is therefore likely that Ahhiyawa was located on the Greek mainland, that Millawanda was indeed Miletus, and that the Lukka Lands are indeed to be equated with Lycia.

It will now be understood that, partly owing to the equivocal dating of available inscriptions, little is to be learnt from Hittite sources about the fortunes of the empire during the final years of the thirteenth century BC, or about contemporary developments in its foreign relations. Certainly no pointers are here apparent to the reasons for its imminent disintegration. If, however, we now turn to the Egyptian records of this period, we learn of historical events which clearly mark the culmination of some prolonged upheaval among the peoples and islands of the Aegean, extending, in the time of Ramesses III (c. 1194–1162 BC), to the eastern Mediterranean. Described and illustrated on the walls of his great mortuary temple at Medinet Habu are battles dated to the fifth and eighth years of his reign, in which he defeated a composite host of unrelated peoples, whose forces had devastated the countries of the Levant as they swept southward to the Nile Delta. He himself says:

> As for the foreign countries, they made a conspiracy in their islands. All at once the people were on the move, scattered in war. No country could stand before their arms. Hatti, Kode (Kizzuwadna), Carchemish, Arzawa and Alasiya (Cyprus), they were cut off. A camp was set up in a place in Amor (Amurru). They desolated its people and its land was like that which has never come into being. They were advancing on Egypt....[7]

So the Egyptians called them the 'Sea Peoples', though they were certainly not a single nation nor by any means all connected with the sea. A generation earlier, in 1220 BC, there had been a similar invasion of the Delta from the Libyan side, by 'northerners coming from all lands', which had been repulsed by Merneptah, the previous Pharaoh. Both episodes must be seen as a huge, historically undocumented movement of peoples in lands bordering the Aegean, coincidental with the destruction of famous cities on the Greek mainland during the aftermath of the legendary Trojan War, and perhaps with the arrival of the first Phrygians in north-west Anatolia.

19. Mural painting of a sea-battle from a building on the volcanic island of Santorini (Thera). Although dated two and a half centuries earlier, the soldiers depicted probably resemble the later Sea Peoples of about 1200 BC. Drawing by Ann Searight.

During Ramesses' land- and sea-battles with the Peoples of the Sea, many prisoners were taken, and on the walls of Medinet Habu his sculptors not only listed their supposed countries of origin but depicted in relief their national dress and other peculiarities. The information thus provided has been studied with great care, notably by N. K. Sandars in a book which is a small masterpiece of patient scholarship.[8] Some of the peoples can already easily be identified from earlier historical texts; for others she has proposed new and remoter

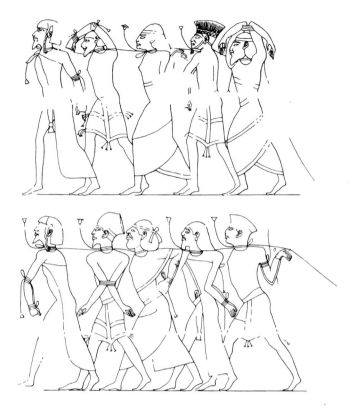

20. Prisoners taken during Ramesses III's foreign campaigns, about 1200 BC. From N. K. Sandars, *The Sea Peoples*, London 1978, p. 136.

provenances. Notable, however, is the high proportion of countries located on the west and south coasts of Asia Minor, lands which are known to have been affected by a widespread famine at this time. It may well be that, in the early stages of the Sea Peoples' migration southward towards Syria and the Levant, the Hittite state was denied access to these countries and its trade routes were dislocated. One authority[9] considers that this may have been no more than a single factor contributing to its downfall. He maintains, with some justification, that the destruction of the actual homeland of the Hittites should not be ascribed solely either to Sea Peoples, or to Phrygians, but is more likely to have been the work of their northern enemies the Kaska, who, in the eighth century BC, are to be found firmly installed in central Hatti.

Only a passing reference has so far been made to the Trojan War of Homeric legend, which, for obvious reasons, we assume to have taken place before the destruction of Greek cities. Attention should now also be drawn to the mention in Hittite texts of the Assuwan League, which included two place-names, Taruisa and Wilusa, which are significantly similar to Troy and Ilium, and to the presence among the Hittite allies at Kadesh of a people called Dardany (*Drdny*), perhaps the Trojans of the *Iliad*. But equally intriguing is the survival elsewhere of a single personal name, apparently known both to Hittite historians and to later Greek writers. This individual first appears in a Hittite document known as the 'Maduwattas Indictment', where the name 'Mukshush' is attributed to a supporter of the Ahhiyawan king Attarissiyas, in his correspondence with Tudhaliyas of Hatti. The name in this form has been firmly identified with that of Mopsus, the well-known sage of Greek legend who, during his wanderings after the Fall of Troy, founded Greek colonies in Pamphylia and Cilicia: traditionally, Aspendus, Phaselis and, of course, Mopsuestia. To add conviction to this story, his name also occurs in the bilingual inscription discovered by Turkish archaeologists in 1946 at Karatepe in Cilicia (see Chapter 7), where he is claimed as ancestor by an eighth-century chieftain of the 'Danuniyim' or 'Danaoi', in fact the Homeric Greeks. Mopsus would thus become the first figure of Greek legend to be authenticated as an historical personality.

Not all of this can be easily equated with the notional chronology of Homeric scholars, who until recently dated the 'Fall of Troy' (like the Hittite *débacle*) to about 1200 BC. First, the Maduwattas text may, as we know, be wrongly dated to about 1220 BC; secondly, Carl Blegen, the excavator of both Troy and Pylos, would never agree to a date later than 1250 BC for the end of the Trojan War. It may therefore be timely at this point to provide some facts about the supposed site of Troy and its excavation.

The truth is that, from an historical point of view, excavations at the site which the Turks call Hisarlık have raised almost as many problems as they have solved. The approximate location of Troy (or Ilium, as it is more frequently referred to in the *Iliad*) was traditionally known and confirmed by plentiful references in the works of Greek and Latin writers long before Schliemann appeared on the scene. During the early years of the last century, Hisarlık was identified as the probable site of Ilium by Hellenistic and Roman inscriptions found in its vicinity. At that time, however, the relationship of the two names Ilium and Troy still remained controversial, and a place further inland, called Balli Dağ, was considered a more likely situation for Troy itself. It was not until 1865 that an Englishman called Frank Calvert, who actually owned part of the hill at Hisarlık, reached the conclusion that the names were in fact interchangeable. Encouraged by the results of some soundings he had made, he showed the place to Schliemann, who accepted with enthusiasm its probable identity with the site of both Ilium and Troy. In 1870 Schliemann began excavating on a large scale.[10]

Hisarlık is situated on a low shoulder of rock, overlooking the marshy valley of a river historically known as the Scamander. The river reaches the sea some three miles to the north-west, where the coast makes an angle at the entrance to the Hellespont. The indisputable significance of Schliemann's subsequent finds was that here, in a position which corresponded accurately with the geographical details mentioned by Homer in his description of the fighting between the Trojans and the Greeks, there indeed existed the remains of an ancient fortress, complete with defensive walls and towers. On the other hand, he himself was the first to realise that, throughout the ages, the place had been many times rebuilt: and in those days, before archaeological stratigraphy was properly understood, it was not easy for him to be sure which of the superimposed layers of architectural remains might actually represent the period of the Trojan War. Guesswork involved him in an almost ludicrous error, for the walls which he called 'Homeric', and the hoard of jewellery which he naïvely christened 'Priam's Treasure', can now be reliably dated almost a thousand years earlier, to a period of antiquity which to him would have been hardly imaginable.

Schliemann's mistaken conclusions about the chronology and interpretation of his finds were not totally or effectively corrected until the years between 1932 and 1938, when his work was resumed by an American expedition under the direction of Carl Blegen. Blegen was able to distinguish the remains of nine successive settlements (each with a number of sub-periods), and to assign to them approximate dates. It was the earliest occupation of the seventh settlement which proved to correspond in time to Homer's Troy, and Schliemann's bewilderment could be forgiven when it was discovered that the greater part of the remains dating from this period had been bodily removed in classical times, in order to obtain a level emplacement for the buildings of a new acropolis. This did not, however, apply to the fortification walls and

21. Schliemann's Greek wife, Sophie, wearing some of the jewellery from a hoard which he called Priam's Treasure. In fact the jewellery probably dated from the late third millennium BC, about 1000 years before the Trojan War. The present whereabouts of most of the Treasure are now unknown.

gateways, which had in fact been built in the time of the sixth settlement and re-used in the seventh. Blegen was able to expose large sections of these, and so to reconstruct the outline of the fortress as it must have existed in the thirteenth century BC. It took the form of an irregular oval with a maximum dimension of almost exactly 200 metres, and would have enclosed an area of something over 5 acres.

So here is the sort of enigma which presents itself when attempts are made to equate the findings of archaeologists with the contentions of historians and the substance of legend. Blegen himself summarises the many flattering references in the Homeric poems to the size and magnificence of Troy as a city. He starts by saying:

> The fortress enclosed an area extensive enough to provide room, not only for its own large population, but also for the numerous allies who assembled to help repel the Achaean aggression and who found place for their chariots and horses and all other equipment. Some scholars have

22. A two-handled silver vessel found near Troy. Similar pottery and metal vessels were found by Schliemann at Troy and he compared them to the *depas amphikypellon*, a two-handled cup mentioned by Homer. This example is now in the British Museum (WAA 132150); it is 15 cm high and dates from about 2200 BC.

> calculated that, as envisaged in the poems, more than 50,000 people could be accommodated. The city had wide streets and an open *agora*, or square, was laid out in the upper part of the citadel, outside the 'splendid' palace of Priam....[11]

All this is of course ridiculous when applied to the little fortress at Hisarlık, since the 50,000 people would have been standing shoulder to shoulder. The explanation which most readily suggests itself is that the fortress was merely the citadel of a much greater city, and indeed Schliemann did succeed in tracing a line of less impressive walls, enclosing a very extensive outer city, which he called 'Ilium', covering the whole summit of the promontory behind. But this dated from what he referred to as the 'Hellenic' period, and no traces have ever been found beneath it of a similar extension of the city in the thirteenth century BC.

So the enigma remains; and it is aggravated by our continued ignorance, both of the political situation which could have prompted the Achaeans to attack Troy and of their victory's after-effects on the peoples of Asia Minor. We shall perhaps be right if we dismiss at once suggestions made in the past that the power of Troy restricted the passage of Greek shipping through the Hellespont. The place was not a seaport, nor was it credited by Homer with a fleet of its own, while the anchorage known to have been used by ships approaching the straits was Lemnos, an island traditionally unconnected with Troy. We should perhaps more usefully consider, first, who these Trojans or Dardanoi were, to whom the Greeks found themselves opposed. The powerful walls which guarded their fortress in Homeric times had, as Blegen discovered, been in use during the lifetime of his 'sixth settlement': a long period of almost undisturbed prosperity which he thought to have lasted from 1800 to 1300 BC. The distribution of pottery types used at Troy during that period seems to be restricted to a province in north-west Anatolia corresponding approximately to the Troad of later times: perhaps a political state of which Troy itself could have been no more than an outpost or coastal stronghold. And here there is an interesting fact which may have some relevance: namely, that apart from Miletus, whose relations with the Achaeans we have observed, Troy seems to be almost the only city on the Aegean coast which shows signs of regular trade relations with the Mycenaeans during the fourteenth and thirteenth centuries BC. One notices in this connection that on a map accompanying one recent study of the Hittites,[12] the Troad is labelled 'Ahhiyawa', although, as suggested above, this is more likely to have been on the Greek mainland.

Perhaps then, one may dismiss this perplexing subject with a quotation from the late G. A. Wainwright, which Sandars rightly considers to be 'eminently sensible'. He concludes that:

> ... the Greeks were only interested in that part of the commotions in Asia Minor in which their ancestors had taken part, and that was in the Trojan War. That proves to have been only an episode in what we know to have been a long drawn-out period of wars, disasters, migrations and so forth. We have therefore to understand 'Troy' as western Asia Minor at the time of the 'Trojan War'.[13]

CHAPTER 6

The Kingdom
of Midas

The Phrygians who invaded Anatolia during the final centuries of the second millennium BC should probably be seen as a federation of tribal peoples from eastern Europe. Their arrival must of course be regarded as an historical event of major importance since, after sweeping across the plateau and aiding the displacement of the Hittites from their homeland, they occupied the interior of the peninsula for several hundred years. Historically, however, we know a great deal less about them than we should like to. Inscriptions using the alphabet which they adopted in the eighth century BC have survived in considerable numbers (Fig. 25): but unfortunately, legible as they are, they cannot at present be understood. References to events in Phrygian history and indications of their chronology have therefore to be sought elsewhere in two different quarters. Greek writers record some traditions about their origin and have more to say about their later history. From a quite different viewpoint, the annals of the Assyrian and Urartian kings refer to political developments at the eastern limits of their expansion.

The Greeks were unanimous in thinking that the Phrygian invasion took place before the Trojan War. Homer includes them in the list of Trojan allies, and even refers to an earlier occasion on which Priam of Troy fought side by side with Mygdon, the eponymous Phrygian leader of the Mygdonians, against a people known as the 'Amazones' who have sometimes audaciously been equated with the Hittites. From the Mesopotamian angle, their first appearance in the Assyrian annals can be dated about 1160 BC, although their Greek name is not used in this context. The Assyrians usually refer to them as 'Mushki', or sometimes as 'Mushki and Tabal', the former appearing to occupy an area which later became the Roman provinces of Lycaonia and Cappadocia, while the latter seem allied to the Kaska tribes in the north – old enemies of the Hittite kings, whom they may have helped to displace.

So here, less than half a century after the fall of the Hittite Empire, is this Phrygian kingdom – or perhaps a coalition of related rulers – occupying the whole of inner Anatolia from the Marmara eastward to the frontiers of Assyria, yet still separated from the Aegean coast by a line of tenaciously conservative aboriginal states, comprising the old 'Assuwan League' from the Troad to Lycia. In the south, too, the kingdom of Cilicia (Que or Khilakku), already perhaps colonised by Mopsus and his Greeks, barred their way across the Taurus into Syria. Where Mopsus had taken the initiative, other Greeks were to follow, and during the eleventh and tenth centuries BC the whole Aegean coast was to be populated by their maritime settlements. So it is in the interior of Anatolia that we should look for traces of the long Phrygian occupation, and they are indeed numerous. To the east, the greatest concentration of Phrygian settlements seems, as might be expected, to cover the already popu-lous area of the so-called Hittite Homeland, from Ancyra (modern Ankara) eastward throughout the great bend of the Halys river and beyond to Cappa-docia. For the most part they take the form of rather modest walled towns overlying the ruins of major Bronze Age cities at such sites as Alaca Hüyük, Alişar, Kültepe, Pazarlı and over the citadel of the old Hittite capital itself at Boğazköy. Painted tiles from the façade of a building at Pazarlı bear figures in relief including a procession of Phrygian soldiers. They carry circular shields and wear plumed helmets, unlike anything previously seen in Anatolia. From the Phrygian levels at Boğazköy there is also a grotesque example of Phrygian sculpture: a half-naked goddess (Cybele?) supported by comic figures playing the lyre and the double pipe. More attractive is the characteristic Phrygian pottery, with intricate designs in several colours, which is found at all these sites.

The western half of the Phrygian kingdom is both historically and archae-ologically better known. Its capital city, Gordium, is situated at the point where a great highway (the 'Royal Road' of later times) crosses the Sangarius (Sakarya) river. Within sight of the huge mound which covers its remains are scores of burial tumuli, some of them marking the rich tombs of Phrygian ruling families associated with names such as Gordios and Midas, familiar to the Greek historians.[1] American excavations in the city-mound itself have revealed the military strength and pretentious character of the town in the eighth century BC. Raised up on the ruins of an earlier Hittite settlement, it was surrounded by powerful stone walls, strengthened with baulks of timber. Deeply recessed between towers of masonry, a fine gateway has been exposed, leading to an impressive group of public buildings, some of them paved with a very early form of patterned mosaic. Of the several tumuli excavated by the Americans, one was the greatest of all; a mound of earth 200 feet high, traditionally known to this day as the Tomb of Midas. The burial chamber itself was located by drilling in 1955 and approached through a horizontal tunnel at ground level. One might have expected this to be a simple task of engineering, but in fact its final stages presented unforeseen difficulties.[2]

The tunnel had already reached a length of almost a hundred yards when

23. The site of King Midas' capital at Gordium. On the right can be seen the tumulus traditionally known as the Tomb of Midas.

it came up against a vertical stone wall about three feet thick. When the late Dr Rodney Young, director of the excavations, made a breach in this, a rubble of loose stones about the size of oranges began to pour out, and continued to do so however much was removed. It then became clear to him that he was actually drawing off the protective mound of rubble piled over the burial chamber. As there seemed no alternative, he was compelled to continue doing so for a whole week – carrying out on his railway about 200 cubic yards of stone. When the fall-out began to slacken, he was able to see that about six feet inside the stone wall there was another vertical barrier, this time built of uncut tree-trunks. Beyond this again was a further three feet of rubble and then the wall of the chamber itself, very neatly constructed of wood, with huge

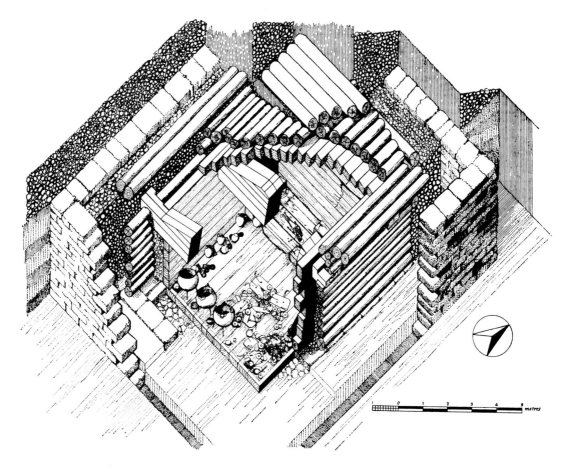

baulks of juniper measuring up to two feet square in section. Meanwhile, after shoring up the rubble on either side, he was able to climb up and examine the roof of the chamber. And here was a really extraordinary sight.

The mound of stone rubble covering the chamber had evidently itself been sealed in with a layer of clay about ten inches thick, before the earth was piled over it. From beneath this the stone had now been drawn away, leaving the clay in the form of a vast, cathedral-like dome, which was all that now remained to support the great weight of earth above. Young was comparatively unworried by this, and he next proceeded to cut an opening through the actual timber wall of the chamber. (When the present author visited the excavations a week later, the whole atmosphere was still thick with the pungent smell of juniper sawdust.) Young's first entry through the opening he had made must have been an extremely dramatic experience; for directly in front of him and beneath where he stood, was the huge collapsed bed on which the king's skeleton lay, half buried beneath the decaying remains of twenty-one linen and woollen coverlets. But what immediately preoccupied him much more effectively was, in the silence of the chamber, distinctly to hear the faint crackle of disintegrating wooden objects, as the outside atmosphere entered through the opening for the first time in 2,600 years.

He was to some extent right to be anxious about the wooden furniture in

24. The 'Tomb of Midas': structure of the burial chamber beneath the great tumulus at Gordium (about 700 BC).

this tomb. In this case he was able to arrange immediate chemical treatment, but the sheer volume of furniture would have proved something of an embarrassment to any museum. The inventory included no less than nine three-legged tables of wood, two inlaid screens and three ornamental stools. The quality and complexity of their inlay was remarkable.

The bronze vessels – of which there were 169 in all – were also of great interest. Along the wall on the right was a row of great copper cauldrons standing on iron tripods; and in front a tremendous cascade of smaller copper vessels, where some great piece of inlaid furniture had collapsed and spilled them on to the ground. But the extraordinary effect was the brilliant colour – a sort of glittering peacock-blue – of the patinated bronze. These vessels are now neatly arranged on shelves in the Ankara Museum and reduced to their normal dull copper colour after chemical treatment. And, in spite of their beautiful workmanship, the impact of their original appearance is now lost. Perhaps the most striking pieces were the three bronze cauldrons, with their rim decorations of modelled human figures, since they were clearly imported from elsewhere and represent the highest standard of Urartian metalwork. Then there were the smaller bronze vessels of widely varying types, one of which was bucket-shaped and beautifully modelled to represent the head of a snarling lion. In a sculptured relief from the palace of King Sargon II of Assyria (now in the Louvre), a figure carries in his left hand an exact replica of this ritual vessel. The date of the relief, in the last decade of the eighth century BC, corresponds well with Young's estimate for that of the Midas tomb.

An extremely peculiar aspect of this Phrygian burial, of which no satisfactory explanation will perhaps ever be forthcoming, is that it contained not a single object of gold or silver, and there were no weapons, such as one seems invariably to find in male burials of early periods. The figure lying on the bed was identified as the body of a man over sixty years of age and little more than five feet high. He was dressed in ornamental boots or 'buskins', and two garments, each of which was fastened at half a dozen points with bronze fibulae. In addition to these, near the head of the bed was a large linen bag containing a further 165 fibulae, which had burst out and spilled over the floor. But there was no jewellery of more precious metals. Remembering the mythical association of the name Midas with gold, it has even been suggested that his more valuable possessions might have been buried in a second chamber beneath that excavated: but Young had reasons for doubting this.

One further point of interest: most of the inscriptions found in the Midas tomb were written on the face of bronze bowls. Three of these, when cleaned, were found to have little panels of wax just below the rim, on which a short inscription was written in the enigmatic Phrygian alphabet. Writing on wax-covered panels of wood or ivory was a common practice at this time in Assyria, as an alternative to stone or clay tablets, and may well have been adopted at a very early period in Anatolia.

Apart from the capital city at Gordium, the greatest number of 'Phrygian' monuments are concentrated in a remote area of rocky uplands to the south-east of modern Eskişehir.[3] These are rock-hewn sculptures, some of them figuring heraldic lions or other, less easily identifiable motifs. They were thought by their discoverers in the last century to be associated with royal tombs, but more recently a new interpretation has been placed upon them. Located in this district are the sources of several important rivers, including the Sangarius itself, and it has been noted that in almost every case the sculptures are to be found in the vicinity of a conspicuous spring of fresh water. R. D. Barnett has accordingly suggested their identification as sanctuaries connected with some water cult.[4] But the most impressive of all these monuments is another so-called Tomb of Midas at Yazılıkaya. (N.B. This is not to be confused with the Hittite shrine of the same name near Boğazköy.) Here a rocky plateau is covered with ruins of a somewhat later date, though often referred to as the Midas City. Nearby, the vertical rock-face is sculptured to represent the end façade of a gabled building, decorated with geometric ornament in relief, probably representing terracotta wall-facings like those found at Pazarlı, while the gable is crowned by a very Greek-looking acroterion ornament. If this can be regarded as a temple rather than a tomb, it would conform with Barnett's further proposal that the rock-sculptures generally may be associated with the cult of Cybele – the Greek version of the Phrygian name for the very anciently worshipped Nature Goddess of Anatolia. The Phrygians also called her Agdistis ('She of the Rock').

Barnett[5] has collected some further information about the Phrygians. He says of their written language, 'It is common knowledge that the Phrygian alphabet, no less than the Ionic and other Greek alphabets, is derived from the Phoenician. But that the Phrygian letters most closely resemble the earliest Greek examples yet known ... has aroused little attention. The system of writing lines in alternate directions, called *boustrophedon* ("as the ox turns in the plough") which is used in early Greek scripts, is apparently derived through Phrygia from the Hittite Hieroglyphs', and he concludes that 'the Phrygian alphabet may well prove to be a parent of those of Greece, and Gordion the place of its invention in the mid-eighth century BC.' Barnett also recalls some minor accomplishments attributed to the Phrygians. The figured tiles already mentioned support the contention that Phrygian architects invented the frieze (Latin: *phrygium*). He noticed that the Latin word for an embroiderer was *phrygio*, and that Phrygian carpets were well known to the Greeks who called them *tapetes* (French: *tapis*). The Greeks also credited Phrygian musicians with the invention of cymbals, flutes and other instruments. Finally, Midas is said to have 'discovered' roses. Perhaps these northern rulers of Anatolia, who have been described as a 'horse-rearing aristocracy', did in the end make a substantial contribution to its indigenous culture. But their rule was soon to be ended by a new wave of immigrants, this time from the direction of the Caucasus. At the beginning of the seventh century BC, a barbarous people from south Russia, known historically as Cimmerians and in the Bible as Gomer, swept westward across the plateau. Gordium was destroyed by fire and Midas is said to have committed suicide.

25. The so-called Tomb of Midas of the eighth century BC, at Yazılıkaya south of Eskişehir. There are Phrygian inscriptions along the top and down the right-hand side of the rock-cut blind façade, one of which mentions the name Midas. The niche probably held a cult statue of the goddess Cybele.

CHAPTER 7

Carchemish and Zincirli

We have seen the Phrygian kingdom of the eighth century BC occupying the whole of what may strictly be called the Anatolian plateau, up to the western borders of Cappadocia and the inner fringes of the Taurus mountains. This has been concluded from the historical testimony of Greek writers and confirmed by the evidence of archaeological excavations. The question next arises as to what prevented its further expansion eastwards, a subject on which one would expect the historical records of the Assyrian kings to provide some enlightenment. And here immediately some confusion arises, because, as we have seen, the inhabitants of central Anatolia at this time are not referred to by the Assyrians as 'Phrygians', but as 'Mushki', or sometimes as 'Mushki and Tabal'. The most favoured explanation of this is that the Phrygian empire was in fact a confederation or coalition of several elements: the western (more authentically Phrygian) element, with its capital at Gordium, occupying the plateau, and the eastern component, consisting of Mushki and Tabal, being centred on the city of Mazaca (later Caesarea Mazaca, modern Kayseri). This being so, a wider problem next presents itself, as to who, in that case, were the inhabitants of the mountainous country separating the Phrygians/Mushki/Tabal from the borders of Mesopotamia and north Syria. And for this we should seek evidence not only in the Assyrian and Urartian records, but in the results of archaeological excavation.

The earliest Assyrian references to the Mushki suggest that their eastward thrust into the Taurus and towards the Euphrates had already become a menace. In about 1100 BC Tiglath-Pileser I defeats a coalition of 'five Mushkian kings' and brings back six thousand prisoners. In the ninth century the Mushki are again defeated by Ashurnasirpal II, while Shalmaneser III finds himself in conflict with Tabal, which he says is composed of twenty-four kingdoms. But when, in the following century, Tiglath-Pileser III once more records a confrontation with 'five Tabalian kings', the spelling of their names reveals the fact that these are no sort of Phrygians, but a semi-indigenous Luwian-speaking people, who must have survived the fall of the Hittite Empire. And now also in the eighth century mention is made for the first time, both by the Assyrians and by the Urartians, of a people referred to as Hatti,[1] occupying a pattern of city-states between the Euphrates and Cilicia, who also speak the Luwian language and write in hieroglyphs. These are the 'Syro-' or 'Neo-Hittites' of modern historical terminology, and whether or not the later Assyrian scribes considered them as part of Tabal is of little consequence. What we do know is that they were the western neighbours of Urartu over whom, as we shall presently see (Chapter 10), the Urartian kings occasionally extended their influence, either by conquest or through alliances against the Assyrians.

A good deal must be said about these Neo-Hittite and Tabalian cities, if only because a number of them have been excavated and much has been learnt from the results. Their art and architecture testify to the posthumous revival of provincial classical Hittite culture, and their inscriptions throw some historical light on the post-imperial 'diaspora' of the Hittite nation. Some of them had been provincial capitals of the old Empire, and there is no doubt that, in the final decades of the second millennium, they were further enlarged and vitalised by an influx of true Hittites, driven by the Phrygians from their homeland on the plateau. Yet it would be a mistake to conclude that they had displaced the earlier population. Rather, they seem to have allowed themselves to be absorbed into the existing political fabric. In particular, the cities in the Taurus and on the fringes of north Syria were hybrid societies, consisting of several different elements. Some, for instance, were Aramaeans, originally nomads from the Syrian desert, now sharing their settlements with Hurrians who had been there for a thousand years. And, further to the north-east, there were Tabalian cities, still only loosely associated with the Phrygian kingdom. In some of these communities the new arrivals would tip the balance in favour of a Hittite monopoly: in others a strong Aramaean element would from time to time become predominant. But of all these cities, it was perhaps Carchemish which remained the most uncompromisingly Hittite and whose conservatism justified its reputation as the political centre of Hatti.

Dominating the approach from Mesopotamia to the west, at a primary crossing of the Euphrates, Carchemish had been the seat of a Hittite viceroy in imperial times. When, however, it came to be excavated by British archaeologists, the buildings and sculpture which appeared beneath the surface of the mound could be attributed to a dynasty of independent kings, who ruled no earlier than the tenth century BC. In Neo-Hittite times, therefore, it was evidently still a city of some importance and, as the texts confirm, had often tended to be the first objective of the Assyrian armies in their campaigns against Syria. Consequently, it is well fortified and protected on two sides by the river, above which it stands in full view of the modern railway bridge. The character of the town at this time is interestingly revealed by the late Sir Leonard Woolley's publications of the work he did there during the years

preceding the First World War, when he was assisted by T. E. Lawrence.[2] Little remained at the summit of the high citadel, but at a point below, where it was approached by a monumental stairway, there was a broad open 'patio', surrounded by public buildings whose walls were decorated with row upon row of relief sculptures depicting deities, royal personages, priests and warriors alternating with explanatory inscriptions in hieroglyphic writing, installed and added to by successive kings. Since the decipherment, now almost complete, of these Luwian pictographs, the texts have proved a rewarding source of historical information. The reliefs, many of which are now prominently displayed in the Ankara Museum, were supplemented by a number of statues in the round – a rarity in earlier Hittite sculpture.

The fate of the Carchemish sculptures after the British expedition left Turkey in 1914 was at one time something of a mystery. It seems, however, to be satisfactorily explained by a passage in a personal letter from Sir Leonard Woolley, dated July 1956. He says,

> We had promised to leave everything to the Turkish Government, and of course, did so. Everything remained *in situ*, or in our magazines until after the war. Then in 1920 a Turkish army officer stationed at Jerablus decided to move the stones (or was about to do so?): many were smashed, the rest put on railway trucks but pitched off on to the embankment, where they remained until 1921 or later. Some pieces were stolen and sold; one lion's head ultimately came to the British Museum by purchase (much to my disgust) and other bits to the Louvre.

26. The 'Royal Buttress' at Carchemish, depicting Yariris, regent of Carchemish, with the young prince Kamanis and the rest of the royal family, including a child who is learning to walk and a babe-in-arms, followed by the goat which provides its milk. The Luwian text, written in 'Hittite' hieroglyphs, identifies the scene. The basalt reliefs, now in the Archaeological Museum at Ankara, are about 1.15 m high and date to about 800 BC.

The lion's head which he mentions belonged to one of a pair, supporting the seated statue of a god. The base only is now in the Ankara Museum, and the missing head has been replaced by a replica.

Woolley's excavations were not the first at Carchemish. As early as 1878 some less methodical investigations had been sponsored by the British Museum, and it was perhaps these which had initially aroused interest in the remains of the Neo-Hittite cities. Ten years later, the Deutsche Orient-Gesellschaft embarked on the excavation of an even larger site of the same sort. This was Zincirli (ancient Sam'al), situated high up in the great valley through which the main-line railway passes on its way southward from Fevzipaşa to Aleppo. Here again there is a fortified citadel, containing a complex of architecturally impressive palaces; but it stands in the centre of a residential town, enclosed by a double enceinte of defensive walls which form an exact circle, 800 metres in diameter. Here also there was a wealth of sculptures – both from the citadel and from the three fortified gateways in the city wall – and these were taken to Berlin and Istanbul. Included among the finds were several inscriptions in Aramaic which now make it possible to reconstruct a genealogy of local rulers, a dynasty of kings corresponding approximately in time to those of Carchemish. But it is clear from their names and from

27. Fragment of a pedestal for a statue from Carchemish, carved with a Luwian inscription in 'Hittite' hieroglyphs.

28. An orthostat, 1.12 m high, which stood in a palace doorway at Zincirli (ancient Sam'al). It is now in Berlin and shows Bar-rakib, ruler in about 730 BC, and his scribe beneath a symbol of the moon god and an Aramaic inscription. From *Ausgrabungen aus Sendschirli*, IV, Berlin 1911, pl. 60.

some details of dress and insignia in the portrait sculptures that this was a preponderantly Aramaean city, though the style of the carving and many of the conventions used are still essentially Luwian-Hittite.[3] A more complicated synthesis of styles becomes apparent in the course of the eighth century BC, when the influence of Assyrian design becomes increasingly evident. Perhaps the most notable work from Zincirli, and the most characteristic from this point of view, is the well-known orthostat relief depicting a Semitic-looking king called Bar-rakib (*c.* 730 BC), seated in a chair of typically Assyrian design and dictating to a scribe.[4] The historical background of figures like this and the character of the city over which they ruled have today been given a greater reality by the written evidence of the Zincirli texts. As Max Mallowan wrote:

> They give us an inkling of the dramatic events, the revolutions and murder of the king and his family which occurred in the confines of the palace. Here too we read of the harvests and the price of corn, of the fat and lean years, and of the renewed aspirations of the rulers concerned with egalitarianism and social welfare. We read of demagogues and of princes belittling the achievements of their ancestors in terms which no Assyrian monarch would ever have employed . . . and other visions which these relatively short inscriptions have conjured up for us concerning

contemporary life in the township of Zincirli and doubtless Carchemish during the first quarter of the first millennium BC.[5]

Here then we have two examples of Iron Age cities; one nostalgically retaining the Hittite culture of its vice-regal days in the second millennium, the other adapting the Hittite conventions of an imposed minority to the prevalent authority of its Aramaean inhabitants. Both retained their independence until the late eighth century BC, when they became subject to the Assyrian Empire. It may now be of interest to consider a third city, this time too far from Syria to be affected by Aramaean influence but adjacent to the region which the Assyrians regarded as Tabal and accordingly occupied by a Luwian element of the old Hittite population.

Ancient Milidia or Milid of the Assyrian and Urartian records lies beneath the mound called Arslantepe, some distance from the modern city of Malatya. This market town was newly sited as recently as 1938, five miles to the northeast of Roman Melitene (Eski Malatya), whose walls and medieval ruins are in part still standing. Its position, dominating an upland province between the Euphrates and the Anti-Taurus gave it a strategic importance which the Assyrian kings could not afford to ignore, and its name already appears as a Hurrian stronghold in the annals of Tiglath-Pileser I (1112 BC). However, it seems still to be maintaining its independence at the beginning of the eighth century, when a new monumental gateway was built and the colossal statue of a king was erected in the gate-chamber. This and other parts of the city were excavated by the French from 1932 onwards and the gateway has been restored in the Ankara Museum. Its walls were decorated with small but very interesting orthostat reliefs, evidently in secondary use since they have been dated stylistically to a much earlier period, a date since confirmed by the discovery of a link with the kings of Carchemish in the second millennium BC.[6]

The Malatya reliefs show no signs of Aramaean or Assyrian motifs, but there are remains of other cities west of the Euphrates which are known, either from the Assyrian records or from the results of minor excavations, to have attained some political prominence during the ninth and eighth centuries BC. There was Gurgum (modern Maraş) where a fine, unexcavated mound may be the source of chance-found inscriptions; Kummukh, later the Hellenistic state called Commagene, whose princes were buried at the summit of Nemrut Dağ (Fig. 56); Unqi, on the shores of the Amuq Lake, near Antioch, with which must be associated the burnt palace and temples excavated by Americans at Taynat on the Orontes; also, not far from Zincirli, the Neo-Hittite 'summer palace' at Sakçagözü, from which in the early years of the present century John Garstang procured a further fine collection of reliefs, though no inscriptions came to light. And finally there is one, rightly famous, rock relief associated with the name of an historical character.

The principal rock relief at Ivriz (near Ereğli, ten miles south-east of the road leading down to the 'Cilician Gates') is one of the most impressive monuments in Anatolia. For the identity of the king who is depicted, we must return to Tiglath-Pileser III's campaigns against five Tabalian kings in 738 and 732 BC.[7]

29. A relief cut in the second half of the eighth century BC on a rock face at Ivriz. King Warpalawas of Tuhana is shown before the god Tarhunzas. Beneath it, a torrent of clear water has been diverted to irrigate the whole valley.

One of these was Warpalawas, ruler of Tuhana, a country which included the fertile oasis of Tyana (modern Bor) astride the ancient highway which reaches the plateau from Cilicia and the Gulf of Adana. In the relief, the smaller figure is Warpalawas who stands in an attitude of prayer and is dominated by his god, Tarhunzas, a characteristically Hittite deity, laden with grapes and corn. Both figures are identified by hieroglyphic inscriptions, and the significance of their confrontation is not far to seek, since from the base of the cliff beneath them a great torrent of clear water gushed forth, now diverted to irrigate broad acres of orchard and vineyard. Certain details of the king's costume are clearly Hittite, but he wears a Phrygian fibula and the general iconography and the inscriptions are Luwian/Hittite.

30. Relief carvings of the eighth century BC from Karatepe, showing attendants and musicians at a banquet. On other slabs were carved the famous bilingual inscriptions in Luwian and Phoenician.

There is a link here with Karatepe, the site of a ruined palace high up in the Ceyhan valley above Cilicia, where a bilingual inscription was found which made it possible to interpret the Hittite hieroglyphs. In the inscription Aza-tiwatas, who gave this place his name in the eighth century BC, refers to the king of Adana – another ruler in the Tabalian alliance.[8] But the Karatepe reliefs which accompanied the inscriptions indicate a much more confused cultural background, in which Phoenician and even Egyptian influences are imposed on the Aramaean and Hittite. The content of the now famous bilingual text would imply that this may also have been one of the few points of direct contact between the Neo-Hittite states and the early Greek settlers, whose fortunes we must presently follow.

CHAPTER 8

The Coming of
the Greeks

In Chapter 5 we saw the Late Bronze Age peoples of the Aegean coast and its islands disturbed and displaced by a wave of conquests or migrations which cannot as yet be satisfactorily explained. Nor, in the obscurity of the twelfth and eleventh centuries BC, can historians at present profess to see more than an interval of confusion, anticipating the repopulation of the area by Greeks from the European mainland. Even the approximate date at which this movement itself began to develop would be hard to estimate, were it not for the evidence provided by archaeological excavations. Significant in this respect is the discovery in the deepest occupation levels at sites such as Old Smyrna of the so-called Protogeometric painted pottery, which can be dated to the tenth century BC. Other evidence suggests that the wave of migration which resulted in the settlement of the Eastern Greeks on the coast of Asia Minor had already begun to subside in about 800 BC, so the whole process may have been completed within a period of about two centuries. As for the identity and antecedents of the new settlers, we are left to accept or reject their own traditional beliefs, as conveyed to us by their later historians such as Strabo and Pausanias. They are in any case largely restricted to the so-called Ionians, who settled in the middle reaches of the coast, between Smyrna and Miletus, and are said to have been refugees from the northern Peloponnese. They appear to have assembled in Athens before embarking for migration overseas.

Of the twelve earliest Ionian settlements which afterwards became important cities or city-states, two were on the offshore islands of Chios and Samos. The others were Phocaea and Clazomenae, on opposite sides of the Gulf of Smyrna; Erythrae, on the peninsula facing Chios; Teos and Lebedos on the southern side of the same peninsula; Colophon, nine miles inland; Ephesus, again south, at the mouth of the Cayster; and Priene, Myus and Miletus, in the estuary of the Maeander. Added to these at some slightly later date was Smyrna, originally

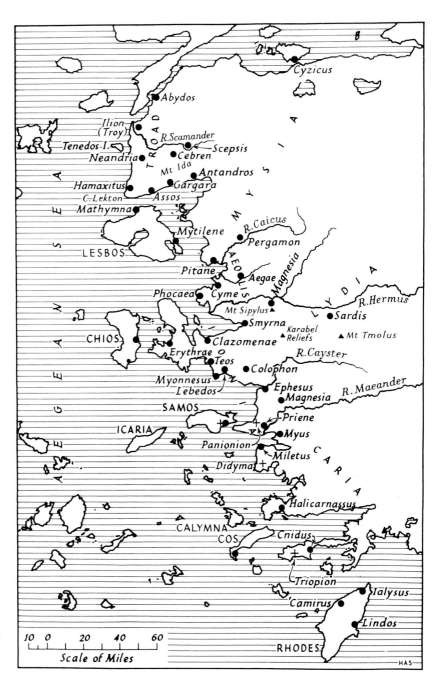

31. Map of Ionia, from
J. M. Cook, *The Greeks in
Ionia and the East*,
London 1962.

founded by Aeolian settlers. Much less is known about the Aeolians who
formed the second branch of the great eastern migration. Their speech in later
times seemed to suggest for them an origin in Boeotia and Thessaly. Their
primary base was in the island of Lesbos, where their first settlement, Mytilene,
was to become one of the greatest cities of the Aegean. The earliest Aeolian

settlements on the mainland occupied the coast to the north of Phocaea, between Cyme and Pitane, and extended up the valley of the Caicus towards Magnesia. Their further extension northwards was apparently barred in these early years by the survival of a Late Bronze Age state which they knew as Mysia. Beyond this, however, Lesbos was able to colonise the Troadic coast as far as Troy itself. To the south of Ionia, it remains to mention the Dorians from Megara on the Greek mainland who, after occupying the islands of Rhodes and Cos, settled on the western peninsulas of Caria and founded two great cities, Halicarnassus and Cnidus.

There is little doubt that a great many other sites were tentatively chosen in the early stages of settlement and afterwards either abandoned or annexed to the territory of some more prosperous neighbour. It has never been difficult to imagine the location and character of these pioneer coastal establishments. If one examines and compares those that are known, it is easy to recognise the cautious attempts of these nautical adventurers to gain a foothold on the coast of a foreign and potentially hostile country. Nevertheless, they were to some extent assisted and encouraged in this by the geographical formation of the Aegean coastline, with its plentiful estuaries and protected fiords. In any of these, a miniature island might suggest itself as a temporary refuge while the adjoining mainland was being investigated. If we are to believe tradition, this happened, for instance, in the case of Ephesus,[1] where the first band of migrant Ionians found an indigenous community (Carians and Lelegians) already established on the southern shore of the Cayster estuary. They themselves first settled on a small neighbouring island, but later took over the native township and adapted it to their own idea of a city. The same situation is to be seen at the site called Bayraklı, on the northern shore of the Gulf of Smyrna, where another band of Ionians established themselves on a small island joined by a causeway to the mainland. Old Smyrna survived there until shortage of space necessitated its removal to the site on which the modern city stands.

J. M. Cook's excavations at Bayraklı in collaboration with Ekrem Akurgal deserve a further mention at this point, because with the exception of a minor sounding at Phocaea (modern Foça), and the German excavations of the deeper levels in the old city at Miletus, they alone have created an acceptable picture of just such a fortified settlement as we have tried to describe: the Dark Age embryo of a Greek city, of a sort which has rarely been revealed by excavations on the mainland of Greece. It is still all very primitive indeed with single-compartment, mud-brick cottages, the smoke from their domestic hearths escaping through vents in the thatched roof. But, by the ninth century BC, the island had been flattened and extended to accommodate 400–500 families and it was surrounded by a substantial city wall, with a stone substructure and a broad walk behind its embattled parapet. After a disaster in about 700 BC when it was destroyed, it was rebuilt to a more systematic plan, with better houses, some of them having more than one storey and a simple shrine for a patron deity.[2]

In his useful book on the Eastern Greeks Cook devotes a whole chapter to what he calls the 'Ionic Renascence' in the seventh and sixth centuries BC, that is 'the expansion of Ionia to its full stature in the Mediterranean world'. But before summarising his account, we should perhaps anticipate a little by considering (since we have not yet done so) the subsequent status of the Eastern Greek cities in classical history, to which all these pioneer activities served as a prelude. It will have been noticed that, except in connection with the Aeolian settlements in the Troad, we have hitherto intentionally avoided the words 'colony' or 'colonisation' when referring to the new foundations, since this would impute to them some sort of provinciality. For in following the development of their civilisation, we may, as Cook himself says, 'note the emergence of certain distinctive qualities of character and intellect among them. But we must bear in mind that they were never isolated from the Greeks of the Greek mainland; the Aegean was always the focus of Greek civilization and, unlike their compatriots in southern Italy and Sicily, these Eastern Greeks were not in any sense colonials.' In a word, they were an extension of Greece itself, destined to contribute as much, if not more, to the aggregate of Greek cultural development as the older cities of the west.

Yet paradoxically it was the 'colonial' policy of the Eastern Greeks themselves which played a major part in promoting the Ionic Renascence. During the eighth century BC, the cities had succeeded in extending their territories some way eastward up the river valleys towards the Asiatic interior, and in doing so they had so far met with little opposition. Lydia, for instance, with its capital at Sardis in the hinterland of Smyrna, seems not yet to have been sufficiently well organised politically to oppose their expansion, while the frontiers of the Phrygian kingdom must still have seemed reassuringly remote. But, as a sequel to the destruction of Gordium by the Cimmerians in about 700 BC, the sudden rise to power of Sardis, under its ambitious Mermnad dynasty, changed the situation completely, creating an effective barrier against further Ionian encroachment. For the Greeks, whose need of living space was becoming increasingly acute, this new frustration must have presented a problem which could only be solved by once more taking to the sea – an expedient which would readily commend itself to the more adventurous spirits among them. By the mid-seventh century, therefore, an ambitious policy of overseas sub-colonisation had been inaugurated, and the initiative in this movement had been taken by the great city of Miletus. For the Milesians, the pitiful inadequacy of their territory had long threatened a crisis in their political development, for which their far-reaching trade connections now served to suggest the most obvious remedy. As a great seaport, Miletus already possessed the requisite geographical information and experienced navigators.

Since a line of Aeolian colonies already occupied the coast as far as Troy, the Milesians went beyond, to the Narrows of the Dardanelles, where they founded Abydus (Çanakkale) on the Asiatic shore. Next came Cyzicus, on the southern shore of the Propontis (Marmara), whose hinterland provided them with a broad agricultural province of the sort which they so badly needed. At about the same time, the Dorians of Megara, no longer content with their

primary foundations in western Caria, planted a group of colonies at the eastern end of the Marmara, of which the most successful was Byzantium; so it remained for the Milesians to interest themselves in the Black Sea coast beyond. Here they founded Sinope, which soon proved its value as a trade outlet for the products of the north Anatolian provinces. The much coveted 'steel' of the Chalybes could be shipped from here to the Aegean; also the red ochre of Cappadocia and hardwood from the Pontic forests, both of which were in demand among the Greeks. Sinope shared these commercial advantages with its own satellite colony at Trapezus (Trebizond/Trabzon) until the foundation of Heraclea (Ereğli) gained the advantage by reducing in length the dangerous sea route from the Bosphorus. After this, settlements along the south coast of the Black Sea soon multiplied, bringing the important provinces of Bithynia and Paphlagonia within the Greek sphere of influence. In due course, many of them are shown by historical records to have become cities, yet to judge by their surviving architectural remains, their alien climate and remote situation may have been less conducive to civil aggrandisement than the familiar comforts of the Aegean and Mediterranean coasts.

Meanwhile, in the extreme south-west the progress of colonisation seems to have been temporarily halted by the inhospitable aspect of Lycia, a mountainous province projecting into the sea with few if any coastal communications. The Greeks found Lycia already occupied by a stubbornly conservative indigenous people, who during the centuries that followed seem to have been prepared to accept the benefits of Greek civilisation while remaining politically

32. The theatre at Miletus was first built by the Greeks in the fourth century BC. In its final phase in Roman times it could seat 15,000. It supports the remains of the Byzantine city wall. Beneath the theatre are the remains of a tower belonging to the archaic city of Miletus.

aloof. Dorians from Rhodes eventually planted a single colony at Phaselis, on its east coast, but it remained hardly more than a convenient seaport facilitating trade with Cyprus and the Levant. In the provinces to the east of Lycia, in Pamphylia and Cilicia, the situation during and after the Dark Age remains historically less easy to define. If Greek tradition is to be believed, both coastal plains had been partially colonised by Achaean adventurers after the Trojan War. If so, by the seventh century their towns must have already become Hellenised, though in the eyes of historians at this time they did not rank as Greek cities.

In this way then, during the centuries which preceded the Persian conquest, Ionians, Aeolians and Dorians populated the northern and western coasts of Anatolia and developed some relationship with the part-Hellenised cities of its Mediterranean seaboard. In doing so, the twelve cities of Ionia about whom most is known temporarily united themselves in a Pan-Ionic League, primarily a religious federation based on a cult of Poseidon whose principal sanctuary was at Melia, on the north coast of the Mycale peninsula which faces the island of Samos. This development was remarkable only as an instance – rare in these early days – of some impulse among the newly founded cities towards mutual association. For although, during the seventh and early sixth centuries, they had grown to attain a hitherto unparalleled degree of civic maturity, collectively adhering to the uniform pattern of political order, ethical convention and aesthetic sensibility which constituted the hallmark of Greek civilisation, yet each at the same time cultivated and jealously maintained a self-conscious individuality of the sort which could only lead to bitter rivalries and perennial hostility between one state and another. For all practical purposes, the cities seem at this time to have been irremediably disunited, and later to have suffered accordingly when called upon to face aggression from the military powers of the Asiatic interior.

The shortcomings of a nation composed of multiple city-states with divided and unpredictable loyalties could be amply illustrated by other historical examples. In the present case one must remember that a similar situation existed among the older states of the Greek mainland, and its results will presently be seen reflected in the tangle of changing alliances which bedevilled the military enterprise of later times.

By contrast, it would next be reasonable to examine the actual accomplishments of the Eastern Greeks at this time and the contribution which they made to the increasing stature of Greek culture. And here, though the literary records that have survived are of some help, material evidence in the form of art and architecture is still regrettably scanty. This must be attributed to a variety of factors connected with the siting and subsequent development of the earliest cities, by which their remains have today been rendered archaeologically inaccessible. The miniature islands or projecting promontories in the estuaries of the great rivers, which so easily recommended themselves to the early settlers, were doomed in a few generations to be overwhelmed by the rising tide of alluvial deposit or isolated by the receding shoreline. They were aban-

doned by their inhabitants when a new site was chosen, and earthquakes and tidal waves have obliterated their remains, so that in many cases they can no longer be located. Cities at other sites chosen with greater foresight survived for many centuries, but with the process of expansion and repeated rebuilding, traces of their original occupation have become deeply buried. Rare exceptions such as the site of Old Smyrna and the ancient citadel at Miletus have already been mentioned, and from these both painted pottery and fragmentary remains of architecture have been recovered in comparatively recent times.

The history of temple building by the Greeks goes back no further than the final decades of the eighth century BC. Earlier forms of worship took place in the open air, and a simple stone altar was the only requirement of a cult centre. This was found to have been the case at both the sites mentioned above, and it was clear that a roofed building only became necessary when a venerable cult-image with votive paraphernalia needed to be enclosed and protected. This appears to have happened first at the shrine of Hera at Samos where, some time before 700 BC, a long rectangular building was erected, its

33. The theatre at Myra, isolated by the rising alluvium which has covered the ancient city and silted up many other coastal sites.

roof supported on a single row of wooden posts. A generation later this was replaced by a more substantial sanctuary of mud-brick on a stone foundation, and the covered 'veranda' which surrounded it, supported on posts, established a precedent for the peripteral (i.e. surrounded by a peristyle or row of pillars) planning of Greek temples throughout the ages. Also, the precinct which surrounded it was for the first time provided with a free-standing porch or *stoa*, another indispensable feature of later Greek architecture. When the first all-stone temples came to be built in the early sixth century, their Ionic proportions and style of ornament distinguished them from the Doric order which was prevalent on the Greek mainland, and in particular the voluted capitals of their columns became a criterion of Eastern Greek design. In the first half of the sixth century, with the canonical details of the Ionic order now fully established, the Heraeum of Samos was once more rebuilt, this time on a gigantic scale. It stood upon a stone platform 117 metres long, with columns 1.5 metres in diameter and almost 14 metres high, supporting a gabled roof above its heavy entablature.

But the primacy of Samian architecture was no longer to remain unchallenged. Ephesus was now competing with Samos for the monopoly of the Aegean trade routes, and the rivalry between the two cities had begun to be expressed in more spectacular forms of ostentation. It was now, therefore, that the first great temple of Artemis – the so-called Archaic Artemisium – was built on the alluvium of the Cayster estuary, on a scale which made it the largest building of the Greek world. Its double rows of external columns were 19 metres high and gave the building an overall length of 115 metres. It was still under construction when Croesus occupied Ephesus in about 561 BC, but he contributed to its completion and it survived until the birth of Alexander the Great. The Samian Heraeum was destroyed by fire during the Persian conquest in about 520 BC.

The Eastern Greeks were late in adapting themselves to the art of sculpture, but early in the sixth century it would seem to have been introduced to them by the craftsmen of Naxos, long noted for their skill in the art of carving marble. From then onwards, both architectural sculptures and votive statues acquired popularity, their style retaining the archaic conventions of the Greek mainland, though acquiring certain individual characteristics. In vase-painting too the Ionians lagged behind their contemporaries in Attica. The orientalising heraldry of the East Greek style persisted long after the evolution in Athens of the beautiful black-figure technique, which came to the Eastern cities fully perfected in the mid-sixth century.

Regarding the social and political development of the Ionian city communities after their Dark Age adolescence, it is surprising to find that our most rewarding source of information is in the Homeric poems. (Any mention of the long-standing controversy concerning their authorship would here clearly be out of place, and it is tempting to content oneself with Mark Twain's conclusion that they 'were written by a blind poet called Homer, or if that was not so, by another blind poet of the same name'.) The Greeks believed that

Homer was born at Smyrna, though he afterwards taught on the island of Chios, and scholars today date his lifetime to the eighth or very early seventh century BC. Many details of his two great epics make it clear that, though the events with which they are concerned took place some five hundred years earlier, their setting has been unconsciously assimilated to the Ionian world of the poet's own time. As J. M. Cook points out,

> In Homer we find cities of the classical Greek type, with walls which enclose the whole urban population, and temples for public worship. Cities like this are something totally different from the Mycenaean citadels of Late Bronze Age Greece, and they imply a new conception of city life in which every citizen has his share. The houses of the gods on earth must also be new.... Kings are an essential part of the Homeric stories, and kingship is therefore nearly always present in Homer. But the idea of citizenship is already well advanced in the poems, and government appears to function with a council of elders (*boule*) and a popular assembly (*agora*).... On the balance of all available evidence, it seems unlikely that there was much left of the monarchy in the Ionic cities of Homer's own day.[3]

Where abstract thought and logical reasoning were concerned, great advances were made by the Greeks of this period, and some of the first thinkers to become public celebrities were born or lived in the cities of Asia Minor. One of these was Thales of Miletus, whose mind seems to have been the first capable of discarding traditional conceptions regarding the origin and purpose of human existence and formulating alternative theories for critical examination. Following this principle of reasoning, another Milesian, Anaximander, postulated a primeval 'infinity' of neutral material from which the elements were constructed, but showed more practical ingenuity in making a map of the earth and inventing the sundial. Many other names are remembered to this day. Pythagoras was born in Samos in the same century. Later came Parmenides with his pupil Zeno, who challenged existing theories of objective observation, and Heraclitus of Ephesus, who substituted intuitive understanding. These and many others contributed to the process of dialectical enquiry which enriched the intellectual climate of Greek thought at this time.

It has been possible in these few paragraphs only briefly to recollect some of the early attainments of the Asiatic Greeks in laying the foundations of a civilisation whose full flowering is to be seen in classical times. More will be said on the subject and their cities revisited when they reach the peak of their maturity in the aftermath of the Persian conquest.

CHAPTER 9

The Reign
of Croesus

We have already had reason to mention the name of Lydia, a state or nation which, under another name, may well have existed long before the arrival of the Phrygians. During the centuries which followed the Trojan War, Lydia would appear to have become separated from the Aegean coast by the barrier of newly founded Greek colonies, yet somehow to have retained a measure of independence during the Phrygian conquest and domination of the plateau. Certainly it survived the Cimmerian invasion which, in about 695 BC, brought the Phrygian empire to an end, for no more than twenty years later, in its capital at Sardis, a new dynasty was founded, inaugurating a line of powerful Lydian kings whose rule brought their country into the mainstream of contemporary history.

And here, from an historical viewpoint, we at last find ourselves on much firmer ground. For we are able to draw on the works, for instance, of Xanthus, a Lydian historian who flourished in about 480 BC and wrote 'Four Books of Lydian History', fragments of which have survived; on Strabo, who adopted other information from the same source; and finally on Herodotus. Herodotus was attracted by and interested in the story of the Lydian kings, which he recounts in great detail, embroidering with suitable dialogue incidents which were the current tradition of his time and have been accepted in later ages as evoking the philosophy and ethics of Greece. First, however (Book I, Ch. 6), he gives a rather credulous genealogy of the Lydian people, listing two dynasties previous to that with which we are concerned. The second of these should be the more informative of the two, since it is associated with the Heraclidae, traditional rulers of the Peloponnese. But as it includes the names of Belus and Ninus – fabulous Mesopotamian kings – its historical value appears to be minimal. From other information which he provides, it has however proved possible to conclude that: 'the country known to the Greeks as Lydia was anciently occupied by a race distinct and yet not wholly alien from the Lydian, who were called Maeonians. This people was conquered by the Lydians, and either fled westwards across the sea or submitted to the conquerors. . . .'[1]

Next, the story itself begins, rather dramatically, with the accession to the Lydian throne of Gyges, the first king of the family called Mermnadae (685 BC). The anecdote about his replacement of the last king of the previous dynasty begins with the intriguing sentence, 'Now it happened that Candaules was in love with his own wife . . .' (Book I, Ch. 8). It then tells at some length how Candaules, anxious to confirm his own rapturous admiration of her beauty, arranged for Gyges, an incredulous friend, to watch from a discreet hiding-place when his wife was preparing for bed. The plan miscarried, and the queen, understandably incensed, secretly compelled Gyges to contrive her husband's assassination. It ends therefore with Gyges acquiring both Candaules' throne and his queen, not without some opposition from the partisans of the Heracli-dae. This quarrel was resolved by an appeal to the Delphic Oracle – a precedent frequently followed by Gyges' successors. All we can say of Gyges himself, once he had become king, is that in other and more significant ways he set the pattern of military aggression which was to be followed by his descendants. He brought to an end the long-standing tradition of tolerance towards the Greek cities on the coast by attacking Miletus, Smyrna and Colophon. While preoccupied in this way, he found himself faced by a new inroad of nomadic hordes from beyond the Black Sea, once more described by most historians as Cimmerians, and on this occasion he took the bold step of appealing for help to Assyria. One is reminded of the great distance separating the Lydian kingdom from Mesopotamia if one observes that Ashurbanipal, who received the message in about 663 BC, had in fact never heard of the 'Luddi' (Lydians). He does, however, seem to have sent some sort of material assistance to Gyges, which enabled him for the time being to repulse the 'Gimmarai'. This new association with one of the great powers of his time seems to have gone to Gyges' head, for a little later one finds him interfering with Assyrian interests by supporting Egypt against them, and this of course ended in disaster. The Gimmarai, having renewed their attack in 652 BC, defeated and slew Gyges before entering and partially destroying Sardis. Its high citadel, however, proved impregnable and the Cimmerian occupation of Lydia must have been short-lived; for Gyges' successor Ardys resumed the war against the Greeks. He in fact became involved in an ineffectual struggle with the great seaport city of Miletus which prolonged itself throughout the reign of his son Sadyattes. It was eventually terminated by the next king, Alyattes. He attributed a breakdown in his own health to the retribution of the Greek gods, whose shrines around Miletus his troops had violated.

Lydia seems, in the meanwhile, to have been extending its political authority over a large part of the old Phrygian kingdom, and in 590 BC Alyattes found himself in conflict with a power far more formidable than the individual cities of Ionia. The Medes, who had destroyed Nineveh in 612 BC and brought to an end the Assyrian Empire, were now moving westward through Cappadocia

34. Tablet recording an embassy of King Gyges of Lydia to King Ashurbanipal of Assyria (668–627 BC). It is written in the cuneiform script on clay. British Museum (K. 2675).

with further conquests in view. Supported as they were by Babylonian and other allies, it seems surprising that they should have met with such determined resistance from Lydia. But the status and extent of the kingdom which Alyattes had inherited and enlarged can be gathered from the fact that the war, after prolonging itself for five years, was satisfactorily terminated by a treaty which established the river Halys as the common frontier of the two powers. The date of this treaty, symbolically sealed by a marriage between Alyattes' daughter and Astyages, son of the Median king Cyaxares, is conveniently dated to 585 BC by Herodotus' mention of a solar eclipse.

After settling his affairs with the Medes, Alyattes seems to have spent a part of his remaining years in building himself a suitably spectacular burial mound, somewhat in the manner of the 'Midas' tomb at Gordium. Its remains, plundered in antiquity and much damaged by illicit digging in later times, occupy a prominent position in the great Lydian necropolis, not at Sardis itself, but six miles to the north at Bin Tepe, between the Hermus river and the Gygean Lake (Mermere Gölü).

The many scores of burial tumuli at Bin Tepe[2] vary in size very considerably, but the Tomb of Alyattes is undoubtedly the largest. It was examined and even excavated by several European travellers in the last century. W. J. Hamilton[3] reported having taken ten minutes to ride round it and estimated its circumference at half a mile. This would give it a diameter somewhat smaller than that of 355 metres measured by Spiegelthal, the 'Prussian Consul at Smyrna', who in 1853 succeeded in finding an empty burial-chamber, probably one of several and not part of the central complex. It has a flat ceiling and is built of finely dressed marble masonry with some of the earliest examples of lead clamps. The mound is surrounded by a retaining wall (*crepis*) of huge limestone slabs. G. Rawlinson[4] reproduces Spiegelthal's (?) engraving of the interior. The American excavators of Sardis[5] worked for a time on a comparable burial mound, thought to be the tomb of Gyges, but failed to find a tomb chamber. Other information of varying reliability is given by Herodotus (Book I, Ch. 93). Some of the tumuli at Bin Tepe are known to have been crowned with phallus-shaped finial ornaments and he says that Alyattes' tomb had five of these, representing the various social classes at Sardis whose work had contributed to the building of the mound. Most prominent were the prostitutes, a fact which Herodotus explains by one of those statements for which he is heavily censured by Rawlinson: 'The daughters of the common people in Lydia', he said, 'one and all pursue this traffic, wishing to collect money for their portions.' One of these finials survived until recently.

Croesus, the last king of the Mermnad dynasty, had already reached the advanced age of 35 when he succeeded his father Alyattes, sometime between 560 and 557 BC. The modest empire which he inherited is said by Herodotus to have included all the peoples of Asia Minor 'within the Halys', except Cilicia and Lycia, which one may suppose to have been protected by their mountains. Like the earlier kings, he at once set about ensuring the subordination of the Greek cities, but one receives the impression that his initiative in this respect lacked the ferocity of his predecessors and in fact met with only token resistance. Clearly his intention fell short of obtaining actual sovereignty over them, being concerned rather with tribute in kind and commercial privileges. Ephesus, for instance, was his first objective, and the story has long been familiar of how the Greeks connected their city by a rope almost a mile long with the sacred precinct of Artemis outside the walls, thus ensuring it divine protection. Croesus also seems to have accepted the canonical implication and reached a settlement with the Ephesians, which required of them little more than the dismantling of their frontier fortresses and the replacement of their current ruler. It is added by one historian[6] that, in order further to conciliate their goddess, he 'gave substantial aid to the restoration of her temple, which had been in progress since the Cimmerian attack about a century before'.

This statement is in fact a little difficult to reconcile with the history of the great Artemisium, as now revealed by excavations. The building which Herodotus himself had seen in the fifth century BC was that now referred to as the Archaic Artemisium and known to have been tragically destroyed by fire in 356 BC. It was replaced by the even more magnificent temple whose remains

35. One of the columns of the Artemisium at Ephesus has been re-erected, but this is all that can now be seen of what was, in Hellenistic times, one of the Seven Wonders of the World.

were discovered by J. T. Wood in 1869 (see Chapter 16). But it is now known that the Archaic temple itself was begun during the decade between 560 and 550 BC and, as Croesus is thought to have succeeded to the Lydian throne in about 560 BC, it may well have been completed before his threat to Ephesus. It is, of course, certainly true that earlier shrines, in one form or another, had already occupied the site for many generations. Our information on this subject we owe mainly to D. G. Hogarth[7] who, in 1904, was sent out to Ephesus by the British Museum to investigate, if possible, what lay beneath the gigantic platform on which the Archaic temple was built. The objects he found provided dating evidence for the architectural remains with which they were associated. The earliest construction, consisting of no more than an altar, was built in about 700 BC, and was replaced a century later by a covered sanctuary or *naiskos*. In the time of Croesus this can no longer have existed.

To return then to contemporary history: we are told that, following the example of Ephesus, all the other Greek cities, both Ionian and Aeolian, now submitted to the military threat from Lydia, agreeing to periodical levies of money and men. They appear to have shown very little resentment on this score. Their historians on the whole speak favourably of Croesus and, indeed, only a few years later one finds them refusing help to his Asiatic enemies. Certainly the improved commercial facilities which he thus obtained contributed to the prosperity of his kingdom; for in the years which followed, its wealth became fabulous and his own name a byword for personal affluence. Clearly his capital at Sardis was advantageously placed as a centre for trade between the plateau provinces of Anatolia and the Greek seaports. Perhaps something further should be said at this point about its character.

The broad valley of the Hermus river (Gediz Çayı) in which the city stood is immensely fertile and agriculturally productive. Apart from the great Artemis temple, which replaced a shrine of the Lydian goddess Cybele, most of the ruins to be seen today date from Roman and later times. They lie astride the main road from Izmir to Ankara, at a point where a minor stream, anciently known as Pactolus and called by the Turks Sart Çayı, after the modern village, flows out into the open plain from between broken hills of soft conglomerate. One of these, rising abruptly from the river bank to a great height, forms the acropolis, from which the city fans out northwards in terraces. Here the work of American archaeologists has mostly been concerned with buildings of the third century AD, but Lydian houses and tombs have also been found and a deep sounding has reached sub-Mycenaean (twelfth century BC) levels which could be equated with the Heraclid tradition. One of their minor discoveries, among buildings on the east bank of the Pactolus, dated between 600 and 580 BC, was a structure identified as an 'installation for refining gold'[8] and this has a special significance because Croesus was said to have owed his great wealth in part to the productive gold-washings of the Pactolus, as well as to the gold-mines in the neighbouring mountains.[9] Herodotus mentions as a Lydian invention the minting of coinage, and gold coins were certainly in use during Croesus' time. But the reality of his wealth in precious metals can in any case hardly be doubted in view of the offerings which he made to the Delphic and other Greek oracles. As Rawlinson reminds us, 'Herodotus had himself seen the ingots of solid gold, six palms long, three broad and one deep (the size of a tall folio volume, of about the usual thickness), which to the number of one hundred and seventeen were laid up in the treasury at Delphi'.[10]

36. Silver stater of Sardis, Lydia, representing the earliest known phase of silver coinage about 540 BC. British Museum (BMC 1982–7–35–1). Width 21 mm.

and he goes on to list some of the other treasures presented by Croesus to various Greek temples. In fact, Herodotus' own detailed account of their history is totally convincing. He refers for instance to 'two bowls of enormous size, one of gold, the other of silver, which used to stand, the latter upon the right, the former upon the left, as one entered the temple (at Delphi)'. And he adds: 'They too were removed at the time of the fire; and now the gold one is in the Clazomenian Treasury.... The silver one stands in the corner of the ante-chapel and holds six hundred amphorae' (about 5,000 gallons).

So, for the time being, Croesus rules peacefully in his capital at Sardis, on increasingly good terms with the Greeks, who, 'not yet thoroughly schooled to set a gulf between themselves and "Barbarians", seem to have regarded him as almost one of themselves.... Seen as he was by his visitors leading a life hardly distinguished from the Ionian except by its greater splendour, the friendship which he showed to the Greek city-states was accepted in the spirit in which it was tendered.'[11] It was at this time that he was visited by Solon, the famous Athenian legislator, who was now almost 80 years old, and we have Herodotus' story of the encounter between the two very different personalities with the apocryphal dialogue which took place between them.

This legend, or at least its details, must have originated long after Croesus' death, when the disaster which eventually overwhelmed him was common knowledge, and Solon's admonitory precepts clearly profit from hindsight. 'Whom', Croesus asked, 'would you consider to be the happiest of men?', to which Solon, avoiding the obviously anticipated reply, responded by citing the names of some obscure acquaintances in Greece; and then, after noting Croesus' understandable disappointment, treated him to a homily on the unpredictability of fate, broadly concluding that 'no man can be deemed happy until the manner of his death is known'. Rawlinson observes Solon's phrase 'The power above us is full of jealousy (*phthoneron*)', but discards the parallel with the 'Jealous God' of Scripture, on the grounds that Herodotus' own conception is that of a capricious rather than an avenging deity. As Rawlinson puts it, 'Prosperity, not pride, eminence, not arrogance provokes him. He does not like anyone to be happy but himself.' He then adds rather interestingly, 'What is most remarkable is, that with such a conception of the Divine Nature, Herodotus could maintain such a placid, cheerful, childlike temper. Possibly he was serene because he felt secure in his own mediocrity.'[12]

Herodotus relates one more incident in this otherwise happy period of Croesus' reign. This was the story of how his favourite son, Atys, was accidentally killed while hunting boar. Croesus is said to have suspended all political activity for as much as two years while he mourned his loss, but it was at the end of this time, in about 548 BC, that he began to be involved in the military adventure which led to his downfall. Once more Lydia was called upon to combat the ambitions of an eastern conqueror, and in this case the initiative was her own.

Sometime before 550 BC the hegemony of the Medes in Iran and Armenia had been challenged and subverted by Cyrus, the founding father of what was to become the Achaemenid dynasty. Alyattes' old treaty with the Medes, establishing their frontier on the Halys river, had apparently worked well and been respected by both sides for a whole generation. But it will be remembered that it had been sealed by a royal marriage, as a result of which the Median king now displaced by Cyrus was in fact Croesus' own brother-in-law. Being, as he probably was, poorly informed about the aggressive strength of Cyrus' army, this may have presented itself to Croesus as a *casus belli*, for he now began to cast a covetous eye upon the attractive province of Cappadocia, beyond the Halys. First, however, since it had become the fashion with Lydian kings, much time had to be wasted in consulting a number of Greek oracles. By the time that convoys of suitable gifts had been sent, their sealed replies assembled for simultaneous perusal, and an arbitrary interpretation made of their ambiguous pronouncements, the summer was over and the winter had to be spent in assembling levies from tributary states to support the Lydian army. In the spring of 547 BC, Croesus crossed the Halys (at a point misleadingly described by Herodotus as being 'near Sinope') and spent much of the summer in unopposed raiding. It must have been autumn by the time that Cyrus' army arrived, and an inconclusive battle was fought near a city called Pteria (which may or may not have been Hittite Hattusas). What happened next may well be regarded as one of the curiosities of military history, for Croesus, having decided that the campaigning season was in any case practically over, packed up and went back to Sardis, where he paid off his levies, intending during the course of the winter to solicit help from mainland Greece, Egypt, Babylon and elsewhere. Cyrus, on the other hand, 'with a nice disregard for the rules of the game as played in his day', leisurely reorganised his army and followed by the same route. According to Herodotus, Croesus remained unaware of this until the Persian army actually made its appearance in the Hermus valley. In the battle which ensued, the famous Lydian cavalry, hastily mobilised, might still have put up some resistance had not Cyrus once more broken the rules of conventional warfare. Exploiting a zoological peculiarity with which he had probably been familiar since his childhood, he protected the vanguard of his attack with a screen of baggage-camels whose smell had a predictable effect on the Lydian horses. In the resulting chaos he secured an easy victory. Sardis was taken.

Croesus himself and his entourage seem to have found time to withdraw into the citadel, which in the time of Gyges the Cimmerians had regarded as impregnable. The Persians, however, scaled the rock by a neglected path, down which one of them had seen a Lydian soldier climb in pursuit of his bouncing helmet. So the citadel too was taken. Of the two incidents described by Herodotus which resulted in Croesus' own life being saved, many consider the first to be the most appealing. It concerns his younger son, to whom he was very much attached though he was deaf and dumb. During the confusion after the capture of the citadel, a Persian soldier, not recognising the king, was about to strike him down, when the boy, finding his voice for the first time, cried out 'Man, do not kill Croesus', and his father was then brought before

37. Croesus of Lydia on his pyre. Design on an Attic amphora of the first half of the fifth century BC, found in Italy in 1829 and now in the Louvre in Paris. From A. Furtwängler and K. Reichhold (ed. F. Hauser), *Griechische Vasenmalerei*, II, Munich 1909, pl. 113.

Cyrus. The second episode, when a sudden storm extinguished the flames around the pyre on which he was to be burnt alive, has too much in common with other classical legends to be plausible. His reputed cry *in extremis*, 'O, Solon, Solon' (which had to be explained to Cyrus), also seems particularly improbable, since Herodotus himself records that Croesus had been glad to see the last of the Athenian, whom he thought 'an arrant fool'. The fact remains, however, if any credence at all can be given to the Greek historian, that Cyrus was much attracted by his prisoner, treated him with great consideration and even, on some subsequent occasions, accepted his advice. Croesus by all accounts seems to have had a magnetic personality and Greek writers other than Herodotus made much poetry out of his life-story.

There was a final attempt to displace the Persians from Sardis, when a Lydian called Pactyas (his name occurs elsewhere in the legend of the birds' nests at the Didyma temple), who had been enlisted to help the new satrap in collecting and packing Croesus' treasure, absconded with the money and used it to raise an army. And then one by one, the Greek cities also submitted to Persian rule.

CHAPTER 10

Urartu: a Long-Forgotten Nation

It must already have become apparent in these pages that the history of Anatolia during the four or five centuries preceding the Persian conquest in 547 BC comprises so many regional developments and such complicated interactions between them, that it cannot easily be condensed into a single narrative. Hittites, driven from the plateau by the Phrygians, creating a barrier of city-states in the Taurus and northern Syria; a Phrygian kingdom in the west, ultimately destroyed by an influx of Cimmerian nomads, but adopted and revitalised by a rich Lydian dynasty; Lydians themselves debarred from the Aegean by a peripheral bulwark of Greek cities and from the Mediterranean by the stubborn independence of older native states; Median armies from Iran, confronting the Lydians on the line of the Halys river – each of these nations has its own individual history, documented in varying degrees by Greek or oriental sources and exhaustively studied in more recent times.

For our own purpose, it has seemed logical to consider each in turn, leaving until last a single nation, hardly mentioned till now, whose cultural attainments and political stability invest it with a unique individuality. This is the kingdom of Urartu, centred on Lake Van, which for almost three hundred years (ninth to seventh centuries BC) resisted the encroachment of its enemies, whether Cimmerians, Medes or Scythians, and watched the recoil of repeated Assyrian invasions.

38. The Urartian citadel at Van (Tushpa) has vanished beneath later rebuildings in medieval and Ottoman times.

We are today so copiously well informed about the ancient state of Urartu that it seems hardly credible that our information should have been so recently acquired. From the sixth century BC onwards all knowledge of its history, and even of its location, seems to have been expunged from the records of human memory with only occasional, distorted survivals in Armenian traditions. Only its name, wrongly spelt as Ararat, survived in the Old Testament. A first step leading to its rediscovery was taken in 1827, when a young scholar called

Schulz reported finding rock inscriptions and other ancient remains near the city of Van in eastern Turkey. Schulz himself had the misfortune to be murdered before he could return home, but the careful copies which he had made of forty-two cuneiform inscriptions safely reached Paris and were published in 1840. The language of these 'Vannic' texts proved to be unrelated to those of Mesopotamia, and a further sixty years elapsed before they were finally deciphered. Van could then be identified as the capital of a state whose name appeared frequently in the annals of the Assyrian kings and whose history could therefore be partly reconstructed. Further indications of its importance were provided by the results of excavations, remotely sponsored by the British Museum, which took place in 1879, being followed by a campaign of illicit

39. Beneath the citadel at Van, Urartian inscriptions and a rock-cut chamber dating from the eighteenth century BC.

digging which brought damaged Urartian antiquities to many European museums. More systematic investigations were made by a German team in 1898, and again by Russians during the First World War; but interest in the subject seemed then to decline. Little more was done until 1938, when Soviet archaeologists discovered the ruins of an Urartian city near Yerevan, north of the Araxes river. When their sensational finds became generally known in the 1950s, a great revival of Urartian archaeology took place. Many sites were excavated in the eastern provinces of Turkey, and today, thirty years later, our accumulated knowledge of this remarkable nation, of its geography, its economy and culture, particularly as affected by its environment, is beginning to present a strikingly complete picture.

First, then, from a geographical point of view, during its maximum territorial expansion in the eighth and seventh centuries BC Urartu was a very large state indeed. In addition to all the Anatolian provinces north or east of the upper Tigris and Euphrates, it occupied large parts of what are now Soviet Armenia and Iranian Azerbaijan. Included in this territory are three important lakes, Van, Urmia and Sevan, all lying at an average of 1,500 metres above sea-level, and a number of extinct volcanoes, of which Nemrut Dağ and Süphan,

40. A seventh-century BC Urartian bronze figure of a human-headed winged bull which decorated the throne of the god Haldi. The ivory face is now missing and the piece was originally gilded. It was found in the last century at Toprakkale (ancient Rusahinili) and is now in the British Museum (WAA 91247). Height 22 cm.

overlooking Lake Van, are hardly less impressive than Mount Ararat (Ağrı Dağ), near the modern Turco-Iranian frontier. Economically, this country had the most obvious natural assets. At the time we are considering it was fairly heavily forested and provided quantities of good timber. It was also, and still is, rich in metal ores, including silver, copper and iron. The grazing capacity of its valleys was almost unlimited and large herds of horses were bred, particularly near Lake Urmia. All the normal cereals of that time – wheat, barley, rye, spelt and sesame – were cultivated and grew abundantly. Estimates of the population are largely guesswork, but in the three principal provinces alone, no less than 750 'towns' are mentioned in the texts. We also know that successive kings dug vast irrigation canals and built reservoirs to increase the country's fertility and supply the towns.

Fine Urartian bronze casting and other metalwork influenced craftsmen as far afield as the Etruscan cities of Italy and suggests a very particular aptitude for this craft; even the surviving masonry of Urartian buildings creates the impression that the mason's tools were of high quality. It is also known that, in addition to beer, which was commonly drunk in Mesopotamia, the Urartians, of all the nations in the Old World, seem to have taken a precocious

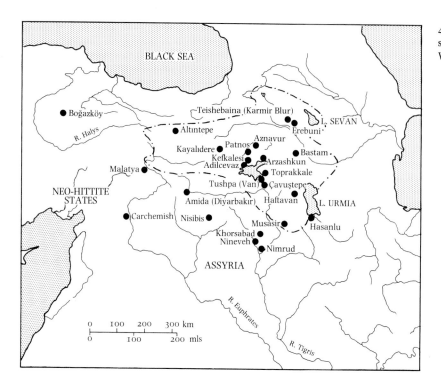

41. Map of Urartu. The sites cluster round Lake Van in the centre.

interest in planting vineyards and making wine. (It has even been pointed out that the Biblical story of Noah's drunkenness is traditionally associated with the district of Mount Ararat, and so with Urartu.)

All these facts could be learnt from the written records of the Urartians, but a great deal more has come to be known about the environmental background against which they lived, as a result of the increased accessibility of their ancient homeland in recent years. For this highland region of eastern Turkey has a character of its own which makes it well worth visiting.

There are several ways of reaching Lake Van, perhaps the least spectacular of which is the modern railway, which brings one to Tatvan at the westernmost extremity of the lake. It is now connected by steamer to Van itself for the continuation of the line into Iran. Alternatively one may approach it by the great Transit Route connecting Iran with the Black Sea, which brings one from Trabzon over the high passes of the Pontic Alps down to Erzurum; or more conventionally by the main road from Sivas, which crosses the old Urartian frontier a little before reaching Erzincan. South from Erzurum, the road follows the course first of the Aras, then of the Murat Su – the infant Euphrates, still a very small river with five hundred miles to go before it reaches Mesopotamia. Here it is part of an alpine landscape, sparsely populated, with a sense of great distances on either side. Reluctantly the road and river part, leaving one hopefully to await the first scattered habitations which herald the approach to Lake Van itself. Then, beyond an upward sweep in the hills, the lake itself appears for the first time – as H. F. B. Lynch once described it, 'glittering in brilliant indigo and streaming with sunshine'.[1] One comes down to it at Erciş from Ağrı along the estuary of another small river, a welcome oasis of rich soil, abundantly planted with trees. Here too, clustering around the outflow of the river, one sees shoals of dareka fish – the only species able to adapt itself to the curious consistency of the lake water. For Van is not a 'salt' lake, but heavily charged with soda. (One analysis has shown it to be the exact equivalent of $3\frac{1}{2}$ ounces of ordinary washing soda dissolved in one gallon of water, which makes it curiously smooth on the skin when one swims in it.)

Lake Van covers an area of 1,300 square miles (as Lynch points out, 'six times the size of Lake Geneva'). Small steamers ply between its coastal towns and there are a number of little islands, one of them, Akthamar, being much visited on account of its tenth-century Armenian church and monastery. Of the two volcanoes close to the northern shore, Nemrut Dağ is the most prominent, and one remembers how Lynch, who surveyed its crater, observed that a complete Urartian army could have concealed itself there (with ample drinking water), to descend upon invading Assyrians. Finally one comes to the city of Van itself (Tushpa of the Urartians), deep in the curve of the easternmost bay, with a smaller mountain behind it. The huge isolated citadel, now crowned by the ruins of an Ottoman fortress, stands up out of flat marshes near the shore, and behind it, irrigated today by natural streams, are several square miles of fruit-gardens surrounding the modern Turkish town. Here, on the citadel rock and on a shoulder of the adjoining hill known as Toprakkale, the palaces of the Urartian kings rose above the streets of their capital city, looking out across this beautiful lake, a sort of 'Highlanders' Nineveh', differing so greatly in its setting from the Assyrian capital on its brown and sluggish river.

This suggestion of a comparison between Van and Nineveh is less irrelevant than it may at first seem. For, in assessing the cultural status of the Urartians, there has in the past been a tendency to concentrate on their art, their religion and the content of their written records. Judged by the testimony of these, their ideas have been considered largely derivative and less than justice has been done to their civilised accomplishments. They have in fact been credited with no more than a pale reflection of Assyrian culture. If, on the other hand, further attention is paid to the architecture of their cities, their engineering works and the complex efficiency of their military and civil organisation, evidence becomes apparent of response to their peculiar environment and intelligent exploitation of its natural advantages, which sets them apart from the plain-dwellers in the south. Particularly one sees in their architecture that they have largely rejected the Mesopotamian traditions of building – square, flat-roofed labyrinths of brickwork, relieved only by occasional ziggurat towers, themselves composed of mud-brick and reeds. All this the Urartian builders had changed, providing themselves with plentiful building stone and adapting their designs to the landscape of their elevated mountain world, with its passes, lakes and fast-flowing rivers. One is tempted to credit them with having created an almost Arthurian atmosphere of terraced and turreted castles or fortresses, connected by roads, over which troops of well-mounted horsemen rode, among villages artificially supplied with water. From this perhaps over-fanciful picture of a people inhabiting a remote region of the Near East during the Iron Age, we may now turn to consider some of the known facts about their history.

There appears to be no reliable evidence to suggest that an actual state of Urartu existed earlier than the eleventh century BC. We do, however, find references in the Assyrian annals, as early as the thirteenth century, to tribal confederations around and to the south-east of Lake Van, against whom the Assyrian kings Shalmaneser I and his son Tukulti-Ninurta I undertook successful campaigns: their country is referred to as Urartu, or alternatively, as Nairi. An expedition of this sort is again described by Tiglath-Pileser I (1114–1047 BC), who claims to have subdued 'sixty kings of the land of Nairi' and to have exacted tribute from them which included 'twelve hundred horses'. He also mentions his arduous march through mountains and forests, where he was compelled to abandon his chariot. Otherwise, in these formal accounts of early Assyrian campaigns there is little to be learnt about the topography of Nairi. The identification of place-names is still largely guesswork, and no capital city is mentioned as such. Later, in the first half of the ninth century BC, it begins to be clear that, out of such earlier tribal groupings, a single and formidable state has begun to materialise, and in texts from the time of Ashurnasirpal II (883–859 BC), it is already frequently referred to as Urartu.

In the year following Ashurnasirpal's death, his successor, Shalmaneser III, undertook the first of several campaigns against Urartu, and at this point a new source of information becomes available which transforms the new state – with its dynastic rulers, armies and fortified cities – into a vivid reality. This is the pictorial account of the Assyrian king's exploits, modelled in relief on the famous bronze gates which have been recovered from his country palace at Balawat, near Nimrud, and are now mostly in the British Museum. Finely drawn, with remarkable attention to detail, they show a sequence of events in Shalmaneser's Urartian wars. Fortress cities, named in the accompanying inscriptions, are assaulted with scaling-ladders and destroyed by fire; loot is removed in carts, while the Urartian defenders, with their characteristic arms and equipment, are seen withdrawing into the hills behind. The Assyrian king 'washes his weapons' in Lake Van and a victory stela is carved on a neighbouring rock-face. Also recorded on the gates is an episode in Shalmaneser's third year, when he boasts of having destroyed Arzashkun, the 'Royal city of Aramu the Urartian'. This place has been tentatively located to the north of the lake, near Malazgirt (Manazgirt), where many centuries later the Seljuk Turks defeated a Byzantine army[2]. But in the last campaign of Shalmaneser's reign, in which he was too old to take an active part, the name is mentioned of a new Urartian king, 'Seduri [Sarduri], Ruler of Urartu', and his capital is now at Tushpa, which is Van itself.

The great citadel at Van, with its vertical rock-faces, is almost a mile long

42. Detail from one of the bronze strips decorating the gates of a palace at Balawat in northern Iraq. It depicts an episode in a campaign of Shalmaneser III of Assyria against Urartu in the mid-ninth century BC. The Assyrians are visiting the stalagmite-filled caves at the source of the Tigris, offering a sacrifice and recording the event by carving a stele representing their king. British Museum (WAA 124656).

and 200 yards wide. At its west end, today some distance from the lake, its summit is approached by a much-weathered stairway, and nearby there is a great bastion of masonry which may have been part of the defences or even a lakeside landing-place. It is built of ashlar blocks, some of them 20 feet long and weighing over 30 tons, on which an inscription is several times repeated, recording that Sarduri, King of Urartu, had 'procured this limestone from the city of Alniunu and erected this wall' (an Urartian quarry has been located near Edremit, south of Van). These earliest inscriptions of Sarduri I are still written in Assyrian. Later kings soon succeeded in adapting cuneiform writing to their own language, as may be seen from their many long inscriptions on the faces of the citadel rock (Fig. 39).

Towards the end of his reign, Sarduri I took advantage of a temporary decline in the political stability of Assyria to extend his frontiers, and the expansion of Urartu thus began. His son, Ishpuini, must have inherited an already impressive state, to judge by his remotely placed border stelae, which include the interesting bilingual inscription at Kel-i-shin, high up on the modern Iraq–Iran frontier. If, as this text suggests, Ishpuini now controlled the whole country west of Lake Urmia, it is easy to understand the apprehensive reaction of the contemporary Assyrian king, Shamshi-Adad V (825–812 BC), who recorded a campaign against Urartu in this area for the purpose of recovering and assuring the supply of horses for his cavalry. Early in the reign of Ishpuini's son, Menua, the balance of military success in these wars began to shift in favour of Urartu, and it was in his time that the state first attained a degree of political and cultural ascendancy which was to assure its status as a major power in western Asia for almost two hundred years.

Inscriptions of the time of Menua (810–786 BC) on rock-faces and buildings are so plentiful and so widely distributed that the territorial expansion of Urartu during his reign can be reliably computed. To the west, a natural frontier must have been provided by the Upper Euphrates and its northern affluent, the Kara Su. An obstacle to further progress in this direction would hitherto have been Malatya (Meliteia in the Urartian records), one of the oldest of the Neo-Hittite states and much valued owing to its strategic position on a main route to central Anatolia. Late in his reign, when Menua made explora-

43. Distant view of the medieval castle at Hoşap, due east of Van. An Urartian canal brought drinking water from Hoşap to Van.

tory campaigns south-westward in the direction of north Syria, he may well have by-passed this city, for it is not known to have been occupied by the Urartians. In a more northerly direction, Urartian territory seems to have been extended to the plains of Erzincan and Erzurum, beyond which a people called Diauehi, whose country is referred to as the Pass Lands, must have defended the mountainous approach to the Black Sea. Whether or not Menua himself succeeded in penetrating north-eastward, beyond the Araxes to Lake Sevan, remains uncertain, though the evidence of objects inscribed with his name in the great fortress built by a later king at Teishebaina (Karmir Blur) suggests that he did. Certainly he maintained the old frontier on Lake Urmia, and may have extended it to the Manaean country south of the lake, since some attribute to him the destruction of the famous palace at Hasanlu (Level IV). His relations with Mana are referred to in an historical inscription – this time on the walls of an Urartian temple. So we should now turn to consider some of Menua's accomplishments as a builder.

Today, throughout the region which was once Urartu, the most characteristic remains are the ruins of fortresses and fortress-cities, many of them founded for the first time during this early phase of its history. Those within the frontiers of modern Turkey were first studied, both individually and collectively, by C. A. Burney.[3] He was able not only to consider their strategic siting and the conventional arrangement of their planning, but also to discuss the defensive and other practical purposes which dictated their geographical distribution. He recognised the traditional composition of the principal cities – a high citadel with a temple and palace buildings, supplemented by a walled residential quarter at a lower level – as already evident at Tushpa itself, where the lower town spread out at the foot of the citadel rock (now buried beneath the ruins of the old Turkish city, destroyed by the Russians in 1916), and he observed the repetition of this arrangement in the smaller fortresses. Later, when reports became available of the Soviet excavations at Erebuni and Karmir Blur, these two great northern fortresses were seen to illustrate the same convention.[4] About the purpose of others, Burney felt less certain. He says:

> Presumably they formed governmental centres in times of peace, in
> addition to their military function. The regular discovery at excavated
> sites of storerooms, usually distinguished as such by rows of enormous
> storage-jars, six feet tall and five feet in girth, suggested the collection and
> safeguarding of tribute and goods levied on the local population as tribute
> in kind . . . Plainly some sites were exclusively military while others included
> a town or residential quarter.[5]

The annals of Menua's reign are inscribed on the walls of a temple at Aznavur, near Patnos to the north of Lake Van. Like most Urartian temples, a heavily built square tower, foreshadowing the Zoroastrian towers of Achaemenid times, it stands at the summit of a conical hill, facing towards Mount Süphan. From it, towered walls sweep down to the plain a thousand feet below, enclosing the town itself and an artificial reservoir. Two miles away, at Gırık

Tepe, a small country palace was found, which had met with some disaster. In chambers behind the throne-room were the bodies of armed guards and a group of young women still wearing their ornamental finery. Menua was also responsible for some of the first great irrigation projects, which later became a feature of the Urartian economy. Perhaps the most striking example was the canal, called by the Turks today Şamiram Su, which brought clean water thirty miles from the Hoşap valley to Van. Still to be seen today are the remnants of its masonry and ruined aqueducts, bearing fourteen inscriptions which describe how Menua built it. One also records the planting of a vineyard for his daughter Tariria, and its terraces are still discernible. Like all Urartians, Menua was also interested in horse-breeding, and another inscription commemorates a record jump of 11.44 metres, which he made while riding a horse called Arsibi.[6]

Much can be learnt about the reign of Menua's son, Argishti (786–762 BC), from a long inscription, perfectly preserved owing to its inaccessible position on the rock-face outside his tomb at Van. One of his main preoccupations was the extension and consolidation of Urartian territory in the north-east, between the Araxes and Lake Sevan. Here at Erebuni (Arin-Berd), on the outskirts of modern Yerevan, he created a regional capital and populated the country with war prisoners, 6,600 of whom he had deported from north Syria after successful campaigns west of the Euphrates. The fine architecture, wall-paintings and treasures of Erebuni have been well described by its Soviet excavators.[7] Of the latter perhaps the most conspicuous group – huge circular shields, helmets and quivers in bronze, decorated in repoussé with human and animal figures – were in fact discovered at Karmir Blur, a nearby city built in the early seventh century, to which they had been brought after the destruction of Erebuni, perhaps by the Cimmerians.

Argishti's conquests in Syria had interfered with the trade–routes and severed the lines of communication between Assyria and central Anatolia. This was a situation which could not long be tolerated. Some form of retribution was inevitable, and it came during the reign of his son, Sarduri II, which, after a good start, was eventually marked by a succession of military disasters. His own annals are inscribed on a pair of basalt stelae set up in niches which created an open-air shrine at the foot of the Tushpa citadel. These were discovered by the Russian scholars Marr and Orbeli during the First World War.[8] But the bare facts can be gathered from the less equivocal testimony of contemporary Assyrian records. The inevitable confrontation between the two powers took place soon after the accession of Tiglath-Pileser III to the Assyrian throne (745 BC), and his first objective was of course the recovery of the north Syrian trade-routes from Urartian control. A major battle was fought in 743 BC north of Aleppo, in which Sarduri II, though supported by the armies of several Neo-Hittite states, was heavily defeated and fled eastwards across the Euphrates. The Assyrians for the moment contented themselves with the rich booty abandoned in the Urartian camp; but eight years later a full-scale campaign was launched against the Urartian homeland itself, and only the impregnable walls of the Tushpa citadel saved Sarduri and his court from total extinction.

An extremely impressive and characteristic fortress, excavated in recent years by Turkish archaeologists, probably dates to the earlier part of Sarduri's reign. This is Çavuştepe (Asbaşin), a few miles south-east of Van, guarding the road to modern Hakkari and Urmia.

Little is known about the remainder of Sarduri's reign. After his narrow escape in 735 BC, the Urartian king must first have concentrated on strengthening the innermost defences of his capital, which he had now been compelled laboriously to rebuild. After this, it remained for his son, Rusa I, to put the country in order again and restore his frontiers, which he appears to have accomplished by good statesmanship and diplomacy.

In this way, during the last quarter of the eighth century the fortunes of Urartu fluctuated between peaceful expansion and the ever-present threat of Assyrian aggression. The year of greatest significance in Rusa I's reign is undoubtedly 714 BC, when the war against Urartu was resumed by King Sargon II. We know a great deal about Sargon's famous 'Eighth Campaign', primarily from the content of a very large tablet in the Louvre, which takes the form of a report to the god Ashur, composed in literary form and bearing the signature of a royal scribe. But in this case something is also known about the activities of Assyrian intelligence agents which preceded it.[9] Surviving among the royal archives from Nineveh and Nimrud are not only the actual reports of Sargon's spies, but summaries of their information made by his son, Sennacherib, to whom they were submitted. These have contributed some minor details of contemporary events in Urartu, including Rusa's first disastrous encounter with the Cimmerians, who were to create so much havoc in western Anatolia. While he was thus engaged, a mutiny was also reported among the troops whom he had left to guard the capital. Perhaps some of these reports contributed to Sargon's confidence, when his army set out northwards from Nimrud in the late summer.

Of the campaign itself the Louvre document gives an extraordinarily detailed and vivid description, with frequent references to the hazardous nature of the mountainous country through which the armies passed and passages which are strikingly evocative of the Urartian landscape.[10] One gains the impression that this must have been, if not the greatest, at least one of the most spectacular military adventures of the Assyrians and that its outcome exceeded all expectations. Although in the account there is no lack of topographical information, the identification of place-names still proves extremely difficult and some controversy persists regarding the geographical interpretation of the narrative. Already for some years, Sargon had been in conflict on his north-eastern frontiers with the Medes, and he now found their increasing power allied to that of Rusa. It was perhaps for this reason that the initial thrust of his army was directed eastwards through modern Kurdistan to the Mannaean lands south of Lake Urmia. This involved 'crossing deep gorges into which the rays of the sun did not penetrate', and rivers 'where the camels and asses of the baggage train were made to leap like mountain goats'. Sargon had already reached 'Mount Uaush' (apparently Mount Sahend on the east side of the lake) when his first major engagement took place, and the combined forces of the Medes and Urartians were there heavily defeated, Sargon having shown greatly superior tactical skills in the mountainous terrain.

After this he turned westward to the Urartian homeland, avoiding Tushpa itself but sweeping round the east and north-west shores of Lake Van in a crescendo of indiscriminate slaughter and punitive destruction:

> To the land of Aiadi I drew near ... Thirty of its strong cities, which line the shores of the terrible sea, at the foot of great mountains, all stand out like boundary stones; Argishtiuna, Kappania, its strong fortresses erected among them, shining about Mount Arsidu and Mount Mahunnia like stars, their foundation walls were visible to a height of 240 cubits ... They abandoned their cities with their possessions and fled like birds into the midst of these fortresses. I sent up large numbers of troops against their cities and they carried off great quantities of their property. Their strong walls, together with 87 cities of their neighbourhood, I destroyed, levelled to the ground.

The account then refers with relish to the looting of granaries and wine-stores, which may have been only less disastrous for the Urartians than the destruction of their orchards and forests. But the greatest booty of all was yet to come. For though the geographical reconstruction of the campaign is still controversial, Sargon would now appear to have turned south-eastward to the upper valley of the Greater Zab river, near which he captured and sacked Musasir, the principal holy city of Urartu. And this episode is illustrated pictorially in certain reliefs from his palace at Khorsabad. (These were among the antiquities lost in the Tigris while being transported by raft to Basrah in 1855, but careful drawings have survived.) One of them depicts the looting of the famous sanctuary and gives a rather misleading impression of the temple façade, with soldiers in the foreground removing its treasures. But it was the palace storerooms which, 'when the seals put on the doors for safe-keeping were struck off', yielded such an extraordinary profusion and variety of treasures. In the Louvre text they are catalogued in detail and at great length, and although many of the Assyrian terms used for this purpose are imprecisely understood, the list and description of 333,500 objects, quite apart from the overall weight of precious metals, have since provided a rewarding subject of study for archaeologists.[11]

After this, one imagines the return journey of Sargon's army to Nimrud through the gorges of the Zab river, and its train of wagons in which military equipment had been replaced by treasure weighing some hundreds of tons. At the end of his account, the Assyrian scribe is able to record with satisfaction the suicide of Rusa on receiving news of the disaster at Musasir.

It has been said of the Assyrians that their policy in military operations of this sort was, like that of the Romans, 'to make a desert and call it peace'. But

44. The sack of Musasir by the Assyrians under Sargon II in 714 BC. From a relief, now lost, found at Khorsabad in northern Iraq.

the state of Urartu was too geographically extensive, too inaccessible and too well endowed with national vitality to be destroyed in a single campaign. So the pattern of political and economic recovery once more repeated itself. Rusa's successor, Argishti II (714–685 BC), rebuilt his cities, repaired his irrigation systems, replanted his vineyards; and Urartu soon regained its position as a primary power in western Asia.

Argishti II was for the time being in no great danger from Assyria, where Sargon's son, Sennacherib, was preoccupied with campaigns in the west against Syria and Egypt. He did, however, find himself continually on the defensive against the Cimmerian hordes who were now becoming a menace to the whole of Anatolia, and it is to his reign that one might well attribute at least one very formidable fortress city on an isolated hill overlooking the plain east of modern Erzincan. Altıntepe, as the site is now called, was the seat of an Urartian viceroy. It was excavated from 1959 with striking results by Turkish archaeologists, after the chance find of a huge bronze cauldron on an iron tripod. This led to the discovery of the first intact Urartian semi-royal tombs: flat-roofed chambers of ashlar masonry, for which deep cuttings had been made in the flank of the hill. The grave furniture, now in the Ankara Museum – weapons, armour, horse-trappings etc., mostly of bronze – makes a very rich collection, and the interest of the tombs is augmented by the architectural layout of the citadel above. The usual Urartian tower-temple here stands in the centre of a colonnaded courtyard, over one corner of which, at a secondary period, a broad columned audience-hall was built (sometimes wrongly described by the Achaemenian term *apadana*). It had been decorated with mural paintings, whose patterns and motifs conform rather monotonously to Assyrian decorative formulae.

Altıntepe is one of several productive sites whose excavation has so greatly enriched our knowledge of Urartian art and architecture in the seventh century BC. Argishti's successor, Rusa II, is associated with the building of another, more remote provincial capital, Teishebaina (Karmir Blur). This was again the seat of a viceroy, built to replace Erebuni, which had been destroyed in the previous century. Here, in addition to excavating the citadel itself, Soviet archaeologists were able to clear large sections of the residential town on the slopes below and to trace the whole circuit of its walls. B. B. Piotrovski describes the citadel as follows:

> It occupied a total area of some 10 acres and contained some 150 separate apartments, together with a spacious courtyard ... Most of the buildings were roofed with a barrel vault of adobe brick; some had roofs formed of large beams of pine, poplar, beech and other timbers. The building of the citadel required some two million adobe bricks; the total quantity of timber required – most of it brought from other areas – cannot be estimated.
> Thus the construction of the citadel involved a vast expenditure of labour on the making and laying of the bricks, the transport of the timber, the quarrying and dressing of the stone used in the foundations and the basalt blocks used in the architectural decoration of the upper storey.

He adds that the citadel 'contained eight wine stores with a total capacity of 9,000 gallons, small storerooms for grain arranged along both sides of a corridor with a total capacity of some 750 tons – and at least as much again was stored in granaries elsewhere in the citadel'. He concludes that the political situation must have been remarkably secure for the Urartians to be able to build such a mighty fortress in remote Transcaucasia. (Rusa also built a castle on a dramatic rock outcrop at Bastam, across the border in Iran; this has been investigated by a team of German archaeologists.)

Nearer home, Rusa built a similar fortress on a mountainside overlooking Lake Van from the north, at a place now called Kefkalesi. Below, near the shore of the lake, a rare find was also made: an Urartian relief carving, depicting the life-size figure of a god, probably Tesheba, broken into fragments, perhaps in transit to or from the castle above. Even more important was the new residence which Rusa built for himself close to his capital, Tushpa (Van). The site he chose was a high shoulder of rock, known today as Toprakkale, overlooking the town on its north side. He named it Rusahinili. Toprakkale has suffered from one of those archaeological disasters which occurred so frequently in the nineteenth century. After a brief investigation by unskilled excavators, its temples and palaces were further pillaged by illicit diggers and their valuable contents torn piecemeal from the ground. Some minor buildings have now been more systematically cleared, but the temple of Haldis is razed to the ground. One may still see the typically Urartian stepped cuttings in the natural rock which carried its foundations. There is also a great water-cistern, through which an entry has now been cut, giving easier access to the summit.

The reign of Rusa II and the cultural renaissance to which his many surviving works testify provide our last detailed picture of Urartu at the height of its prosperity. The succession of four further kings is recorded or to be inferred, but the political decline and eventual fall of their kingdom is documented historically only by obscure references to them in Assyrian and Babylonian annals. Already, early in the seventh century BC, we have seen Argishti II resisting, with only partial success, the inroads of Cimmerian hordes on his northern frontiers. But these prove to be only the vanguard of a more complex migration of related Iranian nomads, pressing southward and westward from the Caucasus. Among these, for instance, were the Scythians, whom Herodotus depicts as displacing the Cimmerians from their pastures north of the Black Sea, to harass the rulers of Anatolia. Certainly in the late seventh century Scythians are to be found dominating the whole of Transcaucasia and what is now Azerbaijan, until suppressed by the Medes whose king, Cyaxares, had welded them into a nation. It is not surprising, therefore, to find great northern outposts of Urartu, like Teishebaina, destroyed at this time, and to learn from its excavators that the weapons of its destroyers were of a distinctively Scythian type. An Urartian king, apparently Sarduri III (c. 645–635 BC), is recorded by the Assyrians as having sent a delegation to Ashurbanipal (668–627 BC) humbly acknowledging him as his overlord. Yet as late as 609 BC, three years after the destruction of Nineveh by the Scythians and Medes, the state of Urartu still existed, for a Babylonian chronicle of that year refers to the annexation by the Scythians of its south-western provinces. The kingdom of Ararat was also called in aid against Babylon (Jeremiah 51:27–8). In fact, the rulership of Urartu may by then have been in a transitional state; for Burney[12] refers to an ingenious suggestion that the name of the king Erimena, who appears to have been the successor of Sarduri III, could fairly be translated as 'the Armenian'.

Historically, the Armenians are newcomers to the political scene at the turn of the seventh century BC, but their identification by Herodotus as an offshoot of the Phrygian peoples must be seriously considered. Clearly their infiltration into eastern Anatolia coincided with the collapse of the Urartian kingdom if it had not, indeed, begun some time earlier. Even if we discount the story, given much later by Xenophon in his *Cyropaedia*, of their settlement there in the time of the Medes and Cyrus the Great, we are left in no doubt that, by the time of Darius I (521–486 BC), they were sufficiently well established for Armenia to become a satrapy of the Achaemenid Empire. A memory of their predecessors is reflected in the great trilingual inscription at Behistun in western Iran, where the Babylonian text gives their country its old Urartian name, though in Old Persian and Elamite it is called Armenia.

As to the fate of the Urartian people themselves, it is now generally supposed that they remained in their homeland and intermarried with the Armenians. In support of this contention, Piotrovski reminds us that 'The resemblance between the dress of the Armenians, as shown in the reliefs from Xerxes' palace at Persepolis, and that of the Urartian emissaries in a relief from Ashurbanipal's palace at Nineveh has long been recognised.'[13]

CHAPTER 11

The Persian Empire

After capturing Sardis in 547 BC and putting an end to the Lydian dynasty, Cyrus left his general Harpagus to complete the subjugation of Asia Minor and himself returned eastward to the conquest of Babylon. Other campaigns carried his armies northward as far as the Aral Sea; his successor, Cambyses, occupied Egypt, and when Darius became king he found himself ruler of a vast territory extending from the Indus and Oxus rivers to the Black Sea, Aegean and Mediterranean coasts, as far as the delta of the Nile. The country which we now call Anatolia formed a part of this great empire, and was to remain so for upwards of two hundred years. During that time, though written records enable us partly to follow the fortunes of the Greek cities, the provinces and older principalities of the Asiatic interior seem to recede into historical obscurity, illuminated only by occasional episodes such as the insurrection of Cyrus the Younger and Xenophon's *Anabasis*. We do, however, know something about the administrative organisation of the Achaemenid Empire.

Cyrus had adopted as his headquarters the old Median capital city of Ecbatana (modern Hamadan), though he afterwards built and briefly occupied Pasargadae, a site nearer to the tribal centre from which his family had emerged. Darius preferred Susa, the old Bronze Age capital of the Elamites, near the head of the Persian Gulf. Later he began the great complex of palaces on an artificial terrace at Persepolis; but Susa continued to be the administrative capital of the Empire, and the Greeks regarded it as the seat of the Great King, the terminus of the 'Royal Road' which started at their own provincial capital, Sardis. For Darius had divided his empire into a number of provinces, each governed by a 'satrap'. Herodotus says that there were twenty of them and gives the amount and form of the tribute which each paid to the central government.[1] But we also have similar lists from two of Darius' surviving inscriptions, one at Persepolis and the other at Naqsh-i Rustam.

Those satrapies wholly or in part located within the frontiers of modern Anatolia are of some interest.

All of the western and south-western states, from Aeolia to Lycia and Pamphylia, were linked with Lydia and Mysia under a single satrap, whose seat was at Sardis. The Phrygian satrapy, which included the Propontis and Paphlagonia, seems to have extended eastward as far as the Halys river, though its capital, Daskylion, has recently been located at Ergili, near Bandırma. Cilicia, probably with its capital at Adana which, as we know from the Karatepe bilingual inscription, had been the seat of an independent ruler, paid tribute curiously in the form of 'white horses'. Next, to the north, came Cappadocia, with its satrap at Mazaca (modern Kayseri), earlier the seat of Tabalian kings, and finally Armenia, which had once been the state of Urartu.

The satraps themselves were usually Persian noblemen, often having close ties with the royal family, and they modelled their palaces and court procedure on that of the king. Safeguards had, however, been devised against their aspiring to complete political independence. Military forces and installations in each province were under the authority of a commander-in-chief, directly responsible to the king himself. The satrap's main responsibility was the collection and transfer to the central treasury of the tribute officially imposed. Beyond that, his contacts with the actual people of his province were extremely limited. The Persian nobility, as one is often told, were 'trained to ride, to shoot and to tell the truth'. But (if some historical parallels be discarded) it is hard to regard these skills as qualifications for imperial administration; and it is accordingly less surprising to find that, in every country with a system of government previously established, the traditional structure of its civil service continued to be maintained by a body of native officials. There was one additional form of control by the central government over the conduct of the satraps. 'Inspectors, called "the ears of the king", were appointed, who were completely independent and in case of necessity had their own armed force. They travelled all over the empire, paid unexpected visits to the administrators and examined their conduct of affairs.'[2]

Cyrus had been the first to profit from the services of Greek craftsmen and of specialists in the application of Greek science. By the time of Darius, a host of Greek masons and sculptors were assisting in the enrichment of his palaces, while rare building materials and luxury goods flowed into the Persian cities from the imperial provinces. Cedar wood was brought from the Lebanon, teak from Gandhara, gold from Sardis, lapis lazuli from Afghanistan, ivory from Ethiopia, and so on. But always the sculptors were Greeks. Also, the Persians encouraged and profited from the mercantile activities of the Greek seaports, though their naval organisation was mainly in the hands of the Phoenicians. Finally, since Cambyses had enlisted the first Greek troops for his attack on Egypt, their military discipline and tactical skill had come to be fully appreciated, and Greek hoplites now acted as the shock-troops of the Persian armies. But there were refinements outside the realm of technical expertise which were now to be transmitted from west to east: 'Only when they had taken Lydia did the Persians become aware of the attractions of "civilised" life, and the Greeks were to serve and instruct the Persians in these matters as they had the Lydians before them.'[3]

From all that has been said above, it will be realised that the integrity and administration of the Persian Empire depended very directly on facilities for communication. The *lingua franca* used for most purposes, at that time, was Aramaic, but a passage from the Old Testament suggests that important edicts could be issued in the languages of the provinces:

> Then the king's scribes were called on the thirteenth day of the first month, and an edict, according to all that Haman commanded, was written to the king's satraps and to the governors over all the provinces and to the

Plate I. The exterior of the rock-cut shrine at Yazılıkaya near Boğazköy (thirteenth century BC). The foundations of the outer gateway and temple can be seen in the foreground and centre of the picture. Beyond, to the right of the clump of trees, lies the entrance to the shrine illustrated in Fig. 13.

45. Fragment of sculpture from the North-West Staircase of the north façade of the Apadana at Persepolis in south-west Iran. It depicts a member of the Persian guard, and it has been claimed that the rosettes above indicate Ionian workmanship. The relief, which is 55 cm high, was presented to the British Museum by the Earl of Aberdeen in 1818 (WAA 118845).

> rulers of all the peoples, to every province in its own script and every people in its own language; it was written in the name of King Ahasuerus [Xerxes] and sealed with the king's ring. Letters were sent by couriers to all the king's provinces. (Esther 3:12.)

Clearly on an occasion like this an efficient postal service was required, and for this purpose Darius had created a network of roads to maintain liaison between the different centres of the empire and its capitals. For the Greeks of Asia Minor, the most important of these was the so-called Royal Road from Sardis to Susa. It was 1,677 miles long and divided into 111 post-stations, each with relays of fresh horses for the couriers. Caravans took 90 days to

Plate III. The citadel of Van in Urartu (see also Fig. 38).

Plate IV. The spectacular Greek theatre built against the hillside at Pergamum (third century BC).

Plate II (*left*). Relief from Yazılıkaya (see Plate I), showing King Tudhaliyas IV embraced by the god Sharruma.

Plate V. Gorgon's head from the frieze of the temple at Didyma (second century AD). It is possible that sculptors from Aphrodisias may have carved the frieze.

Plate VI. Some of the Ionic columns on the north side of the Temple of Athena at Priene (third quarter of the fourth century BC). The architect of the temple was Pytheos: he is better known for the tomb he built for Mausolus at Halicarnassus (modern Bodrum, see Plate X), which was one of the Seven Wonders of the Ancient World. Behind the temple rises the citadel hill.

Plate VII. Lycian tombs of the Roman period at the site of Theimussa, south-west of Myra.

Plate VIII. The newly restored Celsian Library at Ephesus (see also Fig. 75).

Plate IX. A guardian lion at the mountain-top sanctuary of Nemrut Dağ (see also Fig. 56).

Plate X. The harbour at Bodrum (ancient Halicarnassus), seen from the citadel.

Plate XI. Huge storage jars have been found in many Urartian settlements (see p. 103). Here two of those excavated in a storeroom (behind the wall on the right) at Kayalıdere in Urartu are being moved to the local museum in 1965. A bronze relief from the Balawat Gates in the British Museum shows the soldiers of the Assyrian king Shalmaneser III removing a similar jar from an Urartian city in the middle of the ninth century BC.

46. A cylinder seal of the royal Achaemenid Persian administration with a trilingual inscription in the cuneiform script in Babylonian, Old Persian and Elamite, naming 'Darius the Great King'. This was probably Darius I (521–485 BC). The modern impression of the seal shows the king engaged in a lion hunt. The seal is made of chalcedony and is 3.7 cm high, with a diameter of 1.6 cm. British Museum (WAA 89132).

Plate XII. Andriake, the port of Myra, where St Paul landed on his way to Rome.

cover the distance, while royal envoys could do it in a week. Herodotus has a well-known passage in praise of the latter:

> Now there is nothing mortal that accomplishes a course more swiftly than do these messengers, by the Persians' skilful contrivance. It is said that as many days as there are in the whole journey, so many are the men and horses that stand along the road, each horse and man at the interval of a day's journey; and these are stayed neither by snow nor rain nor heat nor darkness from accomplishing their appointed course with all speed. The first rider delivers his charge to the second, the second to the third, and thence it passes from hand to hand, even as the Greek torch-bearers' race in honour of Hephaestus. (Herodotus, VIII:98.)

From Sardis, the Royal Road must have followed the approximate line of the modern Izmir-Ankara motorway to the old Phrygian capital at Gordium on the Sangarius river (Sakarya), then running eastwards and twice crossing the Halys river (Kızıl Irmak) to Mazaca (Kayseri). According to one authority, 'The precise course of the road over Anti-Taurus is a matter of dispute, but it most probably passed from the modern site of Kayseri to Malatya and down the Tigris to Diyarbakır. Thence it would traverse the Tur el Abdin mountains to Mardin and continue over the Tigris at one of the crossings above Mosul, and past Erbil down the eastern edge of the Mesopotamian plain.'[4] A short length of the road was exposed by American archaeologists in 1955, running between the Phrygian burial-tumuli at Gordium. It was five metres wide, and efficiently paved with stone.[5]

If we now return for a moment to the Eastern Greeks, we shall find that their way of life and general well-being was not greatly changed under Persian rule. In the majority of cities direct government was left in the hands of a Greek 'despot', responsible to the Persian administrators only for the regular payment of tribute and the provision of military contingents when these were required. During the second half of the sixth century, the Greeks seem to have submitted fairly complacently to this oriental form of imperial domination. When, in about 511 BC, Darius organised his first great expedition into the countries beyond the Bosphorus, the despots of cities like Ephesus and Miletus came to his aid with substantial numbers of men and ships. Their leadership was, however, unpopular, and at home their tyrannical authority, which was in direct conflict with Greek concepts of political liberty and self-determination, had come increasingly to be resented. As we shall presently see, it was in the city of Miletus, which had been the last to submit to Persian rule, that a struggle for the independence of Ionia was first inaugurated.

Darius' first campaign in south-eastern Europe suffers historically from poor documentation. Its evident intentions were, first, the conquest of Thrace and, secondly, the acquisition of new territory along the western and northern coasts of the Black Sea. Herodotus' narrative is of some interest, because it records the first instance in history of a great army crossing the Bosphorus by a bridge of boats. Herodotus appends a careful description of 'the Straits', including the Marmara and the Hellespont (Dardanelles), though the distances which he estimates are curiously exaggerated and the point chosen for Darius' crossing is described rather uncertainly as 'halfway between the city of Byzantium and the temple at the mouth of the strait'. The bridge itself was constructed by a Samian architect called Mandrocles. Darius was so pleased with it that he loaded him with presents, in return for which Mandrocles 'caused a picture to be painted which showed the whole of the bridge, with King Darius sitting in a seat of honour, and his army engaged in the passage'. The king also erected nearby 'two pillars of white marble, whereupon he inscribed the names of all the nations which formed his army – on the one pillar in Greek, on the other in Assyrian [Old Persian?] characters'.[6]

The scene now changes to the mouth of the Ister (Danube), where another bridge was built. And here a rendezvous was made with a fleet of ships, supplied by the Greek cities, which had sailed up from the Aegean. After the army had crossed over, Darius was dissuaded from his intention of destroying the bridge. Instead he left a detachment to guard it, with instructions that, if he did not return in a given number of days, they should dismantle it and sail home. In the event, Histiaeus, the despot of Miletus, refused to comply with this order (perhaps because his authority at home might have been impaired by the loss of the Persian army), and when, after the time-limit had long expired, Darius in fact reappeared in ignominious retreat, it became clear that his 'wise counsel' had probably saved the king's forces from total annihilation by the 'Scythians'. After this adventure the king himself withdrew to the Hellespont, leaving his general Megabazus to continue the operation in Thrace. This he did with considerable success, assuring the allegiance to Persia of smaller states as far as Macedonia. Herodotus gives no account of this campaign.

Darius seems to have appreciated his indebtedness to Histiaeus, for he insisted upon his returning with him to Susa. In Miletus, meanwhile, the despot's prolonged absence created an opportunity for a widespread anti-Persian intrigue, which rapidly spread to the neighbouring cities of Ionia. This in fact represented the first resurgence of Greek nationalism in protest against the despotic form of government imposed on them by Darius. The insurrection which followed is known as the Ionian Revolt. It was in the end largely abortive, but its significance lies in the fact that now, for the first time, the eastern cities felt justified in appealing for help to those of the Greek mainland.

Histiaeus had, in his absence, deputed his authority as tyrant of Miletus to a relative named Aristagoras. This man is said by Herodotus to have resigned his office after a quarrel with the satrap of Sardis, and to have taken a leading part in organising the insurrection. His first step was to invite help from the increasingly powerful state of Sparta, and the story of his visit for this purpose to the Spartan king, Cleomenes, serves to emphasise how little connection had as yet been established between mainland Greece and Persia. Aristagoras carried with him a tablet depicting the countries of the known world, which he used to illustrate the advantages to be gained by the conquest of the Persian Empire. Cleomenes at first seemed impressed, but asked for an estimate of the distance from Ionia to Susa. Aristagoras replied, with ill-advised promptitude, that it was three months' journey, whereupon the king, without further discussion, sent him home.

In Athens Aristagoras was more successful, and returned with a modest contribution of men and ships – only to find that the Persians had already laid siege to Miletus. He then mustered some additional forces from other dissident Greek cities and, supported by his new Athenian allies, endeavoured to create a diversion by marching on Sardis. His army, as might have been expected, failed to take the citadel, but succeeded (rather vindictively) in setting fire to the town itself – an outrage for which responsibility was afterwards attributed to the Athenians. This was the first occasion on which Darius became aware of their existence. Meanwhile, the revolt had spread southward to Caria and northward to the Hellespont, involving all the cities of the coast and the offshore islands. In the end it failed, owing to the basic political disunity of the Greek states, to their lack of any effective leadership or coordinated strategy. Closing in from the river valleys, the Persian armies isolated and recaptured one city after another, while the Phoenician fleet occupied itself with a recovery of the islands. Miletus itself was finally blockaded by a fleet of 600 ships, which had just reduced Cyprus, and a sea-battle was fought off the island of Lade, during which most of the Greek fleet deserted and returned home. The city was taken and, disastrously, the temple of Apollo at Didyma was burnt to the ground (494 BC). The only gains on this occasion were made by Athens, which obtained possession of Lemnos and Imbros. For the Athenians, the fall of Miletus on this occasion became a memorable disaster. A poet called Phrynicus wrote a play about it, but when it was presented, 'the whole theatre burst into tears and the people sentenced him to pay a fine ... for recalling to them their own misfortunes' (Herodotus, VI:21).

The defiance of Miletus was heavily punished by Darius, who transported the remnants of its inhabitants to a place called Ampe, at the head of the Persian Gulf. His treatment of the other Ionian cities seems by contrast to have been surprisingly lenient and sensible. His son-in-law Mardonius, to whom their pacification was entrusted, started by removing the despots, whose rule had been so much resented, and by substituting a democratic form of administration, more congenial to Greek susceptibilities. He then summoned representatives of each city to a meeting at which they might settle their differences to the advantage of all concerned. The king, however, who had given orders that he should be regularly reminded of his grudge against the Athenians for their part in the burning of Sardis, was now already planning a new expedition against the Greek mainland, with the destruction of Athens as its ultimate objective. There then followed a period of some twenty years during which the Athenians and their allies were compelled to concentrate on the defence of their country against repeated assaults by the land and sea forces of the Persian Empire.

By the Greeks in general, the Persian War was afterwards regarded as the noblest, if not the greatest epic of their history. It would however be wrong to regard it as having been a straightforward conflict between themselves and an alien power, since, as was inevitably the case when fighting took place in the Aegean, there were Greeks on both sides. Yet on this occasion, where the mainland states were concerned, the threat to their existence was sufficiently formidable to evoke among them some measure of pan-Hellenic solidarity. If it be supposed that, under the circumstances, this was a phenomenon which could be taken for granted, one must remind oneself of its astonishing rarity during the remainder of Greek history. Apart from a few decades in the mid-fifth century BC, when the Confederacy of Delos led to the creation of an Athenian empire, the whole story is one of divisive rivalries and conflicts arising out of regional loyalties. One has only to remember, for instance, the absence of the Spartans from Marathon, the strategic quarrels which preceded the naval action at Salamis and the tangle of uncoordinated tactics at Plataea, to marvel that these battles somehow resolved themselves into Greek victories. If matters had been otherwise, and the Greeks had fought as a nation under a single command, the conquest of Persia itself need hardly have been postponed until the following century. Nor, if the significance of common heredity had been respected, would one have seen the greatness and prosperity of Athens foundering in a pointless and self-destructive war with its neighbouring and compatriate kingdom of Sparta. But here already we are touching on events relevant only indirectly to the history of Anatolia, and must restrict ourselves to those aspects and incidents of the Persian War whose repercussions were felt in Asia Minor.

In the years 492 and 490 BC, Darius mounted two expeditions against Greece, neither of which was particularly successful. The first was led by Mardonius, who used his ships to carry the army across the Hellespont and marched along the coast of Thrace. He did succeed in reaching Macedonia, but his fleet met with a storm while rounding the triple peninsulas of Chalcidice (Athos) and was almost completely destroyed. Darius was therefore compelled to abandon the campaign. Herodotus adds that '... the men who perished were more than twenty thousand. For the sea about Athos abounds in monsters beyond all others; and so a portion were seized and devoured by these animals, while others were violently dashed against the rocks' (VI:44). When a recent visitor to one of the famous Basilian monasteries asked why his hosts never bathed in the sea, he was told, 'One of our deacons was eaten by a shark'. Their records showed that this had in fact been the case, but it had happened in 1683.

The second expedition was primarily a naval operation. Under the generals Datis and Artaphernes, the army assembled in Cilicia and embarked in a vast fleet of ships. This time, partly to avoid Chalcidice, they sailed directly across the Aegean from Samos and up the straits between Attica and Euboea. Here, following the instructions of Darius, they paused to destroy the city of Eretria, whose troops had also taken a hand in the burning of Sardis eight years previously. But after the defeat of the Persians by the Greeks at Marathon, the campaign seems to have lost impetus, and the fleet, after anchoring within sight of Piraeus, decided against a direct attack on Athens and sailed home. While planning a third expedition, Darius died, leaving the feud with Athens to be prolonged by his successor, Xerxes.

After much debate and some indecision, Xerxes finally decided on a new western adventure. His preparations were extremely thorough and on an almost fabulous scale: they began in 483 BC, two years after his accession to the throne, and lasted the greater part of four years. In the first place, he seemed obsessed by the memory of the disaster which had overtaken his father's fleet off Chalcidice. For this reason he set himself the initial task of digging a canal, one and a half miles long, across the flat isthmus which separates the mountains of Athos from the mainland. This he accomplished with some difficulty, and traces of the operation are said to be still recognisable.[6] Another preliminary measure was to construct a bridge of boats, this time across the Hellespont (Dardanelles), near the small Greek city of Abydus (modern Çanakkale). This would seem to have been at the point which, during the Gallipoli campaign in the First World War, was known as 'the Narrows'.[7]

Shortly after the completion of the bridge, there was a storm in which the greater part of it was swept away, much to the annoyance of Xerxes, who ordered a ceremonial 'chastisement' of the Hellespont before rebuilding it. This time, a stronger form of construction was used, with two lines of cables, and the details which Herodotus gives (VII:36) are of some interest:

> They joined together triremes and penteconters, 360 to support the bridge
> on the side of the Euxine Sea, and 314 to sustain the other; and these
> they placed at right angles to the sea and in the direction of the current of
> the Hellespont, relieving by these means the tension of the shore cables.
> Having joined the vessels, they moored them with anchors of unusual size,
> that the vessel of the bridge towards the Euxine might resist the winds
> which blow from within the straits, and that those of the more western
> bridge facing the Egaean, might withstand the winds which set in from
> the south and from the south-east. A gap was left in the penteconters in
> no fewer than three places, to afford a passage for such light craft as chose
> to enter or leave the Euxine. When all this was done, they made the cables
> taut from the shore by the help of wooden capstans. This time, moreover,

instead of using the two materials separately, they assigned to each bridge six cables, two of which were of white flax, while four were of papyrus ... when the bridge across the channel was thus complete, trunks of trees were sawn into planks, which were cut to the width of the bridge, and these were laid side-by-side upon the tightened cables, and then fastened on the top. This done, brushwood was brought, and arranged upon the planks, after which earth was heaped upon the brushwood, and the whole trodden down into a solid mass. Lastly a bulwark was set up on either side of this causeway, of such a height as to prevent the sumpter beasts and the horses from seeing over it and taking fright at the water.[8]

While all this was in progress, Xerxes' vast land army had been assembling somewhere east of the Halys in Cappadocia for its march by way of Sardis to the Hellespont. The route which it now followed can be fairly easily recognised from Herodotus' account and is familiar to many travellers in Anatolia – south of the Salt Lake (Tuz Gölü), from modern Nevşehir to Konya, and then by Akşehir to Dinar, which is ancient Celaenae. Here is the main source of the Maeander and the beautiful pool where its water gushes out from beneath the rocks, to flow through the streets of the modern town. It is the fabled scene of the tragic contest between Apollo and the shepherd-boy Marsyas, and must have appealed to Xerxes, for, on his return, he is said to have built a country palace there. Following approximately the line of the modern road from Dinar to Denizli, the army passed Anaua (Çardak) where the salt-pans were till recently still in use, and Colossae, which Herodotus describes as 'a Phrygian city of great size'. Its very extensive ruins are still to be seen, astride the small Lycus river, whose curious habit of disappearing periodically into an underground channel he also refers to. The way would then have led northward, past Hierapolis (Pamukkale) to Sardis.

The army wintered at Sardis, where it was no doubt reinforced with further contingents of troops from the Ionian cities, and in the spring of 480 BC set out for its rendezvous with the fleet at the Hellespont. Once more its route is recorded rather clearly, north-west to Pergamum and then down to the sea at Atarneus, which is modern Dikili. From here it followed the coast to Adramyttium (Edremit) and crossed the Troad to the site of Troy. Xerxes showed some curiosity about the place which Herodotus calls 'the Pergamus of Priam', and one remembers that the Hellenic extension of the city (behind the 'Homeric' mound) must at this time have been occupied. But here the army was in some trouble, because, unlike the Caicus and the Hermus rivers which had already been crossed, the Scamander at Troy proved to be a minor stream and was soon 'drunk dry'. Fortunately there remained only a short march to Abydus.

The host which then assembled, ready to cross into Europe, must have been one of the most impressive sights in the whole history of the ancient world. 'What nation of Asia', asks Herodotus, 'did not Xerxes lead against Hellas?' A short passage from J. B. Bury's *History of Greece* may suffice to convey an impression of those who were conspicuously represented:

The Persians themselves, who were under the command of Atanes, wore coats of mail and trowsers; they had wicker shields, large bows and short spears. Then there were Assyrians with brazen helmets, linen cuirasses, clubs, lances and short swords; Bactrians with cane bows; trowsered Sacae with pointed hats and carrying axes; Indians clad in cotton, Caspians in goat-skin; Sarangians wearing dyed garments and high boots; Ethiopians clad in lion or leopard-skins and armed with flint-headed arrows; Sagartians with dagger and lassoo; Thracians with fox skin caps; Colchians with cow-skin shields. The fleet was furnished by Phoenicians, Egyptians, Cypriots, Cilicians, Pamphylians, Lycians, Carians and subject Greeks. It is said to have consisted of 1,207 warships with 3,000 smaller vessels. Herodotus' total estimate of over 5,000,000 men must of course be treated as fabulous.[10]

In the course of one week, the crossing was successfully accomplished. After which we must leave Xerxes to his campaign, which in the end brought no great glory to the Persian nation.

While Xerxes watched with satisfaction the crossing of his huge army into Europe, the representatives of thirty-one Greek states were meeting at the isthmus of Corinth, under the presidency of Sparta, to bind themselves together in a formal confederation for the purpose of defensive action. This was again one of the earliest instances in their history of anything approaching a pan-Hellenic policy, and an expedient to which only the most critical emergency could have driven them. In the campaign which followed, it is strange, by contrast, to consider the cynical indifference with which an almost equal number of Eastern Greek states were preparing to fight on the Persian side. The passage from Bury quoted above is, of course, no more than a rigorous abbreviation of a long parenthesis in Herodotus' account of the war, in which he lists among others and discusses the contribution of the 'subject Greeks' to the naval force assembled by the Persians. From this one is led to conclude that, apart from a large Phoenician element, the greater part of the 'Barbarian' fleet came from the coastal cities of Asia Minor. Some indication of their indeterminate loyalties may be found in a minor episode of the great sea-battle at Salamis, which seems to have amused Herodotus – perhaps because it concerned one of his own compatriots from Caria. This was Artemisia, Queen of Halicarnassus (a namesake of the fourth-century queen who built the Mausoleum), whose ship, having moved too far ahead of the Persian armada, soon reappeared hotly pursued by a Greek trireme. Finding herself in this way confined between the opposing formations of the two fleets, Artemisia at once rammed and sank an allied vessel in order to escape.

After the Greek victory at Salamis, one would have expected that a part of the fleet might at once have been sent to destroy the bridge of boats across the Hellespont and so to have severed the Persian line of communications. This was not done and, in the event, would have proved to have been unnecessary, since the bridge had once more been swept away in a storm. Xerxes, hurrying back to Asia with a part of his army, was compelled to use the remnants of

47. Detail showing a banqueter, from a painted tomb dated to about 475 BC at Karaburun, near Elmalı, in Lycia. The painting shows both Greek and Persian influence.

his fleet for his return crossing of the Narrows. The pick of his troops were, however, left in Thrace, under the command of Mardonius, and it was they who in the following year were decisively defeated by the Greeks at Plataea, to the south of Thebes (479 BC). Almost simultaneously, a final blow was struck against the Persian reserve force, which had been kept in readiness on the Asiatic coast. It happened, appropriately enough, at Mycale, within a few miles of the Panionium, central shrine of the Ionian League. The Hellenic fleet, which had been refitted and improved since its victory at Salamis in the previous year, arrived at Mycale by way of Samos and effected a landing. The subject Greek element in the Persian camp understandably changed sides and the remainder of the force was easily subjugated. After this, the Spartans returned home, but the Athenians, with other allies, pressed their advantage by vigorous action in the Hellespont, where new bases were established to guard against any further invasion of the European states. It is at this point that Herodotus brings to an end his history of the Persian War.

The half-century following the exclusion of the Persians from Europe and the Aegean must be regarded as the high summer of Athenian greatness and prosperity. It was under the presidency of Athens that an anti-Persian league was now at last created, calling itself the Confederacy of Delos, and practically all the Greek states of the Aegean rallied to its support. The leadership of their combined forces was entrusted to Cimon, the son of Miltiades, who succeeded in liberating the cities of Caria and Lycia, before pressing eastwards into Pamphylia, where a final Greek victory effectively ended the Persian domination of coastal Asia Minor. This battle took its name from the river Eurymedon, in which the Persian fleet had taken refuge, with a substantial army camped nearby. The Eurymedon was the stream known today as the Köprü Çayı, which runs down to the sea from Aspendus. Seen from the Seljuk bridge which crosses it below the Hellenistic ruins, it is difficult to believe that it could ever have been used by ships of any size; yet both Syclax and Strabo maintain that it was navigable as far as Aspendus. Thucydides mentions an episode during the Peloponnesian War when 147 ships sailed up it. On this occasion Cimon perhaps profited from a surprise attack, for the land force was routed and 200 Phoenician ships are said to have been destroyed. After this the liberation of the coastal provinces in the south was completed and the Confederacy became a formidable reality. Almost at once, however, an ominous change in its organisation became apparent. 'From the outset', says J. M. Cook, 'Athens had been the dominant partner. Gradually she became the mistress. For convenience, most of the cities had compounded for their share of fleet maintenance by monetary payments; presently they found themselves in the position of tributaries, and states which attempted to secede were punished as revolting subjects.' By the middle of the fifth century it could be seen that 'Athens was interfering in the internal government of the Ionic cities, establishing democracy after her own pattern and appointing her own commissioners'.[11] Inevitably, in this way the Confederacy soon became transformed into an Athenian empire and began to be openly referred to as such.

The history of these years, during which Athenian democracy was perfected under the guidance of Pericles and Greek civilisation reached the peak of its attainments, is only indirectly relevant to our present theme. All too soon, the even tenor of cultural development was dislocated by wars of the sort which appear to have been an indispensable ingredient in the Greek way of life, and which culminated in the prolonged and disastrous struggle between the conflicting ideologies of Athens and Sparta. Last to benefit from these must have been the cities of Asia Minor, of whose fortunes during this period little can be learnt from the Greek writers. It is clear that their *de facto* emancipation from Persian rule had bequeathed to them an equivocal relationship with the imperial administrators of Anatolia, from whom much of their land continued to be rented. In this way, their loyalties were still to some extent divided between Athens and the Persians, on whom, incidentally, the remoter cities were dependent for protection against harassment by native states of the interior. On the Athenian side they found themselves subject to economic exploitation. By the end of the fifth century, a new symptom of their discontent is to be seen in the ease with which a Persian prince was able to raise an army of Greek mercenaries.

CHAPTER 12

The Journey
of the
Ten Thousand

The story of the Ten Thousand Greeks, who took part in Cyrus the Younger's ill-fated expedition in 401 BC against his elder brother, Artaxerxes II, and Xenophon's account of their epic retreat from Mesopotamia to the Black Sea, make an entertaining chapter in school history books. But they have also in the past provided an endless subject of debate among scholars of classical geography, intent upon reconstructing the route which the Greeks followed in either direction.[1] Until the early years of the present century, those who had travelled at all extensively in Anatolia were surprisingly few; and even today, when the topography of Xenophon's *Anabasis* can be studied by tourists, and the debate shared with Turkish authorities, much of his itinerary remains uncertain. A synopsis of the story presents no difficulties. Cyrus, who had been appointed Viceroy of Asia Minor in 407 BC, planned an expedition to Babylon with the intention (at first concealed from his Greek mercenaries) of dethroning his brother. His army marched unopposed down the Euphrates, encountered the imperial forces at Cunaxa, near Babylon, and fought an engagement during which Cyrus himself was killed. This was a pantomime battle; for the Greeks, fighting in a single body, totally routed the Persian troops facing them, but returned from their pursuit to find their employer dead and the remainder of his army disbanded. Under cover of a truce, the Persians treacherously murdered the Greek officers, and it was then that Xenophon himself took command. Under his leadership, they marched over a thousand miles across the highlands of eastern Anatolia, to reach the Black Sea near Trebizond. From the time of their enlistment by Cyrus, the entire expedition had lasted a year and three months.

When Cyrus set out from Sardis in 401 BC, his army consisted of 100,000 oriental troops and, at first, 13,000 Greeks, of whom 10,600 were hoplites. The early stages of his route corresponded fairly closely to that which Xerxes had taken in the opposite direction eighty years previously, and upon which we have already commented. It carried him south-westward, to cross the Maeander somewhere near Laodicea (Denizli) and from there to Celaenae (Dinar), of which Xenophon says, 'Here Cyrus had a palace, and an extensive park full of wild beasts, which he was accustomed to hunt on horseback whenever he wished to give himself and his horses exercise'. The next place which Xenophon mentions is Peltae, which must have been the modern Çivril. This would imply a march of some twenty-five miles in the wrong direction and since, during the week or so that follows, the itinerary becomes obscure, some deliberate digression has to be inferred. It is tempting to associate this with the rendezvous and subsequent liaison which Xenophon records between Cyrus and Queen Epyaxa, 'wife of Syennesis, king of the Cilicians', which happened at a place called 'the Plain of Caystrus'. The Queen appears to have provided him with enough money to pay his mercenaries, a matter which was already becoming urgent, and in return for this Cyrus arranged a ceremonial review of his army in her honour. This took place at Thymbrium, near Pisidian Antioch (Yalvaç), and Xenophon gives an amusing description of how the

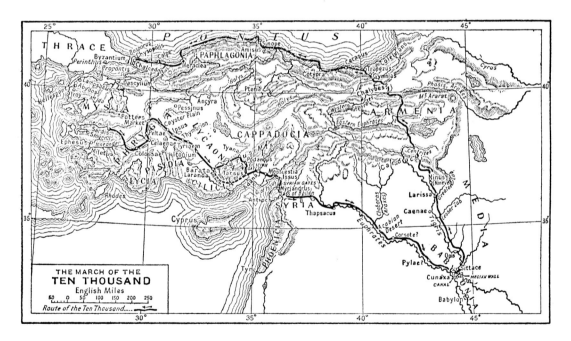

48. The journey of the Ten Thousand. From J. B. Bury, *History of Greece*, London 1929.

Greek phalanx, 'wearing their brazen helmets, scarlet tunics, greaves and polished shields', suddenly made a mock charge against the line of spectators, creating a panic in which even the Queen herself 'fled from her car'.

The army seems now to have been back on the road to Iconium (Konya) and, after spending three days there, to have proceeded by way of Tyana (Bor) to the Cilician Gates, through which its progress into Cilicia was watched with suspicion by Syennesis from the heights above. Later, however, he was

49. The famous pass through the Taurus mountains, known as the Cilician Gates, seen from the Gülek castle above.

persuaded by his wife to abandon his hostility to the Persians, and from his capital at Tarsus, the army was able to march unopposed through eastern Cilicia to Myriandrus (near Iskenderun) and so across the Beylan (Belen) Pass into north Syria.

In the present context there is little point in following the Greeks further into Mesopotamia, or enlarging upon the bewildering situation in which they found themselves after the fiasco at Cunaxa. Deprived of their military leaders, alone in a hostile country, many hundreds of miles from the nearest Greek city, they could only accept the advice of Xenophon, that the retreat should take a northerly direction in the hope of eventually reaching the coast of the Black Sea. Some impression of their ignorance in matters of geography may be gained from the surprise which they showed on learning that there was a second major river running parallel to the Euphrates (as one would have thought to be implied by the name Mesopotamia). In the event, they were able to cross the Tigris at a point somewhere above modern Baghdad, and they reappear in our present story on the frontier of Anatolia, following the east bank of the river, on a line of march which, even today, would present formidable difficulties for a solitary traveller.

As has already been remarked, the itinerary of the Ten Thousand across eastern Anatolia has been the subject of prolonged discussion by many authorities. But after reading them all, one is left with the impression that many of the conclusions reached can still only be accepted with considerable reserve.

50. The fish pools and the Mosque of Ibrahim at Urfa. Xenophon describes the 'large tame fish which the Syrians regarded as gods' (Book I, Ch. 4).

To begin with, Xenophon's own observations and the journal of events upon which the *Anabasis* is based suffer at times from curious omissions and confusion in the identification of landmarks – particularly rivers. This of course is understandable, in view of the many other responsibilities imposed by his leadership of the expedition. Less excusable are equally serious mistakes in the commentaries of nineteenth-century travellers.

While leaving Assyria, the army halted at a place with a 'castle' which is clearly recognisable as Zakho; yet Xenophon does not mention the (eastern) Khabur river which today marks the frontier between Iraq and Turkey, and which so many writers have in the past confused with another of the same name, flowing into the Euphrates below Deir-ez-Zor. The Greeks were now entering the country of the Karduchi, a people who have generally been accepted as the ancestors of the Kurds. It was said of them that 'they lived among the mountains, were very warlike and did not obey the King'. During the days that followed, they harassed the Greeks continually, rolling large stones down the hillsides above them and disputing their passage through the formidable passes which they were compelled to negotiate during this part of their journey. For after passing what is now Jazirat-ibn-Omar (Cizre) and obtaining provisions from the richly cultivated river valley beyond it, they reached a point where the Tigris runs between steep walls of rock and were compelled to take a more direct route northward across the mountains. It has been thought that their line of march would have brought them to the modern market town of Fındık, and to a road which now runs, again northward, towards Siirt. It is certain, in any case, that they returned to the Tigris at a point where its main stream turns sharply westward and is joined from the east by an important tributary, the Centrites of Xenophon, now called the Botan Çayı. It would seem that, in Xenophon's time, the Centrites formed a natural boundary between Kurdistan and Armenia, for, having been guided upstream to a place where it could be forded, the Greeks found their crossing opposed on the west bank by an Armenian army. This was no rabble of banditry like the Karduchi who were still harassing their rearguard, but a well-armed and disciplined force, in the service of the Persian satrap. Under these circumstances, Xenophon's account of the strategic manoeuvres and ruses by which the Greeks succeeded not only in reaching the opposite bank, but in putting the Armenian army to flight without engaging in a pitched battle or suffering serious losses, is one of those passages which make compulsive reading.

In the paragraphs which follow, Xenophon gives some interesting information about the social order of the Armenian state at this early period, important in itself as anticipating the earliest memories of Armenian historians. He tells us that 'The clan constitutes the basic institution, while the chiefs ruled over the fortified rural settlements which were surrounded by walls and ditches. These tribal elders or *comarchs* had charge of the local administration, the satrap being responsible for the whole country.'[2] The Greeks soon met with further evidence of Persian occupation. They saw no villages for some distance after leaving the Centrites, as Xenophon says, owing to the proximity of the Karduchi; but at a place now identified as modern Siirt there was a town of considerable size, 'containing a palace for the satrap'. This appears to have been ungarrisoned, for they were able to obtain provisions and set out again.

There has been much controversy about their route from Siirt onwards, but on balance one would discard Layard's contention that they passed through Bitlis, ignoring the existence of Lake Van, and travelled west of Nemrut Dağ to Malazgirt and Patnos.[3] Ainsworth[4] takes them north-westward to cross the river which Xenophon calls Teleboas near modern Muş. There is no modern road in this direction for obvious reasons, but since the Teleboas is clearly the Murat Su, or east branch of the Euphrates, this identification makes sense. (Both Ainsworth and Layard for some reason confuse the Turkish name of this river with that of the Kara Su or western Euphrates.) At Muş, the Greeks once more encountered Armenian troops under the satrap himself, Tiribazus, whose offer of a *laissez passer* agreement proved unreliable; but they were able to continue their march northwards into the very high mountain range now called Bingöl Dağları. Here, at an altitude of up to 8,000 feet, they were travelling in deep snow, suffering, as Xenophon tells us, from frostbite and undernourishment. Their troubles were somewhat relieved on reaching a richly cultivated upland valley, which one would agree with Ainsworth in identifying as modern Hinnis.

Here Xenophon's description of the army's sojourn in a group of comparatively friendly Armenian villages evokes clearly the timeless conventions of east Anatolian hospitality.

> Their houses were under ground, the entrance like the mouth of a well, but spacious below; there were passages dug into them for cattle, but the people descended into them by ladders. In the houses were goats, sheep, cows and fowls, with their young; all the cattle were kept on fodder within the walls. There was also wheat, barley, vegetables and barley-wine, in large bowls ... the liquor was very strong, unless one mixed water with it, and a very pleasant drink for those accustomed to it ... The chief man ... to show his goodwill, pointed out where some wine was buried. This night therefore, the soldiers rested in their several quarters in the midst of great abundance.

Xenophon accepted a gift of young horses. He says, 'The horses in this country were smaller than those of Persia, but far more spirited. The chief instructed the men to tie little bags round the feet of the horses, and other cattle, when they drove them through the snow, for without such bags they sunk up to their bellies.'[5]

The road northward from Hinnis would have brought the Greeks to the line of the modern road from Erzurum to Horasan, at a point where it would have been necessary to cross the Araxes (Aras) river running eastward to the Caspian. (Xenophon calls it the Phasis, confusing it with the Colchian Phasis, a more northerly stream discharging into the Black Sea.) From here, a modern traveller aiming for Trebizond (Trabzon) would travel westward to Erzurum and take the mountain highway over the two famous passes, Kopdağı and Zigan. This involves two river crossings – the headwaters of the Kara Su (Euphrates) at Aşkale and the Çoruh at Bayburt. But it also necessitates a wide detour to westward. Most authorities accordingly discredit this line of approach to the Black Sea, and prefer a more direct route, across the Pontic Alps. Layard, for instance, even refuses to carry the Greeks as far west as Erzurum, and brings them in sight of the sea 'halfway between Trebizond and Batum'. There is in fact today a minor road, starting a little west of Erzurum, passing by Ispir and Ikizdere, to reach the coast at Rize; but this would imply that their first sight of the sea was still somewhat eastward of Trebizond. It would involve only one river crossing – that of the Çoruh, possibly Xenophon's Harpasus.

However this may be, it was five days after crossing the Harpasus that the episode took place which so many historians since Xenophon have placed among the most dramatic in Greek history. It happened as the army reached the summit of a mountain range, called by Xenophon Theches:

> When the men who were in front had mounted the height, and looked down upon the sea, a great shout proceeded from them; and Xenophon and the rearguard, on hearing it thought that some new enemies were assailing the front, for, in the rear too, the people from the country they had burnt were following them.... But as the noise still increased and grew nearer, and as those who came up from time to time kept running at full speed to join those who were continually shouting, the cries becoming louder as the men became more numerous, it appeared to Xenophon that it must be something of great moment. Mounting his horse therefore, and taking with him Lycius and the cavalry, he hastened forward to give aid, when presently they heard the soldiers shouting, 'The sea, the sea!' and cheering on one another. They then all began to run, the rearguard as well as the rest, and the baggage cattle and horses were put to their speed; and when they had all arrived at the top, the men embraced one another, and their generals and captains, with tears in their eyes.

The army evidently had still some way to go before reaching Trebizond, for, having left the country of the Macrones, they encountered some resistance from the Colchians. They must now have been in the rhododendron forests, whose beauty in the spring so many travellers have admired. For it was here that many of the troops suffered from the disconcerting effects of eating some honey with intoxicating properties, apparently derived from a species of azalea. This seems to have been a phenomenon familiar to many classical writers, for it is mentioned by Pliny, Strabo, Aelian and Procopius.[6] But the worst of the army's troubles were now over and we soon find them celebrating games in the Greek city of Trebizond. As Ainsworth says, 'They recruited themselves till the supplies furnished by the surrounding country were nearly exhausted, and then, only a portion of the necessary shipping having been obtained, they embarked their women and children, with the sick and the aged, under the two oldest generals, Philesius and Sophaenetus, while the remainder proceeded by land.' For the rest of the journey, by Sinope (Sinop) and Heraclea (Ereğli) to the Bosphorus, the army itself seems to have preferred the land route, since it afforded opportunities for looting, which became increasingly attractive as they neared the end of their journey.

When the Ten Thousand eventually reached home, their adventure proved to have been more than a mere epic of bravery and endurance. That an army of Greek mercenaries could defy the forces of the Great King on his own ground and march back through his dominions almost unscathed, appeared to the Greeks as an epoch-making discovery. This pioneer accomplishment had shattered the image of a remote and impenetrable Asiatic empire and to a large extent dissipated the mystery of the Orient. The way was now paved for the Macedonian conquests of the fourth century BC.

CHAPTER 13

Macedon:
a Dream of
Greek Unity

The early decades of the fourth century BC saw the rapid extension of Hellenic culture to western Europe and through the Balkans to south Russia. Yet in Greece itself this would appear to have been a period of increasing social and economic stagnation. The cities of Asia Minor continued to accept with complacency their tributary relationship to the Persian Empire, while, among the older states of the Aegean and the European mainland, regional enmity had become so deep-seated that united action in any major cause had ceased to be conceivable. To the minds of those who still clung to the ideal of pan-Hellenism, it must by now have become clear that unity could only be attained through the enforced hegemony of a single state or the dynamic stimulus of individual leadership. Both these requirements were, as it proved, to become available, though the source from which they were to be derived could at the time hardly have been foreseeable.

Macedon was a large inland state, occupying the mountainous country between Illyria (now Albania) and Thrace. It had been ruled for more than a century by a line of kings who maintained a feudal structure long outdated elsewhere in Greece, and its existence had been hardly affected by the ebb and flow of political power among its more civilised neighbours in the south, for whom it had gained significance only as a potential outer defence against invading armies from Persia. During the final years of the fifth century, however, the state had been reorganised by a king called Archelaos on more up-to-date lines and its aristocracy invested with the attributes of Hellenic culture. Archelaos founded a new capital at Pella, about twenty miles north of Thessalonica, which was connected with the sea by a navigable river and soon became a busy trading centre. From then onwards, Greek writers cease to use the pejorative term 'barbarian' in reference to Macedon and remember only the distinguished ancestry of its rulers. But it was not until 360 BC, when the throne was acquired by Philip II, father of Alexander the Great, that the country's high political aspirations and the possibility of their fulfilment began to become apparent.

Philip's remarkable accomplishment in attaining for his country overall supremacy in the Greek world has tended to be regarded as little more than a preface to the meteoric career of his extraordinary successor. In fact, it is in itself an interesting story. In 365 BC, at the age of 18, he returned to Macedon from the city of Thebes, where for three years he had been left as a hostage.

51. Early posthumous issue by Philip III of a gold stater of Philip II of Macedon. Struck at Magnesia-ad-Maeandrum in about 320 BC. Diameter 17 mm. British Museum (1896–7–3–131).

During that time he must already have learnt much from the Thebans about military science and been impressed by the orderliness and discipline for which they were at the time famous. Culturally, however, he treated them with contempt, having, like all young Macedonians, been taught to regard only the Athenians as completely civilised. Once home, he was quick to recognise the military potential of his tough compatriots. The nobility provided a well-trained corps of heavy cavalry. Farmers and herdsmen contributed to the formation of a sturdy militia, from which in due course there emerged a new and reliable tactical weapon, the Macedonian phalanx. Among Philip's first conquests were the neighbouring Thracians, whose rich gold-mines provided him with a sound basis for future diplomacy. He next intervened in a characteristic contest, at that time in progress between Thessaly and Phocis, over the disputed own-ership of the famous sanctuary at Delphi. The Phocians were defeated and his new alliance with the Thessalians enabled him to annexe the Athenian protectorates along the northern shores of the Aegean, thus obtaining free access to the sea, which Macedon had hitherto lacked. Suddenly the mainland Greeks became aware of a new power confining their northern frontiers from Thermopylae to the Hellespont.

Throughout this period of territorial expansion, Philip had somehow con-trived to avoid any direct military confrontation with Athens, which he still regarded with awe and admiration as the centre of Greek civilisation. The fact was that in Athens itself, political opinion was divided between those who considered the new power as a potential ally, and a party led by Demosthenes, the full force of whose oratory was concentrated upon the Macedonian threat to the integrity of Greece. In the end, ambassadors were sent to Pella and a temporary agreement reached, which afforded time for Athens to consolidate an anti-Macedonian alliance with the city of Thebes. In 338 BC, the combined Theban and Athenian armies were heavily defeated by Philip at Chaeronia, east of Delphi, in a battle during which the young Alexander for the first time greatly distinguished himself. And here again one obtains a glimpse of Philip's character; for though the Thebans were conventionally punished and their city garrisoned, the Athenian prisoners were all sent home unharmed and the Athenian dead buried with honour.

Alexander was able to celebrate his eighteenth birthday at Athens, where he had been sent to negotiate a treaty of alliance. Its terms were once more extremely lenient and scarcely impaired the city's prestige in the Hellenic world. No Macedonian troops were to be quartered on Attic soil, nor warships to enter the harbour at Piraeus, and she was allowed to retain most of her overseas possessions. Upon Greece in general, however, Philip imposed a federal constitution under his own leadership as captain-general, and a meeting-place was fixed at Corinth, where representatives of all the states could meet to settle their differences. He himself set out on a tour of the countries from which they came, and was received everywhere – except by the Spartans – with honour and respect. Uppermost in his mind now was his early dream of a pan-Hellenic crusade against Persia. In recent years, all his preliminary struggles had been directed towards this end, which now seemed capable of fulfilment. To all intents and purposes, Greece appeared finally to have become a nation which, with proper leadership, could measure its strength against its hereditary enemy in the east. His preparations for an invasion of the Great King's territory were already far advanced when, in the late summer of 336 BC, he was assassinated.

Many historians have done less than justice to Philip of Macedon as an historical figure, being content to regard him as an upstart adventurer intruding upon a world to which he did not belong. They criticise the crudity and dissipation of his private life, but ignore his stature as a military leader and diplomatist. Doubtless, in the years after his death, his personality must have suffered from comparison with that of the paragon who was to succeed him. But it was he who had chosen Alexander's tutors, including the great Aristotle, and who had made of his home at Pella a centre of learning to which other great thinkers of his time were attracted. If his self-indulgent behaviour was at times offensive, one must remember the physical disabilities which he had incurred during a lifetime of campaigning. Apart from the effects of many minor injuries, he had lost an eye and the use of one leg.

In recent times, a new degree of tangible reality has been given to the reputed personality and life-style of Alexander's father by the discovery of a royal necropolis at Vergina, near Thessalonica. Its most conspicuous features were two tumulus-burials known as the 'Macedonian Tombs', whose contents have now been unequivocally associated with the royal family. The fabulous riches of gold, silver and other precious materials recovered from their undisturbed burial chambers – particularly that now attributed to Philip himself – have created a new and greatly enhanced impression, both of the king as an

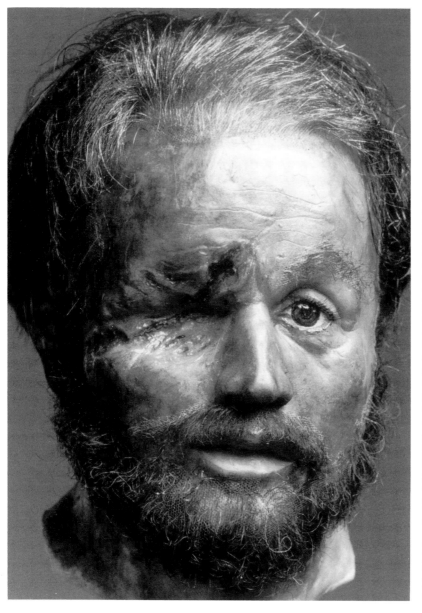

52. The face of Philip II of Macedon, as reconstructed by Richard Neave of the Department of Medical Illustration, University of Manchester. The scarring of the eye wound was probably less horrific than is shown here, for Pliny (*Natural Histories*, VII:124) says that Kritoboulos, Philip's doctor, won great renown for the skill with which he extracted the arrow and healed the wound so that the king was not disfigured. On the reconstruction, see J. N. W. Prag, J. H. Musgrove and R. A. H. Neave, 'The skull from Tomb II at Vergina: King Philip II of Macedon', *Journal of Hellenic Studies* 104 (1984), pp. 60–78; on the eye wound, see J. N. W. Prag, 'Reconstructing King Philip II: the "nice version"', forthcoming.

individual and of the milieu in which he lived. In the words of a Greek excavator, 'This resplendent picture of royal wealth and high cultural standards of the Macedonian court during Philip's reign is here amplified in the most unexpected way by the actual weapons of the dead man.' To add one intriguing detail: some parts of the king's armour had been perceptibly adapted to his known physical deformities.[1]

Here then is the background against which Alexander's great enterprise in Asia was conceived. His father's death must have seemed to him no more than a link in the preordained pattern of events through which he believed that his own destiny would be achieved. From the beginning he had shared Philip's dedication to the pan-Hellenic cause against Persia and his determination that Macedon should play the leading role in the forthcoming war. By his own people he had been spontaneously accepted as Philip's successor and it now only remained to assure the acceptance of his leadership by the rest of Greece. This proved less easy than he had expected.

Alexander started by making a ceremonial round of visits to the principal Greek centres, including Delphi, where he consulted the famous oracle. Finding the 'Pythia' – an elderly priestess who acted as the mouthpiece of the god – temporarily off-duty, his boyish importunity elicited from her the remark, 'My son, you are irresistible!', a pronouncement which, with the adjective slightly amended, could be taken to imply divine approval of his mission. His next step – perhaps less well considered – was a campaign to ensure the security of his remote north-eastern frontier on the Danube, and while this was in progress a report began to be spread that he had been killed. In Greece the news was received with open satisfaction and within weeks the entire Corinthian League repudiated its allegiance to Macedon. Despite the repeated proofs of Greek infidelity to which his father had earlier become accustomed, Alexander was greatly shocked by this development. His reaction was characteristically violent and totally effective. After a forced march, averaging twenty miles a day over mountainous country, he appeared with his whole army before the walls of Thebes, where the people were celebrating his death, having confined the Macedonian garrison to the citadel. Taken completely unawares, they offered little resistance and Alexander ruthlessly destroyed the town, selling into slavery those of its inhabitants who survived the massacre. In after years there were times when this offence against Greek tradition seemed to play upon his conscience. He remembered the words of a Theban lady who had behaved with extreme bravery during the siege, when he politely asked her name: 'I am the sister of Theagenes, who commanded the Thebans at the battle of Chaeronia against your father Philip, and who died there for the liberty of Greece.' But for the moment he had no reason to be dissatisfied with the results of his action. The news of his return and the sack of Thebes created panic among the Greek states, and soon he was faced with the same deputation which Athens had sent to his father on a previous occasion. When he eventually consented to receive them, he was impressed by their sincerity – particularly by the advice of one who was afterwards destined to become his close friend. 'If', said Phocion, 'it is the prevention of unrest in Greece you want, make peace at once; but if it is military glory that you desire, use your army against foreigners, not against Greeks.'[2] Yet it is clear that the time had not yet come for Alexander fully to apprehend the indifference of the Greeks to the high purpose which he intended to serve, or their rejection of his claim to be their leader. Many months later, when his position was fully established, he was still to be deeply shocked by finding Greek mercenaries fighting on the Persian side.

CHAPTER 14

The Conquests
of Alexander

It may now have become clear that some knowledge of the events which preceded Alexander's departure into Asia is necessary if one is to understand his more perplexing attitudes and motivations during the campaign which followed. In the years after his death in Babylon, its progress was documented in great detail by his near-contemporaries, while in more recent times commentaries on his life have continued to proliferate. From these last, one gains the impression that modern scholars have never quite made up their minds how to assess his personality. To quote Arthur Weigall, whom the present writer regards as one of his most intelligent biographers:

> Some have seen him as an idealist, pressing on from victory to victory for what he believed to be the good of mankind. Others have thought his motives to have been purely selfish, and his guiding light a fiery passion for personal glory and power. Some have considered the moves in his tremendous game to have been dictated by an immense intellect. Others suppose that he followed his star with a light heart, being too vain to think himself capable of making a mistake.[1]

It is interesting to note that even the classical authors failed to agree in defining the actual objective which he had set himself during this early stage of his mission. Obviously the liberation of the Greeks in Asia Minor could be regarded as his most immediate purpose, but surely the total conquest of Persia must as yet have seemed geographically impracticable. Weigall emphasises the mystical aspect of the role to which he considered himself appointed; the aura of ambiguity with which his mother, Olympias, had deliberately surrounded the circumstances of his birth, fostering the belief, which he himself now firmly maintained, that his father was in fact the Graeco-Egyptian god Zeus-Ammon. In that case, his campaign was, in a sense, a pilgrimage which would then have been accomplished when he reached the god's shrine and oracle at the Siwa Oasis. But surely again, he was too young to have planned so far ahead.

Leaving this undecided, we must now return to a more actual chronicle of events, which in the present context will be concerned mainly with Alexander's passage through Anatolia, from the Hellespont to the frontiers of Syria. It occupied rather more than eighteen months of the eleven years which remained of his life. When it was over, he could already look back on two major battles against Persian armies and the siege of more than one enormous Greek city. He had been compelled to make tactical decisions of far-reaching importance and obtained his first experience of campaigning in an oriental country. It would be difficult, therefore, to overestimate the importance of this phase in his short career, and it is accordingly surprising to find it dealt with in so few pages by the early historians. One explanation would suggest that, geographically, Asia Minor at that time held little mystery for the ordinary run of educated Greeks. Today, on the other hand, the course of his march and its repeated deviations have gained greater interest, and one may profit from reference to a comparatively recent study by Freya Stark, for the purpose of which she travelled observantly over practically the whole route and formed conclusions well based on historical reading.[2]

Alexander left Macedonia in the spring of 334 BC, marching his army along the Thracian coast and then through the Gallipoli peninsula to Sestus, a small town facing Abydus across the Hellespont at a point where the Narrows of the Dardanelles are less than a mile wide. Here he left his father's most trusted general, Parmenion, to supervise the crossing into Asia, where an advance-guard had already been established before Philip's death. He himself moved on with a party of picked troops down to Elaeus at the extreme tip of the peninsula, since his intention was to pay a ceremonial visit to the site of Troy

53. Gold distater of Alexander the Great, struck in Macedonia about 325 BC. Diameter 21 mm. British Museum (BMC 167a).

before rejoining the army and embarking on his campaign. This he did, having crossed the mouth of the Hellespont by boat and landed at ancient Sigaeum (now identified with a place called Yenişehir on high ground to the south-west of Kumkale where the Scamander reaches the sea). Here he found himself in what he believed to be the authentic setting of legendary events familiar to him since his childhood, among the shades of Homeric heroes with whom he now considered his own destiny to be identified. There ensued a series of almost theatrical performances in celebration of the occasion, sacrifices and ceremonial dances around the reputed tombs of Achilles, Patroclus or Ajax, and a formal visit to the Hellenic city of Ilion which had grown up around the ruins of the old Homeric fortress. Here, in its temple, he acquired a shield and some armour said to have been used by one of the Greek heroes, which he carried with him as a talisman throughout his campaigns.[3] In return for this gift he made arrangements for the rebuilding of Troy itself and, with a promise that its inhabitants should be henceforth relieved of taxation, he finally moved northward to rejoin the main army at Abydus.

On the Persian side, some preparations had by now been made for the impending confrontation with the Macedonian forces. The Achaemenian head of state was at this time Darius III, who had usurped the throne in 336 BC. At his court in Susa he had offered hospitality to a number of political exiles who had left Greece after the collapse of the anti-Macedonian party in Athens and, judging by the information which they gave him, he does not seem to have been unduly disturbed by the news of Alexander's activities. It is clear in fact that Darius at first regarded him as an impertinent young fool, whose behaviour merited no more than a sarcastic and monitory letter. He did, however, at the same time instruct his military commanders in Asia Minor to take precautionary measures, and a powerful concentration of Persian forces had been organised at Zeleia (near modern Gönen at the western end of the Marmara). These now moved westward, to take up a strong position on the east bank of the Granicus river, which flows into the sea near the small modern port of Karabiga.

One is bound to concede that there was some justification for the Persians' underestimation of the threat from Alexander's expeditionary force. In actual numbers his army comprised no more than 30,000 infantry and 5,000 cavalry, while little if any consideration had been given to the question of their pay and provisioning. The Persian forces outnumbered them by approximately three to one. Knowing this, Alexander must fully have understood how much would be at stake during his first critical encounter with the enemy. What the Persians on their side were less in a position to comprehend, was the mood of heroic exaltation which enabled him to make light of all practical realities. For it was in this frame of mind that he now led his army to the Granicus and fought a battle in which his conduct as a general seems to have defied the most elementary rules of tactical prudence. The outcome, however, was a spectacular and overwhelming victory which, as we now know, already distantly foreshadowed the collapse of the Persian Empire.

Unlike the majority of battles in classical times, the course of the engagement at the Granicus was surprisingly uncomplicated. The Greeks reached the river in the early afternoon and were confronted with a massive array of Persian forces, drawn up in close formation along the summit of the steep river bank opposite. Rejecting Parmenion's advice that action should be postponed until sunrise on the following day, Alexander at once set about making the necessary dispositions for a contested crossing. The attack was to be made obliquely across the stream by two columns of cavalry, spearheaded by Alexander's famous 'Companions', the élite of his army. When this became apparent to the Persians, they too brought forward their own aristocratic mounted corps to head the defence, and among them were Darius' two most distinguished lieutenants, Spithridates, Governor-General of Lydia, and Arsites, Viceroy of Northern Phrygia; so the battle began at once with a direct confrontation of the leaders on both sides. As soon as the slippery river bank had been negotiated, Alexander at the head of his Companions burst through onto the level ground above and began fighting with reckless bravery. He himself, in his white-plumed helmet, must have been conspicuous enough, but the Persian commanders could also be recognised, and it was upon them that he at once concentrated a most furious attack. From this point onward the ancient writers have given us what would now be called a 'blow-by-blow' account of what happened. Here for instance is Plutarch's version:

> Alexander, being easily known by his buckler and a large plume of white feathers on each side of his helmet, was attacked on all sides, yet escaped wounding, though his cuirass was pierced by a javelin in one of the joinings. And Rhoesaces and Spithridates, two Persian commanders, falling upon him at once, he avoided one of them and struck at Rhoesaces, who had a good cuirass on, with such force that his spear breaking in his hand, he was glad to take to his dagger. While they were thus engaged, Spithridates came up on one side of him and, raising himself upon his horse, gave him such a blow with his battle-axe on the helmet that he cut off the crest of it with one of its plumes, and the helmet was only just so far strong enough to save him that the edge of the weapon touched the hair of his head. But as he was about to repeat his stroke, Clitus, called the black Clitus [this was the son of Alexander's old nurse], prevented him by running him through the body with his spear. At the same time Alexander despatched Rhoesaces with his sword.[4]

While this was going on, the Macedonian phalanx had finally succeeded in crossing the river and was creating havoc among the Persian infantry. It was probably the courage and discipline of these veteran troops, impeccably trained by Alexander's father, which eventually decided the issue: but, like the death of Cyrus at Cunaxa and the ignominious flight of Darius himself during two of Alexander's subsequent battles, one is inclined to believe that the loss of both Persian commanders – at a moment when the strength of a blow could have ended the war – may already have created a turning-point in the battle.

Last to surrender on the Persian side was a large force of Greek mercenaries who had withdrawn in formation to some high ground. They fought bravely and would not submit until surrounded by the entire Macedonian army. This was Alexander's first encounter with the intransigent militarism of the Eastern Greeks, and his harsh treatment of the few survivors emphasises the tenacity with which he still clung to his old illusion of pan-Hellenic solidarity. Where the Persians were concerned, however, there was no doubt about the magnitude of his victory. Their dead were numbered in thousands, including several close relatives of the Great King, and the spoils from their camp can well be imagined. Three hundred suits of Persian armour were sent to the temple of Athena at Athens, and a tailpiece to the story could be the wording of their dedication: 'Alexander, son of Philip, and the Greeks, *except the Spartans*, dedicate these spoils of the Barbarians of Asia.'

The momentous importance of the victory at the Granicus from Alexander's viewpoint need hardly be emphasised. His expedition, which had until then so widely been regarded as a crazy adventure, had been converted overnight into a well-established initiative with almost incredible possibilities. Weigall reminds one, in terms which are not unduly exaggerated, of the new status which he had attained in the eyes of all Greece, and more particularly in those of his own army:

> The young king's personal prestige after this battle was raised, of course, to sublime heights. The fact that he had employed no strategy, and had given himself no opportunity of displaying his skill as a military leader, was overlooked in the general acknowledgement that he had fought with skill at arms, a physical strength and a death-defying bravery hardly equalled even in the Trojan legends, and that from first to last he had carried himself with almost superhuman heroism and nobility. The whole army adored him as never in memory had a youth been adored before, and all were willing to follow him wheresoever he might lead them.[5]

His ability as a strategist yet remained to be proved. Alexander sent Parmenion to occupy Daskylion (Ergili), where he replaced the Persian governor of Phrygia, and we next hear of the army's arrival at Sardis, after an unopposed march across Mysia. Sardis, as we know, was one of the most important provincial capitals of the Persian Empire, but it was also the ancient capital of the Lydians, whose relationship with the Greeks was traditionally friendly. This may help to explain the Persian garrison's readiness to surrender, for the gates were immediately opened and Alexander soon found himself admiring the city from the summit of its high citadel. Characteristically, he decreed the erection of a temple to Zeus over the ancient ruins of Croesus' palace.

He now turned his attention to the great Ionian cities of the coast, and the Greeks of Ephesus were the first to receive him with open arms. Once again, his first concern was with their famous religious shrine, the Artemisium, which had, as will be remembered, been destroyed by fire on the very day he himself had been born. He decreed that it should now be rebuilt on a magnificent scale and, furthermore, that the entire amount of the tribute hitherto paid by the city to the Persians should be transferred to the temple and its priesthood. When one remembers that, until a few weeks previously, he had been lacking in the wherewithal to pay his troops, this gesture must be taken as a measure of his confidence in the future. Obviously it assured his popularity with the Ephesians, though a small episode related by Pliny suggests that, in their culturally sophisticated society, he was not quite at home. Visiting the studio of Apelles, a famous painter from whom he had commissioned a portrait, he began to discourse, as he imagined knowledgeably, on the subject of art. Presently Apelles interrupted, asking him to speak more quietly as he was making the apprentices laugh.[6]

Alexander's stay in Ephesus ended with the usual religious festival and processions. His next objective was the city of Miletus, thirty miles to the south on the farther shore of the great Maeander estuary. This could be considered one of the most ancient cities of the Eastern Greeks and had, as we know, been a Mycenaean colony as early as the mid-second millennium BC. But here, to his surprise and indignation, his triumphant progress through Ionia was suddenly halted. Indifferent apparently to the prospect of 'liberation', the Milesians closed their gates against him.

The storming of the walls at Miletus involved a great deal of bitter fighting and more casualties among Alexander's own troops than he would have wished. One of those killed was 'Black' Clitus, who had saved his life at the Granicus and of whom he was very fond. It was time now for him to abandon the role of 'liberator' and to face the necessity for some degree of forcible persuasion in acquiring new allies among the Eastern Greeks. Even his attitude to Greek mercenaries had suffered a notable change. When the city had fallen, a party of them took refuge on a small island in the estuary called Lade (now an inconspicuous mound in the alluvial plain), knowing themselves to be in a desperate situation. Alexander merely offered them service in his own army, which they thankfully accepted.

At about this time, Alexander was compelled to consider the naval aspect of his campaign and to make a serious decision. His own small fleet, consisting of about 160 vessels, had come down from the Hellespont following the coast, and arrived at Miletus just in time to prevent the enemy fleet from taking possession of the harbour. The Persians had brought up an immensely larger force of about 400 fighting ships; but they found that the Greeks had jammed their triremes together, bows seaward, at the narrowest part of the harbour entrance and would not be enticed into an open fight. The enemy then sailed away to Samos to obtain provisions. In the council which followed, Parmenion was strongly in favour of risking a sea battle with the Persians on their return, basing his argument merely on the traditional superiority of Greek seamanship. But Alexander had begun to think on quite other lines. He had recently become aware of the great drain on his resources which the very existence of a naval force created. For the maintenance even of his own comparatively modest fleet, it could be reckoned that as many as 30,000 men had to be retained –

for a great part of the time in comparative idleness. Also they needed to be kept supplied with food and water, a requirement which, in the case of the huge Persian fleet, must be creating an even more formidable problem. He also realised that the progress of his army along the Aegean and Mediterranean seaboard would continue to eliminate, one by one, the Persian sources of supply, until the position of their fleet might become untenable. A decision in favour of Alexander's argument – supposedly dependent as usual on a ridiculously equivocal omen – was eventually reached. As soon as the loyalty of the Milesians was assured and the use of their harbour denied to the enemy, the Macedonian fleet was quietly dismantled.

Moving southwards from Miletus, Alexander next turned his attention to Halicarnassus, the capital city of Caria and now the Turkish harbour town of Bodrum. Halicarnassus had been a Dorian foundation in the early days of Greek colonisation, but the Carians were an indigenous people, of whom something is known as early as Hittite times, and they still accounted for the bulk of the population. They had been ruled, at least since the beginning of the fourth century, by a Carian royal family, who persisted in a tradition of female heredity. A king's son could only become eligible for the throne by marrying his sister.[7] This had been the case with the most celebrated king of Caria, Mausolus, who had married his sister Artemisia in 377 BC and was still reigning at the time of Alexander's birth in 356 BC. When Mausolus died three years later, the queen, whose devotion to him had become proverbial (she is said to have mixed a pinch of his ashes with her daily glass of wine), commissioned in his memory the magnificent monument which afterwards became one of the Seven Wonders of the Hellenistic world. When Artemisia herself also died, the rightful heir to the throne was her sister Ada; but at the time we are now considering (334 BC) she had been ousted from her inheritance by a Persian named Orontobates and was living in a remote fortress called Alinda.

Freya Stark, in her study of Alexander's campaign, pays much attention to his encounter with this elderly queen, previous to his arrival at Halicarnassus,[8] and attributes to it some political significance. She recalls that there had been an earlier correspondence between the two of them when Alexander, at the age of 18, had angered his father by proposing marriage to a Carian princess. Whether or not at that early age he had his eye on the kingdom of Caria, it was now at least desirable that he should cultivate the acquaintance of its rightful queen. As it proved, he had no difficulty in doing so. Ada was enchanted by his personality and from then onwards insisted on addressing him as 'My son'. Plutarch even recounts the near-importunity of her consideration for his health and comfort.[9]

Miss Stark was interested in the question of where this meeting took place. Though neither Arrian nor Plutarch specifically says so, she was persuaded that Alexander actually visited Alinda; a city whose site she examined, noting the routes leading to it. In fact, for Alexander this would have meant a complicated detour. His most obvious route from Miletus to Halicarnassus would have been the line of the modern motor road, along the beautiful southern shore of the Latmic Gulf, which is now Lake Bafa. It runs by the site of Euromus to Mylasa (Milas) before turning south-westward to Bodrum. Perhaps, like Queen Epyaxa, when Cyrus was approaching Cilicia, Ada herself came down from Alinda to meet the king.

At Halicarnassus, Alexander was confronted by a walled city, no less well fortified and better garrisoned than Miletus. The citadel on its rocky promontory, today occupied by the great Castle of St Peter (Fig. 65), enclosed and protected the inner harbour, from which the fine buildings of the outer town spread northwards. Concentrated here at the time were most of the Persian forces who had survived the battle of the Granicus. In the harbour lay the Persian fleet, under the command of Memnon, a Greek from Rhodes, committed by his friendship with Darius to the Persian cause. Alexander's assault on the walls suffered a number of quite serious setbacks in its early stages, and Arrian tells us that at one point he temporarily turned his attention to an attack on Myndus at the other side of the peninsula, but met with no better success. On his return, he found the outer city of Halicarnassus in flames, Orontobates and Memnon having withdrawn their troops to the protection of the citadel. Characteristically, rejecting the prospect of a long siege which would have slowed down the momentum of his campaign, he then merely occupied what remained of the city itself, installed Queen Ada as ruler of Caria with a Macedonian garrison to protect her and left the Persian forces to their own devices. He rightly assumed that Memnon could not keep his fleet for long penned up in the harbour, and himself intended to persist in his policy of cutting off its mainland bases.

Winter was now drawing on and Alexander was faced with further strategic decisions. He sent a large part of his army under Parmenion back to Sardis, with orders to make their way inland as far as Gordium on the plateau, which was a primary station on the Royal Road leading to Mesopotamia. Also, he made a gesture which is said to have pleased his troops more than anything he had so far done. He sent back a group of young officers who had been newly married when the campaign began, to spend the winter at home and to enlist new reinforcements on their return. He himself continued on his way towards the harbour towns of the Lycian coast, once more along the line of the modern motor road, visiting Telmessus (Fethiye) and then Xanthus. His object now was obviously to obtain control of the numerous small Lycian cities; but one has the impression that he did not realise what difficult country he was approaching. The province of Lycia comprises a knotted mass of high mountains, projecting into the sea, and such roads as existed in his time must have been extremely precarious.

Miss Stark's careful study of local topography[10] emphasises the uncertainty of his movements from one fortress or city to another before arriving at the fairly large port called Phaselis, on the east-facing coast. He was now aiming for the open coastal plain of Pamphylia, which he would reach at the point where modern Antalya now stands in the north-west corner of its great bay. But from Phaselis there was still a difficult march of twenty-five miles, where the track left the sea and climbed over a precipitous headland, called by historians Mount Climax. The army took this route, cutting steps in the rock where the path became too steep. But Alexander himself found that a shorter way was to follow the actual seashore, where in some places the waves can be seen lapping against the base of the high cliffs. This was only possible when the weather was favourable; but finding the wind in the right direction he took the risk and, with his immediate followers at times wading waist-deep in the sea, covered the distance in a remarkably short time.

It may be that too much has sometimes been made of the king's reckless behaviour on this occasion. Miss Stark quotes Plutarch's reminder that 'Alexander himself in his epistles mentions nothing unusual in this at all....' Describing her own investigations on the spot, when she examined the foot of the cliff from a boat and landed at various points, she concludes, 'As for Alexander's short cut, it is no longer feasible except by two or three hundred yards swimming at the more southerly cliff'. To her this must have seemed to require further proof for (being herself) she swam.

Finding himself now in easier country, Alexander in turn subdued or came to terms with the four great Pamphylian cities, Perge, Sillyum, Aspendus and Side, whose ruins are today familiar to many travellers in southern Turkey. At Side he called a temporary halt to his progress eastward, remembering his intended rendezvous with Parmenion's army at Gordium. The direction of his march was now inland towards the plateau and it brought him at once into Pisidia. Here, the first resistance he met with was from the people of Termessus, a fortress at the head of a deep gorge, perhaps more dramatically situated than any city in Asia Minor.[11] Arrian gives a good description of the difficult approach to the city – not, of course, mentioning the great wall of ashlar masonry across the head of the gorge which was built about a century later – and he makes it clear that although the lightly armed Termessians were defeated in open fighting, Alexander was not prepared to waste time in besieging it. He seems therefore to have swung back to the line of the modern road which runs northward from Antalya, and was not compelled to fight a decisive battle with the Pisidians until he reached Sagalassus, which is near Burdur. Having won this, his way was clear to Celaenae and across the plateau country to Gordium, where, in February 333 BC, he rejoined Parmenion.

The story of how he visited the old shrine of Midas and severed the 'Gordion Knot' is told at some length by both Plutarch and Arrian. This symbolical triumph may in fact have given Alexander less personal satisfaction than the embassies which he now received, offering the submission of great northern satrapies such as Paphlagonia and Cappadocia. At the same time a deputation arrived from Athens, asking for the release of the distinguished prisoners taken at the Granicus. To this he did not at once agree, since he regarded them as hostages against possible Athenian treachery. Of affairs at home, however, he had satisfactory news from the officers whom he had sent on leave and who now rejoined him, bringing with them several thousand Macedonian recruits. The prospects for his campaign must at this moment have seemed extremely favourable. His lines of communication were assured; the Eastern Greeks seemed content with the new régime and the subject peoples of Anatolia disinclined to oppose him. The resumption of his eastward march along the well-trodden route to Ancyra (Ankara) and across the plain to Cilicia presented no problem. Even so, he must have been pleasantly surprised when a midnight reconnaisance, which he conducted himself, showed the narrow defile of the Cilician Gates to be undefended. Once across the Taurus, he made a forced march to Tarsus, where he arrived in time to prevent the departing Persians from looting the town.

Alexander's serious illness after reaching Tarsus must have been as great a shock to his followers as it was to himself, since it was the kind of misfortune from which he had hitherto appeared to be immune. Coming down suddenly into the heat and humidity of the Cilician plain, he had impulsively thrown off his armour and bathed in the Cydnus river which flows through the town towards the sea – in spring still chilled by the melting snows of the Taurus. Unlike the Caliph Ma'mun who, almost a thousand years later, died after making the same mistake, Alexander survived; but his illness and convalescence lasted most of the summer. The trouble seems to have been that, among the physicians accompanying him, only Philip of Acarnania, who had looked after him since he was a boy, dared to prescribe the 'powerful purgative' which in the end saved his life. And there is a story – many times retold – of how, while the dose was being prepared, he received a letter warning him of a plot against his life, but handed it to Philip to read while he himself swallowed the medicine. When he was better he occupied himself with a minor operation against the small city of Soli, whose attractive ruins lie some miles west of modern Mersin. In supporting the Persians, its people appear to have committed the kind of 'solecism' for which they afterwards became famous.

But the time had now come for the army to turn its attention to more serious matters. They had moved eastward to Mallos, at the mouth of the Pyramus (Ceyhan) river, when news was received that the whole Persian army was encamped at a place called Sochoi, beyond the Amanus range, on what is now the Turco-Syrian frontier. Darius had marched up the Euphrates from Babylon in the early summer and was preparing his forces for a major battle. The events which now preceded the engagement at Issus have been variously interpreted by historians. They suggest above all an extraordinary lack of reliable intelligence services on both sides. If one is to avoid the further confusion created by ignorance of local geography in some late accounts, the movements of the two armies may perhaps be best understood by glancing at a modern road map.

Moving up the Ceyhan river, Alexander took the line of the modern motorway running eastward from Adana, which reaches a fork at Toprakkale, one road turning south along the coast towards Iskenderun, the other continuing eastward to Osmaniye and over the Bahçe pass to Fevzipaşa. Alexander took the first of these, continuing southward with the sea on his right, until he reached the port called Myriandrus, a little beyond what was to be the site of

Alexandretta (Iskenderun). His intention was probably to cross the Amanus by the pass now called Belen (or Beylan) into the Amuq plain, where he supposed the Persian army to be. He now discovered to his astonishment that it was in fact behind him, having reached the town of Issus on the narrow strip of land between sea and hills which he had traversed on the previous day. Darius, after impatiently waiting at Sochoi, where he would have been able to deploy his huge army in open country, had decided to take the offensive and had marched by the most direct route into Cilicia, across the Bahçe Pass. Learning the true situation when he reached the Toprakkale crossroads, he had turned southward in the rear of the Greek army.

For Alexander there was no alternative to returning the way he had just come. His army spent the night sleeping among the rocks at a place known as the Syrian Gates, where the foothills of the Amanus come down to the sea, and at dawn set out once more in good order for Issus.

There is no factually reliable record of the numbers who fought on either side at Issus. Certainly the Persians could be counted in hundreds of thousands, and it is equally certain that the Greek army, reinforced by Eastern Greek mercenaries and recruits from Macedonia but depleted by the necessity for leaving garrisons in captured cities, can hardly have exceeded the 35,000 men who fought at the Granicus. Darius therefore should obviously have profited from an army immensely superior in size to that of his opponents. But this was not altogether the case. For now the battle was to be fought on a front strictly limited by the sea on one side and steeply rising hills on the other, so that there was less benefit to be gained from mere numbers. Nevertheless, to the Greek army confronting them across the shallow stream called Pinarus their ranks must have seemed to recede interminably into the distance. In the centre, Darius himself could be seen standing in his chariot, protected by his household troops and a heavy formation of Greek mercenaries.[12]

The progress of the battle at Issus has been recounted in great detail by classical historians, in particular by Arrian, who conscientiously records the movements and counter-movements of individual units in the Greek army, mentioning in each case the name of the officer in charge. Today, therefore, if one observes the battlefield and its setting, as Alexander himself did briefly before the action began, looking down on it from the high ground to the east, it becomes easy to visualise the successive developments and to understand their tactical significance. In doing so, one immediately becomes aware that there is something wrong with the story. One realises that at some unspecified time in the middle of that autumn afternoon, a point had been reached where, as the narrator guardedly admits, the Macedonian army appeared to be not only outnumbered, but out-manoeuvred and out-fought, and one is led to conclude that its chances of victory had become almost negligible. Dramatically, at that precise moment, the 'continuity' is broken, and when the narrative is resumed, the Persians are in flight. Let us then briefly summarise what had happened.

Parmenion on the left, with his wing on the actual shore of the sea, had

54. Alexander the Great (left) and Darius III (in his chariot) at the battle of Issus. Drawing of a mosaic from Pompeii, now in Naples Museum, which was probably based on an earlier Greek painting. From H. Roux, *Herculaneum et Pompéi*, Paris 1862, pl. 23.

been desperately resisting the hordes of Persian cavalry which Darius sent to outflank him. With the enemy already across the river, his distress signals had brought no more than a section of the Companions to his aid. For in the centre too the infantry were in trouble. Approaching the river in parade-ground order, they had engaged Darius' mercenaries with the bitter ferocity of Greeks fighting against Greeks. But the struggle in the water itself and on the river banks had disorganised the famous Macedonian phalanx, so that the crossing had not been effectively accomplished and the outcome of the fighting was in some doubt. On the right, meanwhile, Alexander and the main body of Companions were proceeding with unaccustomed caution. Skirting the foot-hills, he saw Persians manning the heights above, with the intention of descending in his rear. So he detached a company of archers and mobile troops to deal with them and himself finally descended in full force upon the Persian left wing. As at the Granicus, his charge was irresistible and he was soon able to swing left and make a flank attack on the mercenaries, thus enabling the phalanx to cross the river. As the Asiatic Greeks were being cut to pieces, the Persian command was left exposed; and presently the two kings came face to face. This was a 'moment of truth', in which not only the outcome of the battle but the fate of the Persian Empire hung in the balance. The issue was decided by Darius, for he wheeled his chariot and made for the hills, later discarding his royal impedimenta and taking to a horse.

For a modern reader, two aspects of the story tend to remain almost

55. Detail of Alexander the Great from the Issus mosaic (see Fig. 54).

incomprehensible. First, the simple problem of the Persian king's behaviour. Darius III was by no means the craven and degenerate oriental which most Greeks supposed him to be. He was notably good-looking and a head taller than Alexander. He had earned the title 'Bravest of the Persians' for his prowess in single combat during an early campaign. He was also well educated and familiar with Greek literature. Persian ethics should have dictated the deportment required of him under these circumstances. Nevertheless he fled: and the imputation of personal cowardice at Issus was again justified two years later at the battle of Arbela.

But the strangest anomaly in the story is the instantaneous effect of the king's flight on the progress of the battle. Within the space of a few minutes – no longer than it took for the news to spread along the front – the entire force of perhaps a quarter of a million Persians had become a panic-stricken rabble. For that, as Arrian says without further explanation, 'was the signal for a general rout – open and unconcealed'. If one remembers the comparable situations at the Granicus, at Arbela and, for that matter, in an earlier setting at Cunaxa, the question arises as to how the Persian army ever won an empire.

As to events in the aftermath of the battle – the pursuit of the enemy, the discovery of Darius' family in the deserted Persian camp, and their chivalrous treatment by Alexander, the recovery by Parmenion of the Persian treasure which had been sent to Damascus – all these create a colourful postscript to garnish the historian's account of an epic victory. But they adorn a tale rather than point a moral and have little relevance to the subsequent history of Asia Minor. For, after Issus, Alexander and his army pass beyond the confines of our interest in the present context, and throughout the great peninsula of Anatolia the echoes of his campaign fade into the obscurity of an ill-documented historical period.

CHAPTER 15

A Cosmopolitan Culture: Hellenism in Asia Minor

The period of three centuries which followed the death in Babylon of Alexander the Great in 323 BC saw a further prodigious advance in the evolution of world culture. To this end, a significant contribution was made by the peoples of Asia Minor, whose shores and frontiers now included so large a part of the Hellenistic world.

The term 'Hellenistic' deserves a moment's consideration. First it has been satisfyingly defined by M. I. Rostovtzeff in his great work on the period.[1] He says that this adjective should be applied to 'the world created by Alexander's conquest of the East, which existed as long as the states into which it disintegrated retained their political independence, and the Greeks in those states held the leading roles in all spheres of life; that is to say, approximately from the time of Alexander to that of Augustus.' W. Tarn, in his shorter book on the same subject,[2] supports this chronological definition. In his analysis of Hellenism, which, like other writers, he accepts as a convenient substantive, he shows how, during the centuries, the concept was created of *oecumene*, the 'inhabited world', as the common heritage of civilised man, unified by a common speech, the Attic Greek, which now came to be used from one end of it to the other. In order to feel themselves full citizens of this greater world, the upper classes of all nations from the Mediterranean to the Indus now felt it essential to provide themselves with at least the elements of Greek culture. For this implied a share in the privileges which went with it: internationalised commerce, free thought, abatement of race-hatred, and a morality generally dictated by science rather than authority. It was this cosmopolitanism which created the shape in which it was later bequeathed to the Romans and ultimately to ourselves. Let us then examine the part played by Asia Minor in the creation of this new world.

After Alexander's death, his generals found among his papers the plans for further conquests in the west; but not one of them was a man of sufficient calibre to step into his shoes and assume responsibility for the fortunes of the empire as a whole. Soon they were at war among themselves, involved in a complex and interminable struggle where armies of mercenaries from all nations supported the claims of each to the extension of his province at the expense of another. During these disturbances, the surviving members of Alexander's own family, his posthumous son by Roxane, Alexander IV, his witless half-brother Phillip III and even his mother Olympias lost their lives; and the empire became resolved into a number of separate kingdoms, each ruled by one of the great Macedonians who had previously commanded his armies. In this way, Ptolemy became ruler of Egypt and founded a dynasty, with its seat of government at Alexandria, destined to last for exactly three centuries under fourteen successive Ptolemies. Most of the old Persian Empire, as far as the frontiers of India, fell to the lot of Seleucus, who first ruled it from a new city on the Tigris to which he gave his own name, and afterwards from Antioch-on-the-Orontes (Antakya), which he named after his father Antiochus (a name borne by nine rulers of the dynasty).[3] The greater part of Asia Minor had come under the control of Antigonus, the one-eyed general whom Alexander had made satrap of Phrygia. But in 301 BC he was defeated and killed at Ipsus (on the road from Afyon to Konya) by Lysimachus, whose army was supported by that of Seleucus and a great many elephants. Lysimachus then assumed control of the whole country north of the Taurus. Twenty years later Lysimachus himself was eliminated by his previous ally, and this moment, early in the third century, when the Seleucid Empire reached its greatest extent, is perhaps a convenient one at which to survey the circumstances of the Greek and other states of which it was composed.

Alexander, after his first tumultuous passage through the land, pressed for time and urgently preoccupied with further conquests, had no alternative to re-establishing the practical basis of Persian administration: the regional division of the country into satrapies governed by generals, with an overall authority in Sardis, the old Lydian capital. But the free Greek cities of the coast were largely excluded from this authority, while the native kingdoms to the north and the scattering throughout the country of old Asiatic temple-states had yet to be politically incorporated.

The satrapies initially held by the Seleucids started in the north-west with Hellespontine Phrygia (the district bordering the Marmara, of which the centre today is Bandırma). Next came the great central province of Phrygia itself, stretching at that time as far as the Halys; Lydia, inland from the Ionian cities; Caria, in the south-west corner; Cilicia, comprising the whole coast and coastal plain south of the Taurus and, inland from this, Cappadocia, extending from the Salt Lake (Tuz Gölü) to the Euphrates. A longish stretch of the south coast, including Lycia and Pamphylia, remained in the hands of the Ptolemies during much of the Hellenistic period. The great native states of Pontus (then including much of Paphlagonia) and Bithynia accounted for the northern part of the country, and effectively separated the Seleucid world from the Greek cities of the Black Sea coast, whose Hellenic character was consequently from now onwards subject to considerable modifications. The extreme eastern part of what is now Turkey was occupied by the kingdom of Armenia.

Later in the period, Bithynia encroached on Phrygia and settled her allies, the invading Gauls, in its eastern half (approximately the vilayet of Ankara); Cappadocia became a kingdom and, as will presently be seen, Pergamum carved out an independent state from Aeolia. With these and other unsubdued dynasts in Pisidia and elsewhere, the Seleucids were continually in conflict. The most interesting aspect of the Seleucid régime in Asia Minor is its attempt to Hellenise the whole complex of widely different societies which it comprised, by extending the influence of the Greek cities and creating new ones.

Even in the southern satrapies, the old Asiatic temple-states were still numerous and owned much land. Their religion, which was usually based on the worship of the great pre-Aryan fertility goddess, was something foreign to Greeks and Persians alike. The temple-lands were cultivated by 'god's peasants', and from the daughters of these were recruited the female temple-slaves (or prostitutes, as they are often described), who, in their ministration to the fertility goddess, have always so astonished the western mind. These cult-centres made few concessions to the advance of western civilisation, and survived into Roman times. The central figures of their mythology, like Attis of Pessinus or Zeus of Olba, might sometimes acquire the disguise of a Greek association or name, but their orientalising effect on Greek religious beliefs and practice was much more conspicuous than the modifications necessitated by their own adaptation to Hellenism. For example, the early cult of Artemis at Ephesus was presided over by a high-priest known as Megabyzus, the King-bee, who was attended by a swarm of consecrated girls; the bee symbol did not disappear from Ephesian coinage till the time of Lysimachus.

The Seleucids did not attempt to eliminate the temple-states; indeed, they would hardly have had the vitality to do so. But it was their policy to detach from their actual ownership all but such land as was essential to the maintenance of the actual sacerdotal community. The importance of the great priestly families remained undiminished, and, centuries later, they even provided bishops for the Christian Church.

The redistribution of land thus acquired was much facilitated by the foundation of new Greek settlements. Appearing in the first instance as amorphous native communities, dignified by the establishment of Greek military posts, they soon enfranchised their Asiatic population and acquired the semblance, if not the full rights, of free cities. These new settlements, together with some older ones now adopted as Greek provincial centres, were usually renamed after the contemporary Seleucid monarch, so that a road starting from Antioch-on-the-Maeander could pass in succession through cities respectively named Antioch-Mysa, Antioch-Tralles and Antioch-Alabanda. In Cilicia, Adana, Tarsus and the estuary town Mallus all became Antiochs, while Mopsuestia became Seleucia.

Greek culture and Hellenistic methods of administration also spread gradually to the native states. But their Hellenisation was for the present only superficial. Feudal Armenia remained quite unaffected, but one characteristic example was Commagene, near Urfa, whose very identity might today be forgotten were it not for the survival of an extraordinary monument erected by its ruler Antiochus I (69–34 BC). Though partly in ruins and hard of access, it may be seen today at the summit of Nemrut Dağ, an isolated peak near Kahta in the Anti-Taurus.

A tumulus of stone 150 feet high rises from the natural rock, approachable

56. Monumental sculptures and fallen heads in front of the mountain-top burial tumulus of Antiochus I of Commagene (69–34 BC) at Nemrut Dağ. The heads stand over 2 m high.

from three level terraces. Today these are crowded with the damaged remains of memorial sculpture, indifferent in style but all of colossal size (the fallen heads alone of portrait statues are up to 10 feet high). The subjects represented, as may be gathered from fragmentary inscriptions,[4] are the king's supposed ancestors, tracing his heredity on the female side to the Seleucid heirs of Alexander the Great and, among the males, to the great Achaemenid rulers of Iran. Elsewhere an obscure hierarchy of gods and heroes is depicted. The actual tomb-chamber has not been located but was probably carved out of the natural rock beneath the tumulus.

By contrast, then, let us finally turn to the old Greek cities themselves, whose ancient traditions, vast populations and ever-increasing wealth made each of them hardly inferior in importance to a kingdom. For the Greeks who inhabited them, their liberation by Alexander had been the sequel to half a century of subjection to an oriental conqueror. In fact, it had been one of the express purposes of his eastern campaign, and once it was accomplished he set about the task of re-establishing their full status as free and independent political entities. The Seleucids were prepared in principle to recognise their autonomy but adopted the policy of encouraging any form of closer association among them. Old federations were if possible revived, new ones formed and groups of minor cities in certain cases compulsorily amalgamated. In this way there emerged a geographical pattern which was to remain practically unchanged until Roman times.

Occupying the place of honour in this constellation were the three great cities of the Ionian Federation: Miletus, on its small peninsula in the estuary of the Maeander river; Ephesus and Smyrna, each of them now rebuilt on new sites more convenient to their function as seaports. Ephesus at this time, by decree of Lysimachus, absorbed the populations of Colophon (Değirmendere) in the hills to the north and of Lebedos, its neighbouring harbour town. Smyrna became associated in a convenient military alliance with Magnesia-ad-Sipylum (Manisa), which commanded the northern approaches to its valley. Minor Ionian cities also rebuilt at this time included Priene, transferred in the mid-fourth century BC from its old site facing Miletus across the Maeander estuary to a shoulder of the hillside above, and Magnesia-ad-Maeandrum (the only city without direct access to the sea), which was now refounded three miles from the river at the foot of Mount Thorax. Phocaea (Foça) and Clazomenae (near Urla), situated respectively on the northern and southern shores of the Gulf of Smyrna, suffered commercially from the re-establishment of their greater neighbour by Antigonus and thenceforward declined in importance. Erythrae (east of Çeşme) and Teos (west of Seferihisar), neighbours of Clazomenae, on the other hand, continued to prosper, the one as a port from which the island of Chios could most easily be reached, and the other as an important centre of the worship of Dionysus.

North of Phocaea was the fertile coastal district of Aeolis with its three cities, Cyme, Myrina and Grynium, of which Cyme was always the most prominent. Beyond Grynium, Elaea, the port of Pergamum, marked the borders of Mysia, and Adramyttium stood at the innermost recess of the Gulf called by the same name (Edremit Körfesi). The Troad, forming the north-west corner of the peninsula, had in former times been a land of many cities; but some of these had now been amalgamated or merely ceased to exist. Ancient Ilium, from which the district took its name, had been reduced to little more than a village when Alexander restored it to the status of a *polis*. It now continued to be eclipsed by its new neighbour, Alexandria Troas, founded by Antigonus and extended by Lysimachus. Lampsacus (Lapseki) and Parium on the Hellespont, and Assus, facing the island of Lesbos on the south coast, all became members of the new Ilian Federation created by Alexander. Finally, on the southern shore of the Propontis (Marmara) was Cyzicus, occupying the narrow neck of land between modern Bandırma and Erdek.

The districts of the southern seaboard, Caria, Lycia and Pamphylia, remained in the hands of the Ptolemies during most of the early Hellenistic period; but the contribution made by their cities to the advancement of Greek culture was none the less significant. Of the Carian cities, by far the most celebrated was Mylasa (Milas). It was situated at a distance of some ten miles from its port, Passala, and included in its territory the great precinct of Zeus at Labraunda, with which it was connected by a paved Sacred Way. South-west of Mylasa, on the Gulf of Cos, was Halicarnassus, a semi-independent kingdom. Beyond the Gulf, Cnidus, with its two harbours, occupied a unique position at the extreme end of a long peninsula. Like Halicarnassus and Mylasa, it was a member-state of the so-called Dorian Hexapolis.

All these cities, being thus rid of the irksome indignity of imposed rule, could now return to a more congenial way of life and to a form of government

sanctioned by long custom among their ancestors – government by an assembly of the people, the prototype of modern democracy. There can be no doubt at all about the degree of private wealth in the Greek cities of Asia Minor during these centuries. It is reflected in the richness of clothing, the improved comfort of private houses, with their mosaic pavements, elegant peristyle courts, running water and drainage, and in the multiplication of festivals and games, which now involved the engagement of highly paid professional performers. The cities themselves were better planned, sometimes, like Priene,

57. Part of a frieze depicting actors' masks, which decorated the stage building of the theatre at Perge in Pamphylia in the second century AD.

on the grid system, invented in Periclean times by Hippodamus, or at others with a more sophisticated instinct for asymmetrical grouping. The astonishingly dramatic effects obtained by a skilful adaptation of natural settings are referred to elsewhere (Chapter 16). Public buildings themselves, which in the fifth century had consisted almost exclusively of temples, now included council-chambers, theatres, concert-halls, museums and a complexity of spacious porticoes, grouped around a colonnaded agora. To meet the requirements of such buildings, new architectural forms had to be evolved and the rigid conventions of the old Greek builders largely abandoned.

With this material background, the great philosophers and scientists of the Hellenistic world worked and wrote in a congenial atmosphere of public approbation and interest. Human knowledge, the total of which Aristotle had himself been able virtually to encompass in his written works, took a sudden and prodigious stride forward. Many of the spectacular discoveries of the period can be attributed to Archimedes' workshop at Syracuse; it was he who, having devised the launching of a great ship by a system of pulleys, remarked 'Give me where to stand and I will move the earth', and whose cry of 'Eureka' on emerging from his bath heralded his discovery of specific gravity. At the 'Museum' at Alexandria, a group of state-subsidised research workers discovered, for instance, the relation of our world and planets to the sun, and correctly computed the circumference of the earth. This group, which Simon the Sceptic referred to as 'fatted fowls in a coop', included such names as Euclid, Aristarchus and Eratosthenes. But the great Ionian cities and many of their humbler neighbours also produced famous names. Some were botanists, zoologists or specialists in anatomy and medicine, while others represented a new phenomenon arising from the foundation of great libraries like that at Pergamum. These were either 'literary men' who were now able to 'write books about other books', or 'bibliophiles', collectors and translators. The library of the Ptolemies at Alexandria is said to have contained 700,000 volumes, many of them 'standard editions' made possible by the abundance of papyrus and slave-labour in the copying department.

In the realm of religion, a great change had taken place, with the increasing rejection of the old pantheon of conventional gods and goddesses. The Greek citizen, who before Alexander had thought of himself merely as a component of a community, now became an individual with little respect for traditional doctrine. He required a new ethic on which to model his behaviour, and this was supplied by the two great contemporary 'philosophies of conduct', the Stoic and the Epicurean, the former of which at least was perhaps the greatest creation of the age. Such actual religion as remained in Asia Minor acquired a strong oriental flavour from the influence of indigenous beliefs, and a variety to satisfy almost all forms of superstition.

Any parallel with the modern world, however, becomes a false analogy when one remembers the prevalence of slavery. A considerable proportion of the population was naturally and totally excluded from any benefits which may have been implicit in the newly developed way of life described above.

58. The north colonnade
of the precinct of
Asclepius, built in the
first half of the second
century AD in the lower
town at Pergamum.

Having formed a picture of life in Asia Minor under the Seleucid régime, we must now return to observe events following the battle of the Plain of Coros, whereby in 281 BC Seleucus I disposed of his former ally Lysimachus. Seleucus himself was a considerable figure, and had he not been assassinated in the following year, might well have succeeded in incorporating the whole country in his empire. As it turned out, the lesser Seleuci and Antiochi who followed him proved an inferior breed and have left a record only of murderous family feuds and dark harem intrigues. As a result, their territory in Asia Minor was soon lost, and the unification of the country had to await the arrival of the Romans.

The year following Seleucus' death saw the beginnings of an event which must be regarded as one of the strangest in the whole period. This was a migration of tribes from eastern Europe, which resulted in the establishment of a Celtic people in the very centre of the Anatolian plateau. In spite of the formidable resistance with which they had met in Macedonia during the previous year, by 278 BC 20,000 of these Gauls with their families had reached the Dardanelles and had begun to cross into Asia. Failing to obtain any footing among the Greek cities of the Troad, they moved eastwards, and being accepted as useful allies by the two native states, Bithynia and Pontus, were given territory in Phrygia. Here, with the vigour of their raids and general lawlessness, they proceeded to disturb the peace of the western states, and by the imminent threat of expansion to create a general panic among them. It was this threat which brought Pergamum into prominence; and since this state was now to loom so large in the evolution of Hellenism, its history must next be considered.

The great volume of modern literature which has accumulated around the history and antiquities of Pergamum (one standard work[5] has a fifteen-page bibliography) has established its fame beyond all dispute. Yet the story of its

154

promotion from an obscure city-state to the capital of a miniature empire can be summarised fairly briefly. Lysimachus, into whose hands it fell after the battle of Ipsus, deposited in the fortress on its high citadel the treasures which he had amassed during his sojourn in Asia Minor. The contemporary ruler of the city was a Paphlagonian called Philataerus, who was said to have become a eunuch as the result of an accident. He protected Lysimachus' belongings until the latter's defeat and death in 280 BC, after which, equipped with so large a fortune, he felt himself in a position to assert his independence of the Seleucids, and devoted a part of it to improving the defensive economy of his small principality. On his death in 263 BC he bequeathed it to his nephew, Eumenes, who in his turn passed it on, considerably enlarged, to a son called Attalus. Pergamum, in common with all the Seleucid states of the Aegean seaboard, now found itself in conflict with the Gauls, whose aggression had even reached the extent of exacting tribute. Attalus, so far from accepting this situation, took the initiative against them and by a series of military manoeuvres succeeded in defeating and confining them to their own territory. He then turned his attention to the Seleucids themselves, and, taking advantage of a civil war which was in progress among them, mastered their separate armies and drove them southwards until all western Asia Minor was in his hands. The descendants of Attalus therefore succeeded to a very considerable heritage.

The Attalid kings were still reigning in Pergamum when Rome began for the first time to take a hand in the affairs of Asia Minor. It was to her that Eumenes II appealed for help when the armies of Antiochus the Great penetrated to the Maeander, and it was partly as a result of this appeal that in 190 BC the first full-scale Roman invasion of Asia Minor took place. It resulted in the total defeat of Antiochus at the battle of Magnesia-ad-Sipylum (Manisa) and in a peace agreement which robbed him not only of his fleet and elephants, but of all the territory which he had taken from Eumenes. Pergamum thus became a protégé of Rome, and the military support which she thus obtained made possible the subjection first of Bithynia and afterwards of

59. A dying Gaul. Engraving from a copy in the National Museum in Rome of a Pergamene work of about 230 BC. From *Musei Capitolini*, III, Rome 1755, pl. 67.

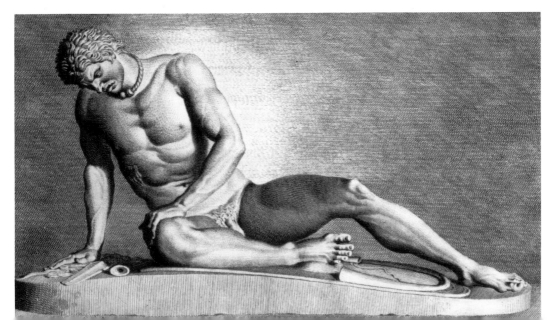

Galatia, the Phrygian province occupied by the Gauls. Her influence was even extended to the kingdoms of Cappadocia and Armenia.

The city of Pergamum itself had meanwhile increased in prosperity and importance, until it had become the greatest emporium of contemporary Asia Minor, rivalling even Ptolemaic Alexandria in its magnificence. The terraced sides of its acropolis rock were covered with palaces, temples, gardens and plantations, while the culture of its citizens was a byword in the Greek world. The ornaments of luxury were supplied by the skill of its own craftsmen, whose cloth of gold, for instance, was considered in a class with the embroideries of Phrygia or Alexandrian brocades. In another sphere their invention is remembered today in the word 'parchment'.

One Attalid ruler followed another; and the direct line of succession acquired such importance that, on an occasion when Eumenes III had visited Rome and his return was inexplicably delayed, his brother Attalus took the precaution both of assuming the kingdom and of marrying his wife, Stratonice. When Eumenes did eventually reappear, he gracefully accepted the return of both, merely remarking (according to tradition) that Attalus had 'married in some haste'. But the end of the dynasty was by this time near. In 133 BC Attalus III died childless, and in a will which came to be considered one of the most controversial documents of contemporary history bequeathed the state of Pergamum to Rome.

Many reasons have been suggested for this gesture. Perhaps the most satisfactory is merely that he realised the vast impetus which Roman imperialism was gaining and accepted it as irresistible. Whatever may in fact have prompted the bequest, it was accepted by Rome, after a somewhat puzzled debate in the Senate. In Pergamum itself, the news was received with less enthusiasm, particularly by the peasant class and slaves, and the Romans in the end found it necessary to suppress an armed rising, led by the heir apparent, Stratonicus, before they could assume full control of their heritage. In 130 BC all the old Attalid possessions were incorporated in the newly created Province of Asia.

For the remaining thirty years of the second century BC the Romans were able to consolidate their commercial footing beyond the Aegean. There was a prodigious increase in trade and an invading army of Roman businessmen further stimulated commerce among the Greek cities by establishing a banking system. Nevertheless, the Romans' hold on the country was, in fact, more precarious than they realised.

Forty-two years later saw the beginning of a struggle which presaged the ruin of Hellenism in Asia Minor. This was the first war between Rome and Mithridates Eupator, King of Pontus. Caught between the imperialist west and a new tide of Barbarian resistance, the Greek cities suffered appallingly, and their sufferings were later increased by the vindictive brutality of rival Roman generals during the civil wars which preceded the end of the Republic. It was during this period that they finally lost their true Hellenic character, and emerged as components of the new Roman Imperium.

CHAPTER 16

Seven Cities

In reviewing the history of the Greek cities in Asia Minor from their earliest foundation onwards, one has primarily been struck by the total absence among them of any impulse towards political unification. Each is revealed as an exclusively independent community reluctant, even in the interests of military security, to enter into any close association with its neighbours. At times, admittedly, there existed arbitrary groupings, dictated for the most part by the paternity of their original settlers. But these tended easily to disintegrate and seldom survived any considerable military setback. In fact, wholesale and effective amalgamations could only be imposed by the imperial ambition of a native dynasty or the despotism of an oriental conqueror. It is also clear that the physical character of the country itself contributed something to the isolation and constraint of the city states. The rocky promontories, which had appeared to stretch out invitingly across the 'estranging sea', prolonged themselves landward into mountain ranges, separating each fertile valley and plain from its neighbour, and effectively segregating its inhabitants.

All this is intelligibly reflected in the Greek and Hellenistic cities whose ruins one can visit today. From Cilicia Campestris to the Plain of Troy and the remoter Pontic littoral, every river valley and sheltered upland bears traces of having once been a conscious political entity, contributing to the balanced economy of a single large city. The limits of the states are no longer certain, and their very identity often in doubt; but the cities remain. Stripped of their ornaments, tumbled by innumerable earthquakes and pillaged to meet the needs of meaner generations, their surviving ruins still emphasise their separate individuality, while at the same time testifying to their common heritage.

Materially their civic attributes show little variety. Some prominent hill has the function of an acropolis, and, grouped near its foot are a theatre, agora, gymnasium, stadium and various temples. Add to these Roman thermae, several Byzantine churches, a Seljuk or early Ottoman mosque, and you have the characteristic elements of a hundred ruined cities in western Asia Minor. Where the traditional prosperity of the state is confirmed by the richness of its material remains, contributory factors are seldom far to seek. Accidents of geography may give commercial advantages. The sanctity of a shrine or the reputation of an oracle may bring material benefits; and wealth creates the leisure necessary to intellectual advancement. But mere wealth and prosperity are no measure of a city's intrinsic distinction, and it will frequently be found that today the less pretentious ruins have a grandeur and dignity disproportionate to their ancient fame. Indeed, the peculiar individuality of almost every site is such, that the modern traveller may visit a score of them in succession, untroubled by the sense of monotony from which he would otherwise most assuredly suffer.

It is perhaps unnecessary here to enlarge upon the incomparable beauty of the setting in which these ruins generally find themselves: it is a subject on which few writers have succeeded in speaking with moderation;[1] and when a travelling scholar of an earlier generation contents himself with the observation that '... the scenery of the Aegaean coast-lands is as bright and varied as that of Greece itself',[2] one is to understand an implied superlative rather than a calculated understatement. Meanwhile, for those already at all familiar with the eastern Mediterranean, it needs hardly more than a few evocative phrases to recapture the sense of life and vigour which one so soon comes to know, in this world of rocky capes and deep fiords, with its prospect of sparkling sea and background of snow-mountains. Whether one disembarks from a sailing-boat or pauses at a turn in some mountain path to glimpse the fine curves of an amphitheatre, the broken shaft of a column and a significant profusion of lichened geometrical shapes among the flowering shrubs, one experiences the diffidence of a guest entering for the first time the house of some cultivated stranger.

But the first isolated shocks of pleasure and surprise give way, with greater familiarity, to a gradual understanding of the historical pattern which governs the present situation and appearance of the various ruin-fields. Considered in this sense, the maritime cities fall into a category of their own, since, in almost all cases, their ultimate fate was already sealed when their sites were chosen by the earliest settlers. For each was soon to discover its own evil genius in the river whose favours it had at first so eagerly courted and beside whose mouth its temples and warehouses had so unsuspectingly been built. The accumulating silt by which each city would ultimately be isolated from the sea was to prove a far greater menace than mere earthquakes, and its later years would be occupied in a perpetual and fruitless struggle against the alluvial tide, beneath which it must be slowly and inexorably buried (Fig. 33).

Smyrna

An interesting example of the drastic measures necessary to avert such a catastrophe is provided by the great modern port of Smyrna. The present city was founded in Hellenistic times, at the mouth of a narrow stream, in the innermost recess of the deep gulf to which it afterwards gave its name. A much larger river, the Hermus, discharged its waters into the gulf on the north side, thrusting before it a promontory of alluvial mud towards the opposite shore. By the end of the last century, the fairway for shipping had been gradually reduced, until the city was in danger of finding itself on an inland lake, deprived of all access to the sea. Finally, in 1886 it proved necessary to divert the course of the Hermus, compelling it to discharge into Ağrıa Bay on the north-west side of the peninsula.[3]

Unfortunately the circumstances which made this possible at Smyrna did not apply elsewhere, and cities like Ephesus and Priene had, early in their history, to be removed to higher ground.

Ephesus

The life-story of Ephesus in particular, as a city, is in this respect a most remarkable one. Today its ruins lie beside the old mouth of the Cayster river, from which the sea has receded five or six miles, leaving a wide, cultivated valley between high ranges of hills. According to Strabo and Pausanias, the first Greek settlers were Ionians, led by Androclus, son of Codrus, the legendary king of Athens. 'They found the region occupied by Carians and Lydians living around a sanctuary of the great Anatolian mother-goddess; with these they came to an amicable arrangement, founded a new city and adopted the native goddess under the name of their own Artemis. This earliest city of Ephesus occupied the northern slope of Mount Pion, now Panayır Dağ – and the land at its foot, which was at that time on the coast....'[4] It was here, or perhaps on the outskirts of this city that, in the sixth century BC, a modest temple was for the first time dedicated to the Asiatic cult of Artemis.

By the beginning of the fourth century BC, Ephesus was already a vast metropolis, and the fame and splendour of the Artemisium (Fig. 35) had increased in proportion. The shrine, which had been several times rebuilt, was now a magnificent temple, and the coincidence of its destruction by fire with the birth of Alexander the Great in 356 BC afterwards enabled the Ephesians to postulate the goddess's temporary preoccupation with, if not attendance at, the confinement of Olympias.[5] It was indeed Alexander himself who, as we have seen, finally liberated the city, but his offer to rebuild the Artemisium on condition that his name should be associated with it was tactfully refused, on the grounds that 'it was unseemly for one god to dedicate a temple to another'. Twenty-two years after its destruction, it was rebuilt by the citizens themselves, in a form which established its claim to be considered one of the Seven Wonders. It may be added that none of the many reconstructions of this building, with its 127 Ionic columns (36 of which had their lowest drums sculptured in high relief, each said to be the gift of a different king), has ever quite succeeded in avoiding a suggestion of vulgarity. Yet Scopas and Praxiteles both contributed something towards its adornment.

At this point it becomes necessary to remind oneself that, up to the beginning

60. Decorated column
drum from the
Artemisium at Ephesus
(fourth century BC).
British Museum.

of the 'archaeological era' in the middle of the last century, not one single
stone belonging to the Hellenic city of Ephesus remained visible above ground.
There are, in fact, still those who doubt its location in the vicinity of its own
Artemisium. For today the ruins of the great temple and the whole area to the
south and west of it, where the city might have stood, are buried beneath
twenty feet of clean alluvial soil. This silting-up process had already begun
when the temple was rebuilt for the last time, and by the middle of the third
century Ephesus, as a result, was facing the imminent loss of its commercial
importance. From this situation it was rescued by Lysimachus, who went to
the length of completely rebuilding the city on a new site, more than a mile
to the seaward side of the old Artemisium, and a second and greater Ephesus
arose, spreading its fine buildings over a saddle between the two hills called
Pion and Coressus and throwing up a coronet of fortifications over the summits
of both.

Lysimachus appears to have had some difficulty in persuading the more
conservative inhabitants of the old city to transfer themselves to their new

quarters, and Strabo tells how he eventually found it necessary to stop up the sewers and flood them out.[6] He then destroyed the neighbouring ports of Lebedos and Colophon and, for good measure, added their inhabitants to those of the new city. From then onwards it became the veritable capital of Asia, and remained so until the third century AD.

It was to this city, in Roman times, that St John is said to have brought the Blessed Virgin after the Crucifixion. Hither came St Paul after his mission in Greece and here, in the great theatre at the foot of Mount Pion, the Ephesians noisily demonstrated against his preaching. In the centuries which followed, many churches were built within its walls by the Byzantine emperors, and one, the Basilica of St John, on the old acropolis hill at Ayasoluk, was in AD 431 the scene of the Third Oecumenical Council.

Also built into the side of the Ayasoluk hill is the beautiful early fifteenth-century mosque of Sultan 'Isa, son of Bayazit I, its twin domes supported on monolithic columns of Egyptian granite pillaged from the ruins of the Roman city. Others from the same source were taken to Constantinople and incorporated in the structure of Hagia Sophia, and these, until the last century, used to be pointed out to visitors as belonging to the 'Temple of Diana at Ephesus'. In fact they had been extracted from the ruins of the Roman gymnasium to the west of Mount Pion, which, being the most formidable building left standing above ground at that time, was generally considered to be the Artemisium.

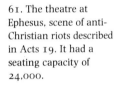

61. The theatre at Ephesus, scene of anti-Christian riots described in Acts 19. It had a seating capacity of 24,000.

This, then, was the situation when Mr J. T. Wood, an English railway engineer, set himself the problem of discovering its real whereabouts.[7] Basing his reasoning on the topographical accounts of actual eye-witnesses such as Strabo and Pausanias, he concluded that it would be necessary to follow the

road which led out from the Magnesian gate of the Roman city in the direction of Ayasoluk, and doing so, he eventually discovered, some metres beneath the present ground-level, a fragment of masonry bearing an inscription which proved it to be part of the temenos-wall, built in the year 6 BC by the Emperor Augustus, to limit the area within which the Temple of Artemis could legitimately afford sanctuary to criminals. Soon after this, on New Year's Day 1869, one of his soundings struck the marble pavement of the temple itself, and his primary object was virtually achieved. He had by then been excavating for no less than six years, two of which had been spent in patiently digging pits and trenches in the clean alluvium.

Wood's work on the rather scanty remains of the Artemisium was continued from 1904 onwards by D. G. Hogarth for the British Museum, working under great difficulties in the muddy water with which the old excavation was now filled. He was rewarded by finding the great foundation deposit of votive objects – many of them of ivory or precious metals – which he brought to London for treatment and study before returning them to Istanbul.[8] Hogarth describes his excavation as 'groping for jewels amid mud and slime', but mentions 'hard on three thousand objects, one with another and greater with less'. Yet, to mark the site of such great discoveries, there remains today no more than a deep and untidy depression, filled with reeds and stagnant water, where the human vanity in the cry 'Great is Diana of the Ephesians' finds an echo only in the croaking of the frogs.[9]

George Bean, in his admirable guide to the Ephesus of today, recalls the melancholy isolation and neglect of the ruins as they appeared in the 1930s – difficult to reach and rarely visited.[10] Excavations by Austrian archaeologists had in fact been undertaken intermittently since 1896;[11] but it is only in more recent years that they have been resumed in earnest. Much interesting architecture has been newly revealed and restored, while commendable works of clearance have been put in hand by the Turkish authorities, benefiting the waves of tourists who visit the place each summer.

Pergamum

From Ephesus, its harbour built by Lysimachus now an unapproachable swamp, the scene is easily shifted to Elaea, the port of Pergamum, where between ruined quays and jetties, the decaying ribs of old ships project forlornly from the mud – not indeed bones of the galleons and triremes of historic times, but abandoned fishing-vessels of a later age; for the harbour was in use within living memory, and the surface of the mud is still covered by an occasional ripple of brackish water.[12]

Elaea's function in Roman times as a commercial outlet for almost the whole of Mysia is perhaps sufficient justification for considering Pergamum (Bergama) in the category of maritime cities, though its actual distance from the sea is considerable. The city itself stands well back, on a tributary of the River Caicus (Bakir Çayı), in the centre of a natural province almost completely enclosed by high mountains. Fertile, self-contained and easily defended, it provided the perfect setting for the maintenance of a city-state, as its Attalid dynasty of rulers soon realised.

When the last Attalid died in the year 133 BC, bequeathing the state to the Roman Empire, yet another civic centre was built outside the walls of the old city, and the town continued to spread southwards. Yet the smoke did not cease to rise from the great Altar of Zeus at the summit of the acropolis, and Plutarch could record how Antony took 200,000 books from the Attalid library for the Queen of Egypt.[13] The Roman city played an important role in the early history of Christianity. Numbered among the Seven Churches of the Apocalypse, it was apostrophised by St John as 'the Seat of Satan' and remembered by many as the scene of the martyrdom of Antipas.[14]

What then were the physical characteristics of the old city at Pergamum, which have caused it to be considered one of the most spectacular achievements of the Greek imagination? Foremost among them one must mention the beauty of its architectural setting. For the most fanciful modern draughtsman, if required to produce a fantasy on a classical theme, could hardly improve on the reality of what was accomplished on the acropolis at Pergamum. With the extravagant caprice peculiar to Aegean peoples, the nucleus of great buildings which provided the focus of the city's public life was flung up on the summit of an isolated rock ('a mountain in the form of a pine-apple', as Strabo described it)[15] rising a thousand feet above the plain. There they were disposed on a series of terraces and rocky platforms, with the artifice indispensable to the creation of a formal composition. The effect, when seen from the residential part of the town below, can at no time have been less than sensational, and in certain lights, when for instance the buildings could be seen emerging from the mists of early morning or transfigured by the setting sun, the impression which they made must have been unforgettable.

No less remarkable than the appearance of the acropolis from below was the prospect from the buildings which crowned it. The great theatre and theatre-terrace were perhaps favoured with the most consideration and ingenuity in the matter of setting; for from the western parapet of the terrace the cliff fell precipitously to a remote valley, while the curves of the theatre itself fitted into a hollow between two shoulders of rock, so that the 30,000 spectators could look beyond the stage, over a wide landscape towards the distant sea.

The Altar of Zeus, which is perhaps the best-known of all the antiquities discovered at Pergamum, occupied the space between the theatre and the agora at the southern approach to the summit. Attention was first drawn to its existence by a chance discovery, for which a European engineer was once more responsible. Within a few months of Wood's great find at Ephesus, a young German, Carl Humann, who was engaged in building a road in the vicinity of Pergamum, was told that a great quantity of loose stone was available among the ruined buildings on the hill-top behind the city. The men whom he sent to investigate returned with stories of a colossal fragment of sculpture, which they had found projecting from amongst the fallen blocks.

62. The Great Altar of Pergamum dates from the first half of the second century BC. It is now restored in Berlin; the frieze is almost 4 m high. From A. Conze *et al.*, *Die Ergebnisse der Ausgrabungen zu Pergamon*, Berlin 1880.

This was the first of many similar fragments which, during the months that followed, Humann was able to 'rescue from the hands of the stone-cutters and lime-burners', and afterwards to transport to Berlin. There the character of the building from which they were derived was gradually understood, and, after a lapse of ten years, Humann returned to Pergamum with a new commission, namely that of 'salvaging and acquiring works-of-art for the Royal Museums of Berlin'. Where the remains of the great altar were concerned, he was prepared to go to considerable lengths, and did not hesitate to demolish large sections of the Byzantine citadel-wall into which fragments of its reliefs had been built. As a result, before the end of the last century, most of the major frieze, of which Humann's earliest find formed a part, had been reassembled and set up in Berlin, and it was already possible to attempt a reconstruction of the whole building.

The Altar, which was built in 180 BC by Eumenes II to celebrate his victory over the Gauls, stood on an enormous stone plinth, which also supported the double colonnade of Ionic columns enclosing it on three sides. On the fourth side, it was approached by a fine stairway, nearly twenty metres wide, and in the centre a column of smoke rose continually from the high pyramid of accumulated ashes. Friezes of two sizes were found, one having ornamented the faces of the plinth itself, and the other, which was smaller, deriving from the colonnaded portico above. The subject of the larger sculptures, namely the battle between gods and Titans described by Hesiod, lends itself to the portrayal of furious action, with the excess of emphasis and detail which are characteristic of the Pergamene School.

Other major buildings within the citadel area include a great hexastyle Doric temple, dedicated to Athena, and a Corinthian temple of Trajan. Little of either has survived the effects of pillage and earthquake, while the library which stands between the two is a great deal less easy to picture in its original state than the Celsian Library at Ephesus (Fig. 75).

The residential part of the Greek city on the southern slope of the acropolis was enclosed by a wall, connected at either end to the citadel fortifications. A second wall, built by Eumenes II, enclosed a much extended area, approachable only by an elaborately defended gateway at its southernmost angle. When the excavations were taken over by the Germans Conze and Dörpfeld at the beginning of the present century, the early discovery of this gate enabled them to approach the city centre along the line of the main thoroughfare, and a nucleus of important buildings was thus discovered. There was first an enormous agora, which had no doubt been the principal trading centre of the town. It is hard, among the disarray of fallen stones which marks its site today, to recapture the sound and colour of a crowded market, but a single inscription discovered among its ruins brings to us across the centuries the flavour of oriental bargaining. For the writer half-humorously complains of the difficulty involved in obtaining a fair price from 'these confounded fish-merchants', when the currencies of half a dozen nations are in use and there is no fixed rate of exchange.

Beyond the agora, a street lined with the mansions of rich merchants leads to the inner gateway, a vaulted building of a kind unique in classical architecture. Then comes the gymnasium, with its separate terraces allotted to the three age-groups distinguished by Greek convention. A very large area of the lower part of the old city has been excavated, and it would perhaps be tedious to continue the catalogue of public buildings which they brought to light. When one has visited them all, there is still the Roman city to see on the west bank of the Selinus river and the charming little precinct of Asclepius, which is so well preserved that plays have been acted in it in recent times.

Priene

To pass immediately from the exuberance and ostentation of Pergamum to the modest elegance of Priene would seem like turning in another sphere from a Last Judgment of Memling to an interior by Van Eyck. Even ignoring the matter of size, the contrast of style must remain poignant in proportion to its subtlety. Yet Priene also is to be numbered among the maritime cities, and the basic shape of its material economy can have differed little from that of its more pretentious neighbours. And indeed, what makes its remains of special importance to the archaeologist is that among them all the attributes of a model *polis* are represented in miniature, neatly and ingeniously arranged in a restricted space.[16] It is perhaps this very miniature quality, combined with the thoroughness of the excavations, which also gives its ruins great charm for the casual visitor. For he finds himself able, with less than the usual effort, to encompass the pattern of the buildings and to apprehend its significance.

Very little is known of the history of Priene from its foundation after a struggle with the Carians in the tenth century until the time of Alexander the Great. The character of the city during these early years must also remain a matter of speculation, since it no longer exists and even its whereabouts are in some doubt. One imagines it as a miniature harbour town at the foot of

Mount Mycale, facing southwards towards Miletus, across the wide gulf which took its name from Mount Latmos at the mouth of the Maeander. The Maeander at this time had two channels, one of which discharged into the sea on the north side of the gulf, within a few miles of Priene, so that its inhabitants must from the earliest times have had some difficulty in keeping their harbour free of silt. There are in fact historical indications that by the end of the fifth century it was already inaccessible to war vessels. A hundred years later the rising alluvium had made it uninhabitable, and a new site had to be sought. Its great neighbour, Miletus, was destined in a later age to suffer the same fate, and today the Latmic Gulf is a wide, cultivated plain, from which the sometime island of Lade rises in the form of a small hill. Priene is now nearly ten miles from the sea.

The site chosen when the city came to be rebuilt was a projecting shoulder of Mount Mycale, several hundred feet up, with a fine view across the estuary (now called Gül Bahçesi). It was dominated by cliff-faces rising precipitously to an almost inaccessible rock, which was to have the function of an acropolis. Its inhabitants at that time can have numbered hardly more than four or five thousand people, and the area enclosed by the city-walls was no more than adequate to accommodate such a population. In spite of the sloping and uneven character of the site, the Hippodamian system of planning was adopted, whereby the streets form a grid, dividing the buildings into rectangular blocks of approximately equal size. At Priene this means that parallel streets following the contours of the hill are intersected at right angles by others which climb so steeply that steps are frequently necessary. The system is therefore by no means ideally adapted to the site, yet with occasional recourse to the expedient of terracing, it appears to have been made to work satisfactorily enough. Several blocks in the centre are occupied by a large colonnaded agora, and the theatre above it is balanced at the lower end of the main axis by a stadium and gymnasium. The resulting composition can be seen most clearly in a delightful model of the city which the German archaeologists constructed in the Berlin Museum.[17] Here the Athena temple also appears, dominating the town on its high platform, and the tiny shrine of Asclepius shines like an architectural gem in its precinct beneath the agora.

Two other public buildings have a miniature perfection of design which one comes to associate with the architecture of Priene. One of these is the neatly proportioned assembly-hall overlooking the agora, known as the Ekklesiasterion. Law-court and council-chamber combined, it was large enough on occasion to hold the whole citizen body of the little town, accommodated in tiers of seats rising on three sides of a rectangular space with an altar in the middle. The third side was open to the stoa flanking the agora.[18]

Another building of exceptional charm and individuality has already been referred to. This is the theatre. Its ruins are approached through a doorway beneath the proscenium, from which one emerges into the sheltered stillness of a minute arena. The ground in the orchestra is at times evenly carpeted with scarlet flowers, and long grass grows around the bases of the six marble

63. The Greek theatre at Priene, built in the fourth century BC, is a field of scarlet anemones in the spring. Note the fauteuils in the front row.

fauteuils which rise in dignified isolation from the first tier of seats. Beyond them the rhythmic curve of the auditorium swings up to meet the sky, like a rendering in stone of a fine musical phrase. The place has a strange atmosphere of suspended animation, which seems to mock the dogma of conventional time. Its effect is a subversion of reality, sufficient to undermine the professional detachment of the least imaginative antiquarian, so that he must feel the air eloquent with the last echoes of the players' voices or vibrant with the applause of an audience, whose physical presence seems hardly dissipated.

Finally, lining the sloping streets beyond the agora, and in a sheltered depression behind the Temple of Athena, one sees the private dwellings of Priene's citizens. It is perhaps these which made Félix Sartiaux compare the site to a 'Pompeii, plus soignée et mieux bâtie', for the quiet intimacy of their interiors have the same appeal. They are so closely set together and their pavements so finely laid, that little vegetation has appeared to obscure them, and today, scoured by the wind and rain of the passing seasons, they remain clean and empty as the excavators left them. Only the crannied rock-plants and Pleiadic groupings of small, starry flowers enrich the discreet simplicity of flagged atrium and columned portico with Pre-Raphaelite ornament.

Miletus

Looking out across the valley of the Maeander on a clear day, one can just distinguish the little peninsula on which the city of Miletus once stood (Balat), and the outline of its ruined theatre. The site is still encircled by a wide loop of the river. In spring, flood-waters fill its four ancient harbours and cover the area excavated by the German archaeologists,[19] obscuring the traces of their work in a mantle of brown slime. Recollecting the description of the site in Murray's guide[20] as 'a fever-stricken spot, which should on no account be selected as a sleeping place', one is grateful to the excavators for removing the beautiful agora façade and other important antiquities to a drier, if not safer place (the Pergamum Museum, Berlin, bombed during the Second World War but now restored).

The theatre, on the other hand, which before the Germans came was the only building remaining above ground, is situated beyond reach of floods and is surprisingly well preserved. It is a gigantic building by any standard, and appears even more so on account of the fact that it is not cut into the side of a hill, but stands free on an almost level site. Over a corner of its ruined auditorium, whose vaulted ramps and passages remind one of the approaches of some great modern stadium, a fair-sized Byzantine structure has been built in later days. The remaining buildings on the site have an atmosphere of melancholy and decay, from which it is a relief to turn to the ornamental elegance of a deserted early Ottoman mosque, dating from the last period of the town's occupation (early fifteenth century).

Didyma

One of the misfortunes attendant upon the destruction of Miletus, as predicted by the Delphic Oracle, was expressed in the words: 'Strangers shall tend my shrine at Didyma'.[21] Through the mouth of the Sibyl, Apollo was of course referring to his famous sanctuary, which fell within Milesian territory. For Miletus, whose prosperity depended to a great extent on its situation at the seaward end of a great trade route, owed much besides to the fame of the Oracle at Didyma and of the priestly caste, called Branchidae, who attended it.

Few traces have ever been found of the early Greek sanctuary, which was plundered after the fall of Miletus and finally burnt down by Xerxes in 481 BC. After a century and a half of silence, the oracle was reinstated by Alexander the Great, and the building of a mighty temple begun. There has been a suggestion – comprehensible when one contemplates the extent of its ruins – that this building was originally conceived on a scale exceeding the practical capacity of contemporary architecture. Certainly there is evidence to show that, in spite of an all-out drive to complete it, as late as the time of Caligula, it was never in the end entirely finished. Yet, even in its unfinished state, Strabo considered it one of the greatest of all Greek temples, and Pliny as second only to the Ephesian Artemisium.

Didyma[22] is situated in the centre of a high promontory whose summit commands a magnificent view of the Aegean, with the islands of Samos, Patmos and Leros visible in the middle distance and the Halicarnassus peninsula far away to the south. But owing perhaps to the location of some natural or unnatural feature which provided the original *raison d'être* for the sanctuary, the temple is built in a shallow depression, from which even the sea could hardly have been visible. Today this effect is exaggerated by the rise in level of the village which still occupies the site, and the temple is half hidden by a stone retaining wall with which the archaeologists surrounded their excavation.

The building is of the Ionic order, with a deep *pronaos* making a forest of

columns at the east end. Approaching axially through the *pronaos*, one is faced
at its eastern end by a prodigiously large doorway, through which one is
clearly not intended to pass, as its threshold is raised more than a metre above
the pavement. From the vestibule, which is visible beyond, a monumental
flight of stairs leads down into the sanctuary proper, but the only means of
access to the latter from outside is by two minute doorways in the *pronaos*
itself, which lead one through dark, vaulted ramps, hardly more than a metre
wide. Whether it was through these that postulants were escorted to consult
the oracle, or whether its answers were delivered by a priest from the great
vestibule doorway to a congregation in the *pronaos*, is not certain.

The miniature building, restored in the German drawings at the eastern end
of the sanctuary, which may be presumed to have housed the oracle itself does
not in fact any longer exist, and one emerges from the dark, sloping passages
into a vast empty courtyard full of flowers and sunshine. The sanctuary was
open to the sky, since no roof could at that time cover so wide a span, and
today, watching the swallows dive and circle against the sky above, one is
reminded of the curious 'bird's-nest' story in Herodotus. A deputation from
Cyme had asked whether they should give sanctuary to a Lydian, Pactyas,
who was endeavouring to escape from the Persians. When the oracle gave a
negative reply, one of their number called Aristodicus 'went round about the
temple and stole away the sparrows and all other families of nesting birds that
were in it', and when a voice from the inner shrine protested, he replied, 'Wilt
thou thus save thine own suppliants, but bid the men of Cyme deliver up
theirs?'.[23]

The exterior of the building is made doubly impressive by the standing
columns, which enable one more easily to conceive of its original proportions.
A minor clue takes the form of a colossal Gorgon's head, fallen from the main
frieze, whose pointed ugliness is clearly intended to be seen only at a great
distance and much foreshortened.

The pilgrimage to Didyma was traditionally made by sea, and a long avenue
of tombs and statues led up to the temple from the ancient port of Panormus.

A direct road from Miletus may not have been constructed until the end of the first century AD.

Halicarnassus

Eastwards of Miletus in the Maeander valley and among the contortions of the Carian coastline to the south, the ruins of a dozen minor cities await excavation. Others, whose traditional fame shone more brightly, have long ago been submitted to the depredations of acquisitive enterprise or to the less devastating effects of systematic investigation. Most prominent among the latter is Halicarnassus (Bodrum), the birthplace of Herodotus, which is to be found near the south-westernmost extremity of the Anatolian peninsula.

The town has a situation of great natural beauty, on a little bay embracing a small central promontory, upon which, early in the fifteenth century, the Knights of Rhodes built a picturesque castle dedicated to St Peter. Its walls, with their fine display of European heraldry, are built largely of material derived from the ruins of the classical city. The rock is also supposed at one time to have been an island, and to have thus provided a favourable *pied à terre* for the earliest Greek settlers.

Halicarnassus was one of the largest and strongest cities in Caria, and a member of the Dorian Hexapolis. It reached a peak of prosperity under Mausolus, a Persian satrap, who acquired for it a large measure of political independence without interfering with its Greek character and traditions. It was his wife, Artemisia, who in about 350 BC erected to his memory a monument afterwards to be considered one of the Seven Wonders of the World.[24] The site of the Mausoleum was excavated by C.T. Newton in the middle of the last century,[25] but the pious symbol of Artemisia's grief and admiration has survived only in the broken sculptures brought by him to the British Museum.

65. Fragments of sculpture dating from the mid-fourth century BC, from the Tomb of Mausolus at Halicarnassus (Bodrum), were built into the walls of the medieval Castle of St Peter. They are now in the British Museum. Drawing by Luigi Mayer (1797), reproduced in J. B. J. Breton de la Martinière, *L'Egypte et la Syrie*, Paris 1814.

CHAPTER 17

Resistance
to Rome

It will be remembered that, under the active protection of Rome, Eumenes II of Pergamum had succeeded in subduing both Galatia and Bithynia, and even in reaching a pacific understanding with Armenia. He had been unable, however, to extend his influence as far as Pontus, the most formidable of all the native kingdoms, whose rapidly expanding territory now comprised the whole coastal area in the north, from the mouth of the Halys to Trapezus (Trabzon) and the mountain country behind. This little realm, under a line of kings whose initial authority derived from the Persians in the fifth century BC, remained an intractable and disturbing element in the remoter background of the Asiatic scene, consenting only occasionally, when circumstances left no alternative, to a formal but unconvincing alliance with Rome. In view of the surprising fact that in the year 100 BC a Pontic king found himself in a position to challenge the very presence of the Romans in Asia Minor and to unite virtually the whole country in an attempt to displace them which only narrowly failed, it will perhaps be well here to take a closer view of a country able to produce both the men and the materials necessary for so ambitious an enterprise.

The lower reaches of the Halys river, where it approaches the sea west of Samsun, are like the handle of a vast sickle, whose crescent blade reaches up to encircle the old homeland of the Hittites on the Anatolian plateau. Eastwards from its mouth, more than two hundred miles of Euxine littoral and the adjacent inland provinces were ruled by the Pontic kings. The geological formation of this piece of country is diametrically opposed to that of western Turkey, where mountain-ridges radiate from the central plateau like the fingers of a hand. For here a single prodigious range runs parallel to the coast at a distance of no more than thirty miles from it, and finds its echo in a series of minor ridges which carry its rhythm inland, like diminishing ripples. Rivers in the valleys between have conformed to this orientation, and themselves also flow parallel to the coast, until a single great rift in the main range enables their united waters to escape seawards.

There is nothing about inland Pontus to distinguish it from most other upland areas in Turkey. For this reason the contrasting climate and character of the country on the seaward side of the mountains is all the more striking. On crossing the watershed, one comes down suddenly, even in late summer, into a world of forest vegetation and flowers. Among the conifers, at a high altitude, there are alpine plants, and in autumn a mauve poisonous crocus (*colchicum*), double the length and size of the familiar variety. Below this come forests of rhododendron and azalea (*pontica*), giving way in the valleys to an extraordinary profusion of deciduous trees and shrubs. To quote Lynch's description of these glens:

> ... the vegetation increases in luxuriance and changes in character, until the scene assumes that almost supernatural appearance which has found such just expression in the weirdness of the Kolchian myths. The foliage, which almost obscures the light of the brightest day, is composed of alder, lime, walnut and elm, of beech and Spanish chestnut. ... Fungus with crimson stools start from the silver lichen, which diffuses an unearthly light. Long streamers of grey-green lichen float on the lower branches, from which a profusion of creepers are festooned. Here and there the thicket opens to an expanse of lawn ...[1]

One is reminded of a comparable contrast in crossing the Elburz watershed above Tehran, which is geographically a continuation of the same range. In the sub-tropical forests which descend towards the shores of the Caspian, one is likely to encounter without much surprise a lynx or, until recently, even a tiger.

The more closely inhabited strip of land between the mountains and the Black Sea is remarkably productive. Today the hazel-nut plantations take precedence over all else, and supply the European market. In Roman times other products were found worth exporting, such as honey and wax, aromatic gums and various drugs such as wormwood and hellebore. But among the coastal villages it was the fishing industry which brought the greatest financial returns. Tunny, on the way from their spawning-places to the Bosphorus, were caught easily and salted for export. They commanded high prices as far afield as Italy.[2]

The economy and even the culture of the coastal strip was much affected, down to Hellenistic times, by the presence of Greek colonial settlements; but these had little influence on the interior. Isolated among its mountains, inland Pontus remained oriental and unchanging, preserving in the feudal pattern of its social and economic structure features which in the west would already have seemed anachronistic. The most important centres were the city of Amaseia (Amasya) which had grown up around the fortified seat of the royal family, and the temple of the great mother-goddess, Ma, at Comana.

66. Orchards near Amasya, seen from the castle above the town.

The city of Amasya today, in its remarkable setting, still retains some of the grandeur and dignity which must have been associated with it as the traditional capital. It stands on either bank of the Iris (Yeşil Irmak), at a point where the river passes through a deep gorge in the mountains. On the left bank it is overhung by an isolated crag a thousand feet high, crowned with a medieval castle. On a projecting shoulder beneath are the ruins of the Pontic royal palace, and, approached by stairways in the rock and hardly accessible terraces, the tombs of Mithridates' ancestors; cave-chambers in the cliff-face isolated from the surrounding rock by deep carving. (An isolated tomb of this sort is to be seen almost at river-level on the left bank of the Iris, some two miles below the town. From time immemorial animals have taken shelter in the narrow passage behind it, so that the rock is polished to the consistency

173

67. Above the houses of Amasya are the rock-cut tombs of the Pontic kings.

of glass. Thus it is known locally as Aynalı Mağara, the Mirror Cave.) The whole mountainside is framed in a tiara of embattled walls, descending on either side to the remains of fortified gateways and bridges across the river. It is here that the modern railway enters and leaves the town by tunnels.

Reflected in the greenish waters of the Iris are the white-painted, half-timber houses of Turkish Amasya, against a counterpoint of tall Lombardy poplars. On the right bank they cluster around the rich architectural relics of the city's medieval prosperity, and climb far up the mountainside behind. Where the houses cease, the famous orchards begin, and, seen from the citadel, the valley appears carpeted with deep green foliage (Fig. 4). Here, beneath the laden branches of the fruit-trees, there is a world of shade and moisture, where the ox-carts wind through rutted lanes bringing the apple harvest to market and the creaking of their wooden axles mingles with the more strident note of tall water-wheels filling the irrigation ditches from the river beneath. There can be few more picturesque cities in Asia Minor than Amasya; yet the city bears the scars of strangely various disasters in recent times. The year 1913 saw one-third of its houses destroyed by fire. Repairs to the beautiful mosque built by Sultan Bayazit II, which lost its portico and the tops of its minarets in the great earthquake of 1939, were interrupted in 1952 by a sudden flooding of the Iris, and the whole lower town was left standing in more than three feet of water.

The ruins of Comana[3] are also on the banks of the Iris river, about six miles north-east of modern Tokat, near the village of Gümenek. Here the road crosses the river on a wooden bridge with stone piers, and, as one modern traveller remarks,[4] 'as if to label the site and rescue the holy city from oblivion, the builders of the bridge have inserted in the nearest arch two inscriptions bearing the city name'. The famous temple stood on a low hill overlooking the river, which is now no more than a vast ruin-field. It was supported on huge columns of greyish marble, eight of which seem to have survived and been transported to Tokat, where they support the entablature of the principal mosque.

The story of the Pontic kingdom's epic resistance to Rome brings into prominence one of the most extraordinary and picturesque characters ever to

68. Silver coin of Mithridates I Eupator, King of Pontus, about 100 BC. Diameter 33 mm. British Museum (BMC 4).

appear in the history of Asia Minor. Mithridates Eupator, who had hardly come of age when he became ruler of Pontus in 110 BC, combined in his person many curiously conflicting characteristics. He was of abnormal stature and strength (he is said to have habitually ridden 120 miles at a stretch and to have driven a chariot with sixteen horses). He was totally unscrupulous and without pity (as is shown by his initial elimination of his mother and younger brother in order to give himself a free hand to rule), and his ambition gave him an indomitable capacity for perseverance. As a result he has often been thought of merely as an abnormally intelligent Barbarian. Yet this view, as Magie points out,

> ... is founded on the belief that ruthlessness and cruelty were un-Hellenic traits and that a complete disregard for the lives and rights of others was confined to those tyrants who ruled over Barbarous nations. The tastes of Mithridates were those of an educated Greek – his love of music and for works of art, his power as an orator, his study of the religious cults of the Hellenes and his interest in letters and philosophy which caused him to invite poets and scholars to his court.[5]

The first ten years of his reign were spent in deliberate and systematic expansion of the Pontic state and in the building up of economic and military reserves. Eastwards he extended his control of the Euxine coast beyond Trapezus (Trabzon) to the Caucasus, and even established a most profitable colony beyond the sea in what is now the Crimea; westward he compacted with Nicomedes, the ruler of Bithynia, for a joint annexation of Paphlagonia, taking what remained of the coast on that side as his own share. Inland to the south he recovered Galatia from the Romans, who were temporarily preoccupied with an insurrection in central Europe. At the same time it is said that he personally travelled incognito throughout the province of Asia in order to spy out the land for a campaign which he already had in mind against the Romans themselves. It was possibly in this way that he became aware of the rising discontent with Roman rule which existed among the Greek peoples of Asia Minor, and conceived the idea of appearing as the champion of Hellenism against the Roman invader.

By 100 BC, Mithridates had become by far the most powerful monarch in Asia Minor; but for the following ten years, during which he was engaged in building up an army equal to the great purpose which he had in mind, the policy which he pursued vis-à-vis the Romans was one of alternate provocation and withdrawal. The kingdom of Cappadocia was during this period the principal bone of contention, and Mithridates repeatedly ejected its pro-Roman ruler and replaced him by a protégé of his own. Even when the symbol of Roman authority appeared for the first time in the form of an army led by Lucius Cornelius Sulla and formally reinstalled the rightful king, Mithridates hardly waited until his back was turned before repeating the process.

War was now inevitable, but by the time it came in 89 BC, Sulla had returned to Rome to face his political enemies, and the Roman armies, such as they were, had been assigned to the command of less experienced generals operating in three widely separated parts of the country. Mithridates, who was by then said to dispose of a quarter of a million infantry in addition to cavalry and scythe-chariots, found his march southwards a triumphal procession rather than a campaign; and the end of the year saw him established in Ephesus with the province of Asia in his hands. Later he added Thrace, Macedonia and almost the whole of Greece to his ephemeral conquests; seized the island of Mytilene and only failed to take Rhodes when a siege engine, consisting of a tower and drawbridge mounted on a ship, collapsed under its own weight and the assault had consequently to be abandoned.

In this moment of a triumph whose completeness can hardly have been less surprising to Mithridates himself than to his enemies, there came from him a gesture which filled the whole Mediterranean world with astonishment and horror. As we have seen, forty years of imperial exploitation had brought into the province a host of Italian officials, businessmen and merchants both great and small, now said to number as many as 100,000. Mithridates ordered a mass extermination of these individuals, together with their families and servants, and so thoroughly were his orders carried out that only one-fifth of their number were said to have escaped. But it was not only the Romans who were to suffer from the arrogant brutality of the new conqueror. The Greeks of the province, whose liberation had ostensibly been his objective, were soon to find themselves subjected to a new tyranny no less oppressive than that of the invaders whom he had thus exterminated. Mithridates in fact abandoned the role of liberator and appeared in his true colours as a rapacious despot.

At home in Italy, meanwhile, the Romans were unhappily divided against themselves. It was the old class struggle which had never completely subsided during the whole history of the Republic, and the people, under the inspiration of their first great popular leader, Marius, were in conflict with the aristocracy as represented by the Senate. But the most recent developments in the province of Asia could clearly no longer be ignored. The Senate entrusted Sulla with the reconquest of Greece and Asia Minor, but no sooner had he and his legions departed from the city than the people, led once more by Marius, rose in open revolt and successfully re-established their control of the government; Sulla's military appointment was officially rescinded and a people's army created to oppose him.

The events which followed could hardly have happened in any other historical setting, and were significant of the increasing emancipation of Roman military commanders. With the function and authority of the central government at home reduced by civil war to chaos and impotence, two rival armies in the field, acting in complete independence of each other, could nevertheless jointly bring about a political and military triumph whose completeness was hardly less surprising than the dispatch with which it was accomplished.

The commander appointed to oppose Sulla was assassinated and replaced by an adventurer called Fimbria, who, ignoring the mandate of his predecessor, set off across the Bosphorus with the two legions at his disposal to try his hand against Mithridates. Sulla, meanwhile, who had succeeded without much difficulty in reconquering Greece, merely remained in Thrace to await events, and occupied himself with the pacification of the states north of the Aegean. More by good fortune than strategic skill, Fimbria succeeded in routing the armies sent by Mithridates to oppose him, and invested the harbour town of Pitane at the mouth of the Caicus, where the king had taken refuge. Having no fleet, he could not, however, prevent him escaping to Lesbos, and was soon disconcerted to find him negotiating for peace not with himself but with his rival, Sulla. It was Sulla, therefore, who now dictated the terms of Mithridates' surrender. In 85 BC a meeting took place between king and general at a place called Dardanus (near the city of Troy, which Fimbria had pointlessly plundered during his recent campaign), and an agreement was reached by which Mithridates surrendered his fleet and all his conquests, retaining only the small northern domain over which he had originally ruled. Sulla then proceeded purposefully to the elimination of Fimbria. The two legions, whose loyalty had been greatly tested by their leader's incompetence, were easily coerced into a change of allegiance, and with Fimbria driven to suicide by their desertion, Sulla at the head of a united Roman army was able to march southwards and set about enforcing the terms of his settlement with Mithridates. The spring of 83 BC found him landing in Italy preparatory to dealing with his own political enemies.

The victory over Mithridates had clearly been no more than superficial: the 'snake' scotched rather than permanently disabled. Yet this first great nationalist movement in Asia Minor was also to be the last. The western part of the country at least could now see how little there was to choose between the extortion of Roman tax-gatherers and the irresponsible tyranny of a native king. Nevertheless, the twelve years which followed the re-establishment of Roman rule were destined to bring the Greek cities to the verge of social ruin and economic bankruptcy. They were heavily penalised for their submission to and collaboration with Mithridates, and their exploitation (rather than administration) was entrusted to a succession of increasingly unscrupulous provincial governors. Among them one need no more than mention Murena, who flouted the authority of his own government by making raids into Pontus, now officially a friendly state; Verres, with his unfortunate passion for collecting works of art and contempt for the long-established rights of ancient sanctuaries,[6] and Dolabella, who was subsequently brought to trial in Rome for fraud and extortion. No sign of relief in fact came until the appointment in 71 BC of Sulla's old lieutenant, Lucius Licinius Lucullus, to control the affairs of the province.

Realising that drastic steps were necessary to save the country from the demoralisation of total insolvency, Lucullus instituted a series of far-reaching economic reforms, checking once and for all the compounding of interest and usurious rates charged by money-lenders. The implementation of these measures earned him the eternal gratitude of the province, which was thus enabled during his term of office to reduce its great burden of indebtedness to manageable dimensions. At home, however, among the tax-farmers and their dependent shareholders it created a storm of resentment which ultimately undermined the security of his position in Asia.

Before his appointment Lucullus had already been in Asia Minor for more than two years, during which he had brought to a successful conclusion a much more formidable task. This was the conduct of a new war against the indefatigable Mithridates.

For some years it had been known that the Pontic king was rearming. He had enlisted and equipped a very large army indeed, and with the help of a Roman renegade called Marius had trained it on Roman lines, eliminating much of the cumbersome display and oriental ostentation which had characterised Pontic armies in the past. A formidable new fleet had also recently come into existence. In the spring of 73 BC Mithridates formally reopened hostilities with a symbolic gesture. At Sinope, which had become his naval base, a sacrifice was made to Zeus Stratius and a chariot drawn by white horses driven headlong into the sea.

Westwards of Pontus, the state of Bithynia had recently come under direct Roman rule. Its last king, Nicomedes, had, perhaps in emulation of the last Attalid ruler of Pergamum, bequeathed his country to the Romans, and it was in the process of being assimilated by them. It was through Bithynia that Mithridates now advanced, and his army met with some initial success. One part of the Roman forces was at Chalcedon (Haydarpaşa) on the Bosphorus, and in a combined attack upon this city by land and sea he was able not only to destroy the greater part of the Roman fleet which was lying in the harbour, but to take prisoner the Roman commander, Cotta, and scatter his army. Lucullus meanwhile was at Ephesus, where he had been engaged in training the main body of Roman troops, and he now marched northwards to take the situation in hand. He was too good a general to risk an immediate encounter with an army of superior size emboldened by recent victories, and accordingly contented himself with keeping it on the move by alternate threats and evasions. Mithridates had clearly made no provision for supplying his great host with food under these conditions, and was soon compelled to regain contact with his fleet in the Marmara. This made it necessary to invest the pro-Roman stronghold of Cyzicus, and having misjudged its strength, he was soon involved in a prolonged and costly siege.

Cyzicus occupied the small island connected with the mainland by a narrow isthmus, just north-west of modern Bandırma. It had twin harbours on either side and a powerful wall protecting both them and the city. Mithridates, who had thrown a cordon across the entrace to the isthmus, soon found his own army blockaded by Lucullus, who established a fortified camp on a hill in the rear. He was again therefore in trouble with the problem of supplies and compelled now to rely exclusively on his ships. This became serious when, over a long period, his assaults on the city proved unavailing, and a large section of his forces, while attempting to withdraw inland by night in order to relieve the supply situation, was caught and cut to pieces by Roman mobile units. In the end he was compelled to abandon the siege and withdraw the remainder of his army by sea. Lucullus was now unable to follow up his success until a fleet had been collected to take the place of the Roman ships lost in the disaster at Chalcedon. Contributions both from the cities and the islands appear to have made this possible, and the next spectacle was of half the Pontic fleet being caught and defeated by a Roman squadron at the entrance to the Dardanelles, while the remaining half was battered to pieces by a storm in the Euxine. The king himself escaped almost alone in a small pirate ship and eventually reached Sinope.

This time the Roman commanders seem to have been under no illusion about Mithridates' capacity for recuperation. In a council at Nicomedia (Izmit) they decided to carry the war into the enemy's country by invading Pontus. The king had now taken refuge in one of his private strongholds, Cabeira (Niksar), which stands high above the north bank of the Lycus and is commanded by a citadel on a spur of the mountains above; and here, sure enough, they found him already engaged in raising a new army. Lucullus could not take the field against him until the spring of 71, and by that time he was once more in command of a formidable force. Fortunately the Romans were spared the necessity for any serious engagement by one of those inexplicable occurrences which are usually attributed to supernatural intervention. It took the form of a sudden nocturnal panic in the Pontic camp, which reduced the entire army in a few minutes to a stampeding rabble, and left its arms and equipment in Lucullus' hands. This time the king took sanctuary in the temple at Comana and afterwards escaped to Armenia.

Lucullus had now only to secure the submission of the Pontic garrisons in Amisus (Samsun) and Sinope, and this, out of consideration for their status as Greek cities, he intended to do with as little violence as possible. Unhappily, in the former case this good intention was thwarted by the garrisons themselves, who fired the city preparatory to escaping by sea, and his troops, preoccupied with loot, could not be persuaded to estinguish the flames. Lucullus, who is said to have actually wept with grief and humiliation, could do no more than compensate the citizens and take steps to ensure that the same thing did not happen at Sinope.

Armenia, where Mithridates had now found sanctuary, has already been referred to as one of the native kingdoms which had so far remained outside the sphere of Roman conquest. The country, to which this name came first to be applied in Achaemenid times, comprises the high mountain district limited on the west by the upper waters of the Euphrates (as opposed to its tributary, the Murat Su), to the south by the Tigris and to the east by a line running approximately due north from Lake Urmia. It is a land of bleak heights dominated by snowy peaks, and its bitter winter climate makes life only tolerable in the protected valleys between.

The most striking geological feature, and in a sense the focal point of the Armenian highlands, is Mount Ararat (Ağrı Dağ). As a mountain it is all the more impressive for the isolation of the situation in which it stands, and which allows an uninterrupted view of it from three sides. There are really two adjacent peaks, known as Greater and Lesser Ararat. The plain from which both rise itself has an altitude of nearly 9,000 feet, while the higher summit is computed at nearly 17,000 feet. The ascent is not difficult. It is in fact made regularly today by a unit of the Turkish army. It has also been made in recent times by a succession of semi-scientific expeditions. But the best description of the whole setting and structure of the mountain is that by Lynch,[7] whose expedition to the summit in 1893 represented the fifteenth ascent by Europeans. He says that both summits are formed by eruptive volcanic action and describes how the greater of the two is rent almost from the peak downwards by a deep vertical chasm. It was here that a landslide, resulting from an earthquake in his time, carried away bodily the only village which had found a lodgement in it and so weakened the structure of the summit itself that, in the event of such a shock recurring in the future, 'the massive roof may tumble headlong into the abyss which now yawns beneath its cornice of snow'.[8] Lynch also discusses the possible identity of Ağrı Dağ with 'mountains of Ararat' upon which, according to the Book of Genesis, the Ark rested, a tradition which is at least as old as the conversion of the Armenians to Christianity. But he reminds one that, 'Mount Ararat could scarcely have been known to the people of the lowlands, among whom the Biblical legend of the Flood originated'. For the rest, he is one of the many visitors whose imagination has been captured by the beauty and individuality of the mountain. Having seen it in May, when it is covered with snow, he remarks that 'the appearance of this immense white sheet from the blooming campagna of the valley of the

Araxes is one of the fine sights of the world'. The present writer saw it for the first time in September, when its mantle is reduced to the perpetual snow upon the highest peak; his recollection of it soon after dawn, against a sky empty save for a private cloud of vapour rising like a tiny plume from its summit, makes it easy to endorse this opinion.

Lynch visited and surveyed the summits of two other famous Armenian peaks. One of these was Sipan (Süphan), which like Ararat carries perpetual snow. The other was Nemrut Dağ (Şekil Dağları), which has a weird lake in its old volcanic crater. Both mountains stand within a few miles of the shores of Lake Van, in whose limpid waters they are to be seen reflected. This lake, which was in a sense the innermost sanctuary of Armenia, has been described in Chapter 10. The lowlands between the lake-shore and the mountains provide the best pasture in the province, and the rivers irrigate wide areas of fruit and vegetable gardens. Yet the most characteristic aspect of Van is the view from the hills above, which embraces neither cultivation nor other signs of contemporary activity. From here the whole scene has the remote unreality of a prehistoric landscape, and the sight of an occasional small steamer plying from shore to shore is a discord from which one's attention turns gratefully to some more timeless phenomenon such as a flock of grey cranes circling slowly over the water.

To the Roman mind the almost fabulous remoteness of Armenia is reflected in Strabo's geographical fantasy, where he imagines the underground course of the river Tigris from Lake Van to its present source.[10] Yet he was not ignorant of the country's natural resources. In fact, it abounded in minerals such as copper, iron and even borax, while the industry of its populous valleys produced woollen fabrics, silks and textiles for distant markets. The famous *kermes* dye (made from a creature resembling a silkworm, found on Mount Ararat) had even then a wide reputation, and the products of Armenian goldsmiths and craftsmen in leather were much in demand.

This, then, was the country which the inhabitants in Lucullus' time had inherited from Urartian forebears. The true Armenians among them were a people who had arrived in Asia Minor early in the first millennium BC, perhaps simultaneously with the Phrygians, of whom, according to Herodotus, they were an offshoot. They settled finally in these eastern highlands but their fusion with the indigenous people seems not to have been complete; for throughout the centuries which followed, they can be recognised as one of two distinct social groups into which the country was broadly divided.

After the fall of Urartu, Armenia went through a period of domination, first by the Medes and then by the Achaemenid Persians. But the weakening of Seleucid power after the advent of the Romans at the end of the second century BC finally enabled them to assert their independence. Artashes, the first Armenian prince, was indeed closely allied to the Parthian Arsacid dynasty, but his successor soon repudiated this connection. Tigranes, the contemporary and son-in-law of Mithridates who inherited the kingdom in 95 BC, even found himself in a position to match his strength against the Parthian kings, and greatly increased the extent of his territory at their expense. The Armenian capital had until then been at Artaxata, north of Mount Ararat; but when, in addition to northern Mesopotamia, Tigranes had succeeded in annexing both Syria and eastern Cilicia, this place began to appear too remote. He accordingly founded a new capital in a more central position (modern Silvan or Mayafarikin not far to the east of Diyarbakır), which he named Tigranocerta, and transferred thither the inhabitants of twelve Greek cities which now fell within his dominions. He was thus able to impose some semblance of western culture on the life of his court and the conduct of his state affairs. He even assigned to himself the title 'King of Kings'.

When in 71 BC Tigranes' father-in-law entered Armenian territory as a fugitive he was not at first officially received, but merely provided temporarily with one of the royal residences. In the following year, however, when the Romans demanded his surrender under threat of military action, Mithridates was immediately summoned to court and invited to assist Tigranes in the training of an army on Roman lines. To this, having some previous experience of such matters, he readily agreed, and in 69 BC Lucullus was compelled to implement his threat of war against the two kings. This time victory was not long delayed. He inflicted a total defeat on Tigranes' army outside Tigranocerta, and being assisted in the destruction of the town by the Greeks whom he found in forced residence there, was able to return to arrange for their repatriation. In the words of Strabo, he 'pulled down the city, which was still only half finished, and left it a small village'. Then, turning his attention to the captured provinces in the west, he proceeded to the liberation of Cilicia and Syria.

Not content with these successes, Lucullus, in the following year, continued his advance eastwards into the heart of Armenia, where Tigranes had now joined Mithridates. But finding that the two kings refused (as he himself had done so effectively when opposed to Mithridates' army in Bithynia) to be forced into an open engagement, and hampered by discontent among his troops who feared to be stranded among the mountains on the advent of winter, he was eventually compelled to leave the subjugation of Armenia incomplete. Turning southwards, however, he was able to besiege and capture Nisibis (Nusaybin on the modern Turco-Syrian frontier), the strong fortress-city from which Tigranes was maintaining a hold on his newly acquired Mesopotamian possessions, and here he spent the winter.

Having brought the war with Mithridates to a successful conclusion and carried the symbols of Roman authority as far as the frontiers of Parthia, one would have supposed that Lucullus had earned the gratitude and approbation of the Roman people. On the contrary, much of what he had accomplished was now to be promptly neutralised by the intrigues of his enemies at home. By appointment or right of conquest he was now governor of five provinces: Asia, Cilicia, Bithynia, Pontus and Armenia, and jealousy of this multiple distinction was now added to the already considerable resentment created by his economic reforms in Asia, to which we have previously referred. Under these circumstances, there seemed to be no limit to the treachery of which the

Senate was capable. In 67 BC, with Armenia still incompletely pacified and Mithridates still at large, a bill was passed not only deposing Lucullus from his command, but authorising the discharge of his legions. By the time he reached Rome in the following year, Mithridates had already returned to Pontus and Tigranes was once more engaged in an attack on Cappadocia.

Confronted with the great general in person, Lucullus' enemies in Rome proved less formidable; and with an inconsequence characteristic of the Republic in its declining phase the Senate ultimately granted him a triumph. The spectacle was an impressive one. To symbolise his defeat of Mithridates, 'there passed by a few horsemen in heavy armour, ten chariots armed with scythes, sixty friends and officers of the king's, and a hundred and ten brazen-beaked ships of war, which were conveyed along with them, a golden image of Mithridates six feet high....'[11] For Lucullus himself, however, the sense of failure and personal disillusion seems to have been complete. The remainder of his life was devoted to literature and art and to the refinements of luxury with which his name is today still associated.

While Lucullus' campaign against the native states of Pontus and Armenia was proceeding, the Romans nearer home had found themselves confronted by a problem of increasing magnitude, whose origin was also in Asia Minor. This was the threat to their Mediterranean trade and communications created by the Cilician pirates.

It will be remembered that during the greater part of the second century BC, the maritime provinces of the south, from the Gulf of Issus almost to the

69. Coracesium (Alanya), where the Romans defeated pirates. The octagonal tower in the centre dates from the Seljuk period (thirteenth century AD).

borders of Caria, had remained in the possession of the Ptolemaic kings (see Chapter 15). Sulla's successors, after ejecting them from Pamphylia (approximately the vilayet of Antalya), had extended the rule of Rome westwards into Lycia and to the east as far as Isauria and the valley of the Calycadnus. But Cilicia remained in their hands; and it was the western portion of this province, (Cilicia Petraea or Aspera as opposed to Cilicia Campestris, today the plain of Adana), which had been adopted by a group of seafaring outlaws as a homeland and base for their raids on Mediterranean shipping. In their early ignorance of the role played by sea power in imperial tactics, the Romans had failed to appreciate the function of the Seleucid fleets as police of the seas, and on destroying them had provided no substitute. A clear field was thus left for these maritime brigands. In the country which today lies between Mersin and Silifke they had found a perfect headquarters and base for their far-reaching raids. Where the rocky foothills rose sharply towards the Taurus they built fortified strongholds from which the approach of hostile shipping could be seen at a great distance, and along the shore, which is indented with little bays and secret anchorages, they built harbours and warehouses. Timber was to hand for shipbuilding and the amenities of life were supplied by captive craftsmen and forced labour. By the year 67 BC, they had already extended their activities to the western Mediterranean and were even able to make daring raids on the Italian coast. When the Romans found their grain ships bound for Ostia captured or sunk, some drastic measures had finally to be taken.

It was this crisis which brought into prominence an individual whose full name was Gnaeus Pompeius Magnus. A measure was enacted by the Senate creating a completely new command with unprecedented powers and authority, solely for the purpose of suppressing the pirates, and it was he who was chosen to fill the post. Pompey's approach to the task was on a dynamic scale and his immediate success almost phenomenal. Less than three months after the start of his campaign, he was able to report that he had captured 120 settlements, more than 800 ships had either been seized or destroyed, and numerous prisoners had been taken. In addition he had laid hands on the pirates' weapons and building materials for their ships.

But Pompey's political sense would not allow him to rest content with mere destruction and punishment. Realising that the fertile district of Cilicia Campestris, where a feeble dependent of the decaying Seleucid dynasty had until recently shared his authority with the pirate chieftains, could now be reorganised as a Roman province and play an important role both commercially and strategically in the future settlement of Asia Minor, he at once recognised the purpose to which the newly acquired material could most profitably be devoted. Even among the captured pirates, it was possible to see that there were many whose resort to lawlessness had been in protest against treachery and injustice suffered at the hands of inept administrators, and who, in return for more equitable treatment, could contribute effectively to his own purpose. He accordingly proceeded to a systematic settlement of the whole area, creating where necessary new cities to accommodate those who were now prisoners of war. One new foundation was made on the ancient site of Soli, and received the name of Pompeiopolis. The attractive ruins of this little port, with the stone quays of its small oval harbour projecting from the sand, and one colonnade of its central street still partially intact, will be familiar to those who have explored the outskirts of modern Mersin.

Pompey had thus shown himself capable of courageous and energetic action, and his name seemed highly to recommend itself for the command recently relinquished by Lucullus. Owing to the incompetence of the latter's immediate replacements, Mithridates was once more in possession of an army with which to threaten the peace of Roman Asia Minor and a settlement with the kingdom of Armenia was long overdue. Clearly any general to be entrusted with the task of remedying this state of affairs would require full support and a free hand, but few can have anticipated the nature of the appointment which the Senate would approve when Pompey was finally selected. For, as Supreme Commander, he was now vested with unlimited powers over all Asia, the governors of whose various provinces were to be officially displaced in his favour.

Having thus availed himself of such military resources as existed within reach of his Cilician base, Pompey marched directly against Mithridates. Once more his success was immediate and spectacular. Somewhere near the sources of the Euphrates, the Pontic army was caught by the Romans in a deep defile and, in the panic which ensued, their defeat became a massacre. Men, horses and camels trampled one another to death in their attempt to escape to the open country, and 10,000 Pontic troops were said to have been slain. With a remnant of his army, the king reached a stronghold called Sinoria (probably the citadel of Bayburt on the road leading westwards from Erzurum to the Kop and Zigane passes), where he had accumulated a vast hoard of treasure. Here he paid off his men and, pausing long enough to collect 6,000 talents for his own use, set off once more into exile. accompanied only by a few companions and a concubine dressed as a man. Being this time rudely refused sanctuary by Tigranes, he was compelled to make his way by gradual stages to the northern shores of the Euxine where he still had possessions. He was destined never to return to Pontus.

Having in this way disposed of Mithridates, Pompey turned his attention to Armenia, and after a rapid march across the mountains, presented himself before the walls of the old capital, Artaxata, to which Tigranes and his court had withdrawn after the destruction of Tigranocerta by Lucullus. Being already involved in a war with the Parthian king Phraates, Tigranes was under no illusion about the folly of resistance, and accordingly made a complete capitulation. Though permitted to retain his kingdom, he was stripped of all his previous conquests and his new status was defined as 'Friend and Ally of Rome', a formula with whose implications he must already have been familiar.

At Artaxata Pompey found himself already over a thousand miles from the Hellespont, but, still unsatisfied with the extent of his conquests, he continued to march eastwards, subduing the remote tribal principalities which he encountered. Winter found him in what is now Azerbaijan, whence he finally returned in the spring of 65 BC and set about the task, now somewhat overdue, of reducing the Pontic fortresses which still remained loyal to Mithridates. One of these, called Taulara (now considered to have been Sivas), proved to have been the richest of all the king's treasure-houses. In it was found such a vast store of vessels, furniture and horse trappings ornamented with jewels and gold, that it took a whole month to remove it. In the following year, while residing temporarily at Amisus (Samsun), Pompey devised a plan for the disposal of his conquests, laying the foundations of a political settlement which was to remain substantially unchanged for many years.

After this, it only remained to consolidate the new Roman possessions in Syria and Palestine, from which the last remnants of Seleucid authority had now been withdrawn. When he returned to Asia Minor with this task successfully accomplished and a treaty with the Parthians awaiting ratification, Pompey could be satisfied that the whole 'Orient' was finally pacified. Among the exhibits which he had accumulated for the purpose of his eventual triumph in Rome were specimen tribesmen from such outlandish regions as Colchis on the shore of the Euxine and the Nabatean kingdom of Petra, south of the Dead Sea. As though to put the final seal on his success, he now received tidings from the Crimea which most dramatically symbolised the accomplishment of his central purpose. Mithridates was dead. During the twenty-five years in which this turbulent individual had troubled the people of Asia, his character had become almost legendary and the news of his death was received at first with superstitious incredulity. Yet it was true. It appeared that the indomitable old man had spent a part of his time since his flight from Pontus in planning an expedition up the Danube with the secret objective of ultimately invading Italy itself from the north, but had more recently found his plans frustrated by treachery and opposition on all sides. On hearing that his son Pharnaces had succeeded in usurping his throne and authority, and possibly visualising a personal appearance in Pompey's Roman triumph, he resolved to end his life. Having drunk a quantity of poison without any noticeable effect, he was compelled to obtain the assistance of a bystander in the act of regicide.

In Asia Minor, then, Rome was once more without an enemy, and, dimly conscious of what had cost so much blood and treasure, she could now give some thought to future security.

CHAPTER 18

Roman Rule

The account in Chapter 16 of the Aegean coast and some of the Greek cities as they appear today reached only as far as the province of Caria and the south-westernmost extremity of modern Turkey. More briefly referred to in Chapter 1, in the discussion of Anatolian geography and ancient trade routes, was the coast which meanders eastwards for 600 miles from the borders of Caria to the Gulf of Alexandretta (Iskenderun). Since this Mediterranean seaboard assumed a role of some importance in the political settlement which Pompey contrived after the death of Mithridates, it may be convenient at this point to say something further about its character and to remind ourselves of the extent to which its earlier history is reflected in the monuments and ruin-fields which attract the attention of a modern traveller.

In its centre, the vast bastion of the Taurus, supporting the Anatolian plateau, thrusts southwards into the sea, and its rocky foothills rising almost directly from the shore make coastal communications difficult and agriculture on a large scale impracticable. Here was the province called Cilicia Aspera (Rugged Cilicia), which we have seen in early Roman times providing a chain of strongholds for the Mediterranean pirates. Over its whole length it is seamed with steep-sided valleys, where torrent-beds have eaten deeply into the lime-stone, and a single considerable river, the Calycadnus (Gök Su) cuts diagonally across the whole range from the north-west, threading its way through prodigious gorges. At some time in the remote past, its stream must have found an underground course into which the whole valley bottom eventually subsided, creating a canyon with almost vertical sides, sometimes more than 1,000 feet high. Today, the burden of silt carried by its water has created near its mouth a basin of alluvial soil in a recess of the hills, which constitutes the only cultivable area of any appreciable extent in the whole province. Dominating this little plain is the city of Seleucia-in-Cilicia (modern Silifke), where the road coming down through the mountain passes from Laranda (Karaman) finds a bridge over the Calycadnus and meets the coastal highway.

West of Seleucia, Cilicia Aspera extended as far as Coracesium, which is today Alanya, but there were few towns of importance on this stretch of coast. The rocky country had little attraction for settlers, and the coastal road was tedious to negotiate. To the east, however, it was for some reason quite otherwise; and as one travels by car from Mersin to Silifke, one is seldom out of sight of classical ruins in one form or another. Innumerable sculptured tombs project from the undergrowth, rocky eminences are crowned with the broken columns of temples, and stately aqueducts cross and recross the line of one's journey. The official boundary of the country on this side was the river Lamus, which reaches the sea through a gorge comparable with that of the Calycadnus. Not far from its mouth is Elaeusa-Sebaste (Ayaş),[1] a 'sacred and autonomous city', which was for a time the residence of a king. Elaeusa, like Tyre, has the peculiar charm of a ruined city which was once an island. The channel separating it from the sea has long since silted up and the whole site is swathed in drifting sand.

Between Elaeusa and Silifke is Corycus,[2] also a sometime Greek *polis* but now remarkable for the ruins of a magnificent medieval fortress. Standing on a small promontory beside a sandy cove which was once a harbour, it faces across a narrow strip of water a second castle on a more miniature scale,

70. A twelfth-century Armenian castle on an island off Corycus on the Cilician coast, seen from a contemporary castle on the mainland.

known as Kız Kalesi. The whole setting today is almost theatrically picturesque, for the wooded valley behind is studded with ruined temples, churches, sculptured sarcophagi and the façades of rock-cut tombs. Scarcely three miles inland, and approached over the remains of a stone-paved street, is the so-called Corycian Cave,[3] in whose depths the ancients imagined the giant Typhon to have been imprisoned by Zeus. A subsidence caused by an underground stream, such as we have mentioned in the Calycadnus valley, has created a canyon with almost vertical sides about 200 feet deep. The bottom is thickly wooded, predominantly with judas-trees which create a lake of brilliant colour in the spring, and at one end the cave itself, vaulted with stalactites, plunges steeply down towards the clamour of an invisible torrent in the depths of the earth below. There was once a classical temple at its entrance, but this has been replaced by a tiny, roofless Byzantine chapel, which, seen from inside the cave, makes a striking silhouette against the rich foliage of the canyon beyond. Travelling Yuruks (nomads) who visit the place refer to it as Paradise and apply a more opprobrious term to a second and quite inaccessible canyon some hundred yards away, in which animals are often lost.

Corycus was the terminus of a road running some twenty miles inland to the temple-city of Olba, whose site is near Uzuncaburç.[4] Olba, as the centre of a priestly state, similar for instance to Comana in Pontus, owed its sanctity to some obscure association with the pre-classical mythology of Asia Minor. The great temple itself, some remains of which still survive, was rebuilt in about 300 BC and at this time, if not before, the patronage of some earlier and outlandish deity was exchanged for that of Zeus.

East of the Lamus Gorge, the Taurus mountains begin to recede inland, and soon become separated from the sea by a wide coastal plain. The Amanus range, striking northwards from the Syrian coast and abutting against the Taurus barrier, completes the encirclement, and a vast, crescent-shaped province of extreme fertility is contained between the mountains and the sea. This was Cilicia Campestris (Level Cilicia), which corresponded approximately to the modern vilayet of Adana. It is traversed from the north by three rivers, known to the classical world as Cydnus, Sarus and Pyramus and to the Turks as Tarsus Çayı, Seyhan and Ceyhan, each of which, by the deposit of silt, has contributed something to the seaward extension of the province. Across the axis of these three streams, the plain is also traversed by a road with perhaps more historical associations than any other in Asia, the great highway descending from Anatolia through the Cilician Gates and afterwards crossing the Amanus into Syria. For centuries it carried the main traffic from the Aegean to the Levant, and watched the passage or return of invading armies.

Of the two passes called Pylae (the Gates) leading into Cilicia, the most famous is that to the north of Tarsus, which creates a passage through the main Taurus range. The road follows a stream through a gorge, which narrows until it is less than fifty feet wide. At this point, in the days before blasting, it had to be cut out of the wall of the rock or, where a cutting was impracticable, carried along on wooden planks. Today the place is known as Gülek Boğazı after a castle perched on a rock a thousand feet above and owned by a well-known Cilician family of that name.

Coming down by the modern road into the plain, one is conscious of the transition from the stimulating altitude of the plateau to the more relaxing climate of the coast. But this pass and these mountains have in the past been a barrier in more than a climatic sense. At times in history they have contributed to the political as well as geographical isolation of Cilicia from Anatolia and its consequent affiliation with countries to the south. In the time of Ibn Hauqal, an Arab geographer of the late tenth century AD, they were 'a barrier between Islam and Christendom', and in the eleventh century the frontiers of an independent kingdom.

At the crossing of the Cydnus was Tarsus, which had been a market and trade centre from the earliest times. It was not itself actually on the sea, and a lagoon, which served as a harbour, reached inland to within a few miles of it, so that it acquired the status of a seaport as well as a caravan city. St Paul, who in his profession as tent-maker no doubt profited from the skilled weaving for which the place was famous, referred to it with some justification as 'no mean city'. But in the Turkish town there is hardly a building which survives from his time, and archaeologists have been constrained to interest themselves more in the Bronze Age and prehistoric settlements which preceded the classical city. Much the same may be said of Adana, which has little architectural heritage from antiquity and a civic aspect which is hardly compatible with its dignity as third city in modern Turkey. Yet it is the centre of an immensely prosperous vilayet. Prodigious harvests of grain and rice are now augmented by the production of citrus fruits and cotton in quantities which would have been unmanageable before the recent improvements in communications.

Adana and Tarsus, with their seaport Mersin, are the modern cities of Cilicia; but in Roman times there were half a dozen others. These were all situated in the eastern part of the plain, on or beyond the Pyramus river, and have for the most part long since ceased to be inhabited places. Only Mopsuestia, whose foundation, as we have seen, was traditionally associated with a mythical hero of the Greeks, has retained some importance on account of its position where the road crosses the river. Under the modern name of Misis, it was still a large village as recently as 1952, but in the summer of that year suffered almost total destruction during an earthquake. Hieropolis Castabala (Tecirli) on the upper reaches of the Pyramus, Mallus and Magarsus near its mouth and Aegeae (Ayas) on the coast further to the east are long since deserted. Finally there is Anazarbus (Anavarza), high up on a western tributary of the Ceyhan, where today a few cultivators' huts and the tents of migrant nomads are the only signs of human habitation.

Anavarza has as strange a situation as any fortified city in Asia Minor. From an otherwise flat plain, an isolated limestone ridge rises abruptly to a height of over 600 feet, forming a line of vertical cliffs occasionally interrupted by deep clefts and shadowy caves. It was here, at the foot of the cliff on the west side, that the city lay, a double line of strong walls swinging out into the plain

71. The ruins of the citadel dominate the Roman city of Anazarbus (Anavarza).

at one end and returning at the other to create a crescent-shaped enceinte. A theatre and hippodrome were ingeniously disposed at the base of the cliff, their seating accommodation cutting deeply into the face of the rock. Wide streets and public buildings can be imagined, and until recently the remains survived of two fine stone aqueducts, approaching the city from the north. Where the cliff-face fell away to a more negotiable escarpment, a rock-cut stairway led to the summit of the ridge. Here there must always have been some sort of military stronghold, and today the rock is crowned by the well-preserved ruins of a castle, last inhabited by the Armenian kings. One peculiar aspect of the lower city in ancient times must have been its echo. Today a single human voice raised among the ruins returns from the cliff-face with its volume hardly diminished, and it gives one pause to imagine the reverberations of a populous city where every sound was prolonged and duplicated in the same manner.[5]

Sixty miles east of Misis, the Cilician highway reaches the fork at Toprakkale, where we saw Alexander hesitate before taking the southern route into Syria. Here the Amanus mountains and the sea-coast converge towards the site of Issus and the Syrian Gates, a narrow corniche by which the road and a branch-line of the railway reach the harbour town of Alexandretta (Iskenderun). The main line follows the northern route over the Bahçe Pass towards Aleppo and the Euphrates.

In Pompey's time, this corner of Cilicia east of the Pyramus, with the sea before it and the mountains at its back, was virtually an independent state under a ruler called Tarcondimotus, who had his capital at Castabala and was held in some respect by the Romans. In the resettlement which took place after the death of Mithridates, it was the only portion of the coastal plain which was allowed to remain a client-principality. It became one link in the chain of similar states protecting the new Roman province of Greater Cilicia. Others were Commagene, with its capital, Samosata (Samsat), at an important crossing of the Euphrates; Cappadocia, whose king, Ariobarzanes I, had patiently supported the Romans throughout their wars with Pontus and Armenia; and Galatia, then newly organised into three divisions under tribal princes or tetrarchs. Within this political barrier, so characteristic of Roman imperial policy, the Campestris and Aspera divisions were consolidated into a prosperous administrative unit, in which Tarsus as capital city acquired a new metropolitan dignity.

During the years immediately following Pompey's settlement, considerable territories north of the Taurus were added to Greater Cilicia, so that its area was nearly doubled, and in 55 BC even the island of Cyprus, recently annexed by a high-handed gesture of the Roman Senate, was placed beneath its jurisdiction. After an initial period of indifferent administration, the new province was rescued from stagnation and insolvency by the orator Marcus Cicero, who served as proconsul in the year 51 BC. Cicero brought to this appointment a talent for administrative reform and a capacity for disinterested public service which might well have served as an example to other provincial governors of that time.

Pompey's resettlement of Cilicia had been in progress ever since his defeat of the Mediterranean pirates in 67 BC. Five years later he was faced with the much more formidable task of reorganising the vast territories which the defeat of Mithridates had delivered into his hands. Here again the 'client' status could be reserved for peripheral kingdoms, such as Armenia on the one side and Paphlagonia on the other, but Pontus itself, with the parts of Bithynia annexed to it by the late king, was too rich and important to become anything but a Roman possession. The device by which Pompey transformed this most intractable of native states into an obedient dependency, and the ordinance known as *Lex Pompeia* by which it was implemented, created an historical precedent, and the resultant régime remained substantially unchanged for two hundred years.

Three Greek cities on the coast, whose rights had recently been restored to them by Lucullus, provided a stable element on which to build, and with them the capital at Amaseia (Amasya) was soon brought into line. For the rest, it was merely a matter of regrouping the old feudal villages into new communities, and investing them with the dignity which, in the experience of the Hellenic world, led to responsible emancipation. This conspicuous policy of Hellenisation is reflected in the names – Diospolis, Magnopolis, Nicopolis, Neapolis and Pompeiopolis – which were assigned by Pompey to five of them.

Pompey returned to Rome at the end of 61 BC and his triumph was held in the following year. When it was finally over, he was naturally anxious to arrange for the official ratification of his recent political settlement in Asia, but to this he found the most surprising and formidable opposition, particularly from a faction in the Senate which still loyally supported Lucullus. It is at this point that another popular hero of the Roman people appears in the story for the first time. This was Julius Caesar, who had just returned from Spain and in 59 BC was made consul. When he also found obstruction in the Senate to measures which he wished to take, he formed a political combination with Pompey and Crassus, and with the support of these fellow triumvirs, brought joint proposals before the assembly. In this way, both his own projects and the ratification of all Pompey's Asiatic settlements were successfully passed. As time went by, however, it unfortunately became clear that the association between the two great generals rested on expediency rather than on mutual confidence. There were quarrels about the distribution of legions, and the year 50 BC found Pompey intriguing with Caesar's enemies in Rome to deprive him of the consulship. A trumped-up charge should have sent him into banishment, but Caesar refused to submit, and his crossing of the Rubicon symbolised his opposition of military force to the Senate's authority. In the civil war which followed, Asia Minor was spared the actual fighting; but its people, to whom the conqueror of Mithridates was still something of a hero, rallied to the support of Pompey, and it was consequently they who in the end were bound to pay a great part of the cost. Pompey was defeated in Thessaly and fled to Egypt, where, a little later, he was treacherously murdered. Julius Caesar sailed down from the Hellespont to Ephesus to receive the submission of Asia.

Caesar in fact treated Pompey's more penitent supporters with remarkable clemency, and during his short stay at Ephesus even found time to institute certain reforms in the principle of Asiatic taxation. The Ephesians dedicated a monument in the usual fulsome terms to 'the descendant of Ares and Aphrodite, a god made manifest and the common saviour of all human life'. The 'god' was as usual short of money, but this was remedied largely by contributions from individuals who would have expected a harsher treatment. Not having heard the news of Pompey's assassination, Caesar set sail for Egypt in his pursuit. He remained there until the following spring, when he received an urgent summons to defend Asia Minor from a new menace.

Pharnaces, the son of Mithridates, whom Pompey had allowed to maintain the rulership of his remote Crimean kingdom beyond the Euxine, had been encouraged by Pompey's supporters to reconquer Pontus. By the time Caesar, hurrying northwards, had reached the Cilician Gates, Pharnaces had already met with some initial success, having even succeeded in defeating a Roman legion under a commander called Calvinus, who had been left in charge of the military forces in Asia Minor. Further troops were now hurriedly collected and, encouraged by the example of the veteran Sixth Legion which accompanied Caesar, confronted Pharnaces' army at Zela (Zile). Here, only twenty years before, Mithridates himself had defeated one of Lucullus' legates.

The battle that followed was hardly less curious than some of those which the old king himself had fought with the Romans. Caesar had taken up position at the summit of a steep hill, facing Pharnaces' camp across a deep valley, when to his amazement he saw the king's army charging up the hill towards him. As Magie[6] remarks: 'So extraordinary was the manoeuvre that the ancient[7] historian did not know whether to attribute it to Pharnaces' conviction that the locality was a lucky one, to encouragement by favourable auspices ... or contempt for the Romans, inspired by his previous victory.' Whatever the explanation, the attack was easily repulsed by a discharge of missiles, the Crimean army thrown into total confusion and their camp plundered. The battle took only four hours and the whole thing was over by the evening of the fifth day after Caesar's arrival in Pontus. The episode has been immortalised by his own reputed comment: 'I came. I saw. I conquered.'

Caesar now only waited to see the proper liberation of cities like Sinope and Amisus, which Pharnaces had besieged and captured, before leaving Asia Minor to return to Italy. But he took the significant step of planting properly constituted colonies of Italian settlers in these and other Hellenic *poleis* through which he passed on his way. He did not again visit Asia Minor before his assassination at Rome in 44 BC. But he left as governors of the provinces men who could be relied upon to pursue the policy of liberalism which he had himself instituted at Ephesus.

Unhappily this promising régime was to be short-lived. After Caesar's death, civil war blazed up once more between his two assassins Brutus and Cassius on the one hand, and on the other Mark Antony, whose eloquence had inflamed the resentment of Rome against the conspirators and who was now supported by Caesar's great-nephew, Octavian. Again Asia Minor was spared the actual fighting, but the provinces were impoverished by Brutus' and Cassius' ruthless extortion of arms and money, and demoralised by the treachery and oppression of adventurers like the notorious Dolabella who were enabled by the temporary relaxation of the Senate's authority to displace and even murder its appointed governors. In 42 BC, the defeat of the so-called Republican forces by the triumvir army at Philippi in Macedonia and the death of both conspirators created a temporary respite, but for Asia a new form of tyranny was in store. Mark Antony, like Caesar before him, now arrived in Ephesus to take command of the East, with a mandate which amounted to the absolute power of a monarch.

The story of Antony's sojourn in Asia Minor, his initial demand for ten years' taxes in advance from a country already impoverished by previous exactions, his leisurely redistribution of political authority and its associated perquisites to his supporters and favourites, not to mention his own autocratic and luxurious mode of living, make a depressing picture. Gestures of ill-conceived patronage, like his extension of the criminal sanctuary around the Artemisium, may have brought tributes from the practised sycophants of Ephesus, but the provinces could only resign themselves to a further period of oppression and exploitation.

Moving eastwards from Ephesus, in the autumn of 41 BC Antony, with his now formidable entourage, arrived at Tarsus; and it was hither that he summoned the young Egyptian queen, Cleopatra, ostensibly to rebuke her for her collaboration with the conspirators. The pageantry surrounding her arrival by boat in the lagoon below the city, and the accomplished seduction by which she disarmed the Roman leader's firmest intentions, have captured the imagination of historians and others throughout the ages and need not here be dwelt upon. From Tarsus, Antony followed her to Alexandria, and the years which followed saw his transformation, through the influence of this extraordinary young woman, into an oriental despot on the pattern of the old Hellenistic kings. The process was completed in 37 BC, when the two were married and Antony acknowledged the paternity of the queen's twin children. This was the occasion for his bestowal upon her and them of dominion over some of Rome's choicest territories in the East, and of titles such as King of Kings, with which, as prospective ruler of the world, he himself could now dispense. All this led to a complete breach with the West and so by gradual stages to his defeat by Octavian in the sea battle at Actium and the total collapse of his oriental empire.

After Actium, Antony's suicide followed by that of the queen left Octavian, at the age of 32, undisputed master of the Roman world. This was a turning point in Roman history, for, in 27 BC, when he was elected consul for the fifth time in succession, the Empire was reconstituted on a completely new basis. Having fulfilled the task assigned to him, described at the time as 'restoring the Commonwealth to the Roman people', he resigned the emergency powers given to him for the purpose and emerged with much greater authority veiled under the discreet title of Princeps or Foremost Citizen. As emperor, indeed, he was now invested with supreme command of all the armed forces of the state, but his new position was distinguished from the crude dictatorship of his immediate predecessors by his relations with the Senate, which could at least be said to be based upon interdependence and mutual respect. Octavian's policy was to implement the Senate's authority, in return for the political support of the conservative faction within it, which was still reluctant to abandon the old Republican formula. He assumed the name of Augustus.

Thus ended a period of civil war which had lasted almost without inter-ruption for a hundred years. With the salutary re-establishment of a single authority, and the encouraging signs early shown by Augustus himself of unique organising ability, hope revived throughout the Empire. The subject peoples, whose territory and belongings had so long been a prey to the contentious rapacity of rival militarists, could now at last pause to review their losses and plan the reconstruction of their economy. In Asia Minor, the Augustan Age heralded an interlude of unbroken peace lasting more than two centuries, during which gradual changes and developments, like the spread of western civilisation and the popularisation of Christianity, were destined to assume greater significance than isolated historical events.

CHAPTER 19

The Legacy
of Augustus

One important step taken by Augustus soon after his accession to the Principate was to appoint a deputy as administrator of the eastern provinces. The choice for this extremely responsible post fell upon Marcus Agrippa, who had commanded his fleet at Actium. Agrippa spent two years (24–23 BC) in Asia serving in this capacity and returned there in 16 BC for a further spell. His conduct of the appointment, concerning which comparatively little is known, is considered to be of less interest than the fact of its having been made, since it involved a division of power between the emperor and a representative in the East with supreme civil authority and unlimited military command. It was during the interval between Agrippa's two periods of residence that Augustus himself paid his only visit to Asia Minor. This took the form of an inspection in 20 BC, from which he must have returned with his mind full of the praise and gratitude accorded to him by the cities. Above all, he had made reparation to them for the oppression which they had suffered at the hands of Mark Antony, and the intelligent measures which he had taken for their welfare seemed to herald a veritable golden age of prosperity and liberal administration. Everywhere temples had been dedicated to him in his deified capacity, often in conjunction with the goddess Roma.

The privileges which Augustus had obtained from the Roman Senate were limited to his own lifetime, and one of his greatest hopes had consequently been that of founding a dynasty. Yet this hope was destined to be frustrated by a succession of domestic and other misfortunes. The first heir appointed was Gaius Caesar, the son of Agrippa and Augustus' daughter Julia. In the year AD 1, at the age of 19, this young man was sent with suitable advisers to a consular appointment in Syria. One of his first duties was that of negotiating with the Parthian king, Phraates V, for the withdrawal of Persian troops from Armenia. In this he was successful and a meeting was arranged on a small island in the Euphrates, where, with their troops and retinues facing each other on opposite banks of the river, the Parthian king and the Roman prince signed the treaty. On this occasion also, Tigranes III having recently died, the succession to the Armenian throne was amicably settled; but when, in the following year, Gaius visited Armenia in order to be present at the coronation of the accepted candidate, he found fighting in progress between the supporters of rival claimants. On becoming involved, he received a wound whose serious-ness necessitated his return to Italy. But he only got as far as Limyra in Lycia, where he died.

Thus tragically robbed of his appointed heir, Augustus began to look else-where for a successor. The imperial power was in fact to remain in the hands of his family for a further half-century, but the succession was relegated to its distaff side. After his death in AD 14 he was deified in Rome, as he had already been in the provinces. He had himself drawn up, during his later years, a detailed account of his own accomplishments. This was engraved on metal tablets outside his tomb in Rome, and after his death the government of Galatia decided that it should also adorn the walls of his temple at Ancyra (Ankara). The text was accordingly inscribed in Latin on both inner faces of the *antae* in the *pronaos* of the temple, while, for the benefit of the Graeco-Galatians it was repeated in Greek on the south-east outer face of the *cella* wall.[1] This is the great Monumentum Ancyranum, which still survives in the heart of modern Ankara and impresses one as much with the beauty of its incised lettering as with its importance as an historical document.

In the resettlement of the Empire after the accession of Augustus to the *principium*, a new and rather curious procedure was adopted in determining the status of the various provinces. They were now divided into two distinct categories, some being assigned to the jurisdiction of the *princeps* himself, and others to the Senate. For this purpose, it seemed natural that the older provinces, whose security could be considered as already established, should remain under Senatorial control, while others, which might be likely to require military protection, should be subject to the direct authority of the emperor. In both categories, Augustus avoided any direct policy of discrimination against administrative officials appointed by his predecessor, realising that any further changes might be fatal to the continuity of their political existence. For the moment, also, he was prepared even to persevere with the precarious experi-ment of maintaining client princes in the native states.

One puppet ruler whose sovereignty came thus to be provisionally confirmed was Amyntas, King of Galatia; but his death in 25 BC created a political crisis which resulted in the eventual incorporation of his kingdom in the Roman Empire. This event marked an important step in the Romanisation of Anatolia, since the new Galatian Province comprised the greater part of the central plateau. With the elimination of the Galatian monarchy, it needed only the integration of Cappadocia, which in fact took place ten years later, for the whole of Asia Minor west of the Euphrates to acquire a new political identity as a component of the Commonwealth.

With the process of unification so nearly complete, one would expect to find little difficulty in formulating a coherent shape for the history of this great territorial unit during the period of the Roman Imperium. But the task in fact proves less easy, owing to the absence of great historical events or tangible epochs upon which to hang the narrative. If one seeks to trace some recognisable process of evolution in the social or political structure of the country as a whole, one can detect no more than the prolongation of a slow movement, whose progress had already been far advanced in Republican times. This was the gradual spread of western civilisation and the Europeanisation of a hitherto oriental population. Furthermore, it must be remembered that the source of this movement was in the cities, whether of Greek or Roman foundation, and that there, perfected by the ingenuity and experience of many generations, political life had reached an equilibrium which required little improvement. The prospect of further development under the aegis of the emperors depended accordingly on the government of the provinces into which the cities were grouped, and on the benevolence or otherwise of the provisions made for their administration. It is therefore with the fortunes of the individual provinces that the historian of this period should really be preoccupied. The history of the cities is a mere record of favours and penalties, whose proportion varies according to the character or temperament of the ruling emperor.

As the burden of supreme authority passed from one Roman to another, the early developments of each reign were watched with uneasy concern by the people and cities of the Empire. They had to be prepared to see the challenge of this prodigious responsibility either accepted with sober understanding or whimsically ignored, as it came to be with increasing frequency when the principle of selection began to deteriorate. In the eastern territories, the rumour of a change in emperors would roll across the country like the sound of distant thunder, and set the city councils to preparing new petitions or to considering the blandishments with which they would seek to solicit the new ruler's patronage. In the case of Augustus' immediate successors, the older and more settled provinces could usually rest assured that little would be expected of them save their acquiescence in some administrative innovations, and they could usually anticipate an equitable disposal of their revenues. Only the remoter principalities and the native kingdoms beyond the Taurus would see reason for serious anxiety. For the death of a puppet ruler could stimulate the rapacity and ambition of an emperor too young to appreciate the equivocal effects of political annexation. In the case of the border states on the eastern frontier, it might necessitate the installation of a new Roman protégé at the cost of some disastrous military campaign. For the rest, the transition from one régime to another would involve only minor disorders and adjustments, comparable, as one would imagine, to the situation created in some large school by the appointment of a new headmaster or in a joint-stock company by a change of ownership.

In these circumstances, it is surprising to find what a vast amount is known and has been written about the individual provinces of Asia Minor during these three first centuries of the Christian era. A small part of it we owe to Latin writers like Strabo or Pliny the Younger, but an enormously greater proportion is derived from the study of contemporary coinage and the inscriptions on surviving monuments. And here above all we are indebted to the tradition of classical learning in Europe and the long saga of field-exploration by travelling scholars. Throughout the whole of the nineteenth century, great men like Texier and Hamilton were to be found in remote parts of Anatolia, recording and preserving the testimony of classical inscriptions, a work which was to be amplified and extended by younger antiquarians such as Humann, Ramsay, Hogarth, Chantre and many others. Soon the need arose for some degree of specialisation. An ultimately comprehensive catalogue or corpus of inscriptions could even be envisaged. So the work continued during the first half of the present century on a more systematic basis, groups of scholars like Keil and Wilhelm, Buckler, Calder and Guthrie or Cox and Cameron contributing to a joint assemblage of *Monumenta Asiae Minoris Antiqua*. Today, as new monuments are discovered or fresh inscriptions exposed, there are classical epigraphists of a still younger generation to maintain the tradition of scrupulous study.

It was almost exclusively from evidence of this sort that in 1957 Calder and Bean were able to construct their wonderfully detailed map of classical Asia Minor to supplement A. H. M. Jones' great inventory of topographical information published twenty years earlier.[2] But when it comes to reconstructing from this plethora of isolated texts some indication of political and social developments during the period, the task is bound to be more formidable, and one is amazed at the results obtained by writers like Ramsay or, in more recent times, Magie.

This is more than ordinarily true in the case of Asia, which takes precedence in our list of provinces. It would plainly be absurd to suggest that, from the time of Augustus to the reorganisation of the Empire under Diocletian, nothing of any importance happened in this advanced and opulent eastern dominion, yet Pliny is silent on all subjects save the regional organisation of its administration at the time of his inspectorate; and when we turn to the inscriptions, the information which they give in this case is tantalisingly fragmentary and concerns only individual cities.

Take for instance Ephesus, the greatest of all Asiatic cities. There are naturally many details of the construction and consecration of buildings and the dedication of gifts, such as statues, presented by individuals for their adornment. One emperor intervenes to suppress abuses arising from the sanctuary for criminals traditionally afforded by the Artemisium; another devises a remedy for the silting up of the city's land-locked harbour. Compliments are exchanged, official honours accepted and imperial cults instituted in return. Then there are the city's finances to be subjected to periodical auditing and adjustment by senatorial agents, and, on one occasion, a miscarriage of justice to be rectified in connection with the affairs of the Elders' Association. Finally, with surprise and disapproval a strike of bakers is recorded.

Or again, as an example of a much smaller city, at the opposite extremity of the province, take Aezani,[3] if only because its ruins are better preserved than those of most inland cities in Anatolia, and easily visited. It stands on the Rhyndacus river to the south-west of Kütahya, among windswept farmlands, in the clear air of the plateau's full altitude. There is an Ionic temple of great beauty built in the reign of Hadrian (AD 117–38) on a wide artificial platform, and, facing it on a nearby hillside, a small theatre and stadium. Here at once is evidence of the musical, dramatic and athletic contests which took

72. The Ionic Temple of Zeus at Aezani (Çavdarhisar) in Phrygia, dating from the first half of the second century AD, photographed by Kim Philby.

place in such a city, for the endowment is recorded by a wealthy individual of an annual festival for this purpose. Another, this time unspecified, gift to the city was made in honour of Nero and appears to have been of such prodigal munificence that the emperor himself wrote to acknowledge it. A delegation sent to Aezani to congratulate Septimius Severus on his defeat of Niger is similarly approved in a letter which speaks of the city as 'honoured and long of service to the Roman Empire'.

Although the inscriptions are not much help in attempting to fill the historical gap, new material is constantly being added, not least from the remarkably beautiful ruins of Aphrodisias, west of Denizli. There, in a prosperous landscape of poplars and olive-groves, the surviving columns of the goddess's own temple are still to be seen, rising above the remnants of other huge public buildings with much carved enrichment, all skilfully exposed during a quarter-century of excavation. Also recovered, and today preserved in an ever-expanding site museum, is a great profusion of fine sculpture, exceeding both in quantity and variety the total finds at any other excavated site (Fig. 74). Furthermore, among its most impressive pieces, evidence has been found

73. Columns rising among poplar trees at Aphrodisias.

supporting the claim of Aphrodisias to have been, during the early centuries AD, the centre of a distinctive 'school': the products of its workshops, and even its craftsmen themselves, are now seen to have been distributed throughout the Roman Empire. For art historians this astonishing display of carving – both in the round and in relief – must be one of the greatest archaeological revelations of recent times.

The neighbouring province of Galatia has always been a subject of great interest to historians and particularly to Bible students, since it formed a background for one of St Paul's most famous epistles, a document of great importance both for the picture which it gives of the early stages in the Christianisation of the Roman Empire and for its reflection on contemporary social conditions in Asia Minor. There is accordingly no lack of literature on the subject, and Sir William Ramsay's own commentary fills a complete volume,[5] with topographical and historical speculations.

One of the most remarkable aspects of Galatia at the time of St Paul must have been the vast size of the province and its consequent geographical composition. By the time of Amyntas' death, Galatia had become the largest of all the vassal-kingdoms. In addition to the ancient territory of the three Galatian tribes which occupied approximately the western half of the plateau, including the upper valleys of the Sangarius and the Halys bend, Lycaonia had been attached to it: that is, the Konya plain, with the lip of the plateau to the south and the famous cities Derbe (Kerti Hüyük), Lystra (Hatunsaray) and Laranda (Karaman). Pisidia and its lake-district had been granted to Amyntas in 39 BC, and, since the Turkish excavations at Side (Eski Manavgat) have shown that he struck coins there, he must also have received Pamphylia (Antalya vilayet) and so extended his kingdom to the Mediterranean. Added to this, after the battle of Actium, was Cilicia Tracheia, which had previously belonged to Egypt. In the north the Galatian frontiers marched with the dependent kingdoms of Paphlagonia, Pontus and Cappadocia and in the west with the province of Asia. As Syme points out,[6] 'this fantastic conglomeration of territories' resembled that of Cilicia in its moment of maximum inflation in late Republican times.

74. The young Nero being crowned by his mother Agrippina. Sculpture from the Sebasteion at Aphrodisias. First century AD.

In Galatia proper, the Gauls themselves had always remained a minority of the population. The older native element, Phrygians and Cappadocians, still filled the towns and large areas of the countryside. Among them the invaders had at first formed a small military aristocracy, speaking their own language and living in castles or fortified villages, surrounded by their tribal retainers. By the time of Amyntas, they had begun to intermarry and otherwise adapt their ways to local conditions. But their national idiosyncrasies and distinctive social customs gave a peculiar twist of character to the mixed race which resulted. Their language also continued to be used side by side with Greek until Byzantine times, and their principal cities, like Pessinus (near Sivrihisar) and Tavium (south-west of Boğazköy) were not completely Hellenised until long after St Paul's time. Ankara, on the other hand, having been adopted by the Romans as provincial capital in 25 BC, at once assumed a mantle of western sophistication, afterwards sustained by the priests who administered the cult of Augustus and Rome. Its great temple had been given a prominent site on the southern slope of the citadel hill, and the agora, hippodrome, gymnasium and baths which grew up around it were now enclosed by a city-wall.

From Ankara, let us shift our attention for a moment to the city of Cyzicus (Erdek), on its little peninsula projecting from the southern coast of the Marmara. It twice became conspicuous during this period, once in the reign of Augustus, when it lost its status as a free city as a punishment for scourging and executing a group of Roman citizens, and secondly when it dedicated to the Emperor Trajan a temple whose ruins show it to have been of a most unusual size. Cyzicus belonged to the province of Asia; but a few miles to the east along the coast was the frontier of Bithynia, which included the whole north-western corner of the peninsula. Pompey had annexed to it the *Ora Pontica*, including the whole coast from Amisus (Samsun) in the east to Heraclea (Ereğli), and many Greek cities, some of them sub-colonies of Sinope, which was itself a colony of Miletus. A double province thus came into being, known as Bithynia-Pontus, which, for two years from AD 111 to 113, was governed by Pliny. The remainder of Pontus, including the greater part of Mithridates' original homeland, was given by Augustus the status of a client-kingdom. Its king at this time was an individual called Polemo, who had ruled over Lycaonia before it was added to the realms of Amyntas. The story of Polemo's family and the services which it rendered to successive Roman emperors has a peculiar human interest, if only on account of the loyalty and affection which its members appear to have inspired in whatever milieu they were called upon to rule.

Polemo himself died during a visit to Russia in the early years of the Christian era. His kingdom was thereafter considerably reduced in size by the annexation of Amaseia and the upper Halys to Galatia, but the remaining parts, consisting of the Euxine littoral and the Lycus valley, continued to be ruled over by his wife, Pythodoris, who appears to have been a woman of great ability. Her capital was at Cabeira (Niksar) on the Lycus, which she renamed Sebaste (Greek for 'Augusta') in honour of Augustus, and from here she controlled her little principality with the help of her eldest son, who nevertheless maintained throughout her reign the status of private citizen. Her younger son, on the other hand, later became king of Armenia and attained the distinction of being the first Roman protégé to remain so for long, with the full approval of his subjects. Pythodoris' daughter Tryphaena was married to Cotys, king of Thrace, who is described as a mild-mannered and kindly ruler. He was treacherously murdered in AD 19 by an ambitious member of his own family, but on being brought to justice his murderer was accused before the Senate by Tryphaena in person and banished. She herself thereupon retired to Cyzicus, where she became a priestess and also apparently interested herself in the improvement of the city's two famous harbours. Her name finally appears rather curiously in the *Acta of Paul and Thekla* (see Chapter 20), as the latter's protector when she was condemned to death in the arena.[7]

Pythodoris meanwhile had been remarried to Archelaus, king of Cappadocia. After her death in AD 34, the Emperor Tiberius further reduced her own kingdom of Pontus by annexing the temple-city of Comana to the Empire, and left it for the time being without a ruler. But his successor Caligula, finding that her two grandsons Cotys and Polemo, grown-up sons of Tryphaena, were still living in Rome, made them respectively kings of Pontus and Thrace. On the death of the younger Polemo in the time of Nero, what remained of the kingdom of Pontus was incorporated in the increasingly unwieldy province of Galatia. This small family saga seems to illustrate the way in which imperial expediency dictated the manipulation of minor native royalties.

Mention of King Archelaus brings us next to Cappadocia, which, as has already been said, became a province after his death in Rome, early in the reign of Tiberius. Here again, we are dealing with an eastern dominion about which a good deal is known, partly, in this case, owing to the survival of a report on the subject made to the Emperor Hadrian by his legate Arrian. Relying on this and other evidence, Magie[8] gives a most interesting description of the province. He first mentions the strategic routes whose convergence at the capital, Mazaca (Kayseri), which Archelaus renamed Caesarea, gave it so much importance. They included the southern highway from Lycaonia, which led by way of Melitene (Malatya) to the Euphrates crossing at Tomisa, the old road leading from Ancyra across the Halys bend to Tyana and the Cilician Gates, and another running northward to Sebasteia (Sivas) and Pontus – all highways familiar to the modern traveller. Next comes a note of the country's natural resources; olives and grapes in the great mountain-girt upland of Melitene above the Euphrates, and a wine which 'was said to rival the wines of Greece'. Excellent grape-vines must also already at that time have been grown in the volcanic area between Mount Argaeus and Hasan Dağ. Here too, and in the whole district of Mazaca, the shallow soil produced an abundance of grass, and the breeding of all sorts of cattle brought considerable wealth to the province. Magie recollects that much earlier, in Achaemenid times, Cappadocia paid a yearly tribute to the Persians of 1,500 horses, 2,000 mules and 50,000 sheep. One is also reminded that in the Ürgüp district Turkish palaeontologists have found, trapped and buried in volcanic ash, the remains of tertiary mammals including many varieties of antelope and even giraffe.

Cappadocia was also rich in minerals. Red ochre was carried northward and exported from the Euxine ports. There were alabaster quarries and a very hard, translucent marble from the middle Halys (Hacıbektaş), which is still today in considerable demand. The country also produced sheets of mica or talc, used for glazing windows. The silver mines at Maden near the Cilician Gates fell within the frontiers of Archelaus' kingdom.

Archelaus had contributed something towards the Hellenisation of Cappadocia. One city which gained greatly in importance in this way was Garsaura (Aksaray), which he renamed Archelais after himself, and another was the local cult-centre at Comana in the Anti-Taurus. Augustus added to his kingdom some parts of Armenia Minor (an ill-defined region to the west of Erzincan and Bayburt), and the whole dominion became a prosperous and well-integrated state which, particularly after Archelaus' marriage to Pythodoris of Pontus, shared with that country the function of protecting the north-eastern frontier of the Empire. Partly perhaps for this reason, when Cappadocia became a Roman province it was placed under the control of a procurator, directly responsible to the emperor himself, to whom also its revenues became returnable, as though to a private proprietor. This being so, it is curious, twenty years after Archelaus' death, to find a son of his, of the same name, still bearing the royal title but retaining out of all his father's possessions only a tiny kingdom in Cilicia Aspera, where he had employed himself in beautifying the little island-city of Elaeusa-Sebaste (Ayaş).

The subsequent history of Cappadocia is obscure and, in view of its character as a frontier-province, largely military. Its fortunes were much influenced by political vicissitudes, connected with the perpetual struggle to maintain a Roman client-ruler in neighbouring Armenia. This policy had been initiated by Augustus through his patronage of Tigranes II, and was persisted in by the emperors who followed him with increasingly disastrous results. The Armenian people would not acquiesce in the role chosen for them by Rome, nor submit to exploitation as a buffer-state protecting her from Parthia. Again and again successive Roman protégés were displaced from the throne, and rare interludes of peace occurred only when *force majeure* dictated the temporary acceptance by the Romans of a Parthian prince as ruler.

Cilicia was another province which, during most of this period, came under the personal jurisdiction of the emperor. It consisted at first only of the Campestris plain, but Tarcondimotus' little Amanus kingdom was added to it by Vespasian, and Cilicia Tracheia – one part of which was ruled by Archelaus' descendants and the other by the priestly dynasts of Olba (near Uzuncaburç) – became gradually incorporated. The great cities of the plain, Tarsus, Adana, Mopsuestia and Anazarbus, had become immensely rich as a result of trade passing through the Cilician Gates and the great productivity of the soil. In addition to grain and wines, they grew flax, which provided the raw material for a flourishing linen industry, and one notices for instance the existence of a linen weavers' guild at Anazarbus and a union of linen merchants elsewhere. A. H. M. Jones describes how the cities 'expended their wealth and energy in feuds with one another', competing for ever more pompous titles and official designations such as 'the first, the greatest and the most beautiful' (Tarsus), or 'metropolis of the race', 'the most precious' and 'the triumphant' (Anazarbus).[9] Such diversions must have been rudely interrupted in the middle of the third century, when the Emperor Valerian was defeated and captured by the Sassanian Persians, and Shapur's armies swept across Cilicia to the Taurus passes, to return loaded with booty from its treasuries and warehouses.

Squabbling and rivalry between individual cities seem at this time not to have been limited to the province of Cilicia. In AD 43 they provided an ostensible reason (or perhaps a pretext) for the Senate, on the instructions of the Emperor Claudius, to put an end to the independent federation of Lycian cities. Added to the new province of Lycia on this occasion was the coastal plain of Pamphylia, which, since the time of Amyntas, had curiously been included in Galatia. The two together were placed under the direct jurisdiction of the emperor, though in Lycia the fabric of the old federal organisation was retained as an instrument of provincial administration. In AD 57, a Roman governor of Lycia having been indicted for extortion, some measure of freedom seems to have been restored to the cities. But Vespasian completed the process of annexation and, during the two centuries that followed, they lost the distinctive character which unity and independence had previously given them. They had also considerably increased in number, to judge from a list given by Pliny. He mentions thirty-six cities, among which five, Myra, Patara, Tlos, Xanthus and Telmessus, share the title 'Metropolis of the Lycian Nation'.

Having once approached the subject of the province Lycia-Pamphylia and its Greek cities, it becomes impossible to content oneself with a brief reference to the dry bones of its contemporary history. For here, where the Lycian alps face their reflection in a summer sea, and the Taurus withdraws from the shore to embrace the Pamphylian plain, one is confronted with an access of natural beauty unparalleled elsewhere in the Mediterranean. And, just as the last vestiges of architectural elegance enhance the setting chosen by the Greeks for their cities, so, one feels, must the people of these cities have acquired some special virtue from the poetry of their surroundings. Let us then for a moment abandon our search for a sequence of historical events, and indulge in the relaxation of an imaginary journey in the Turkish vilayet of Antalya. Antalya itself will be a good point of departure, since it is a harbour town and today easily accessible from the interior.

Attalia (its older name) was founded by an Attalid prince and afterwards bequeathed, with the rest of the Pergamene state, to the Roman Republic. It stands on a limestone terrace overlooking the sea, and is surrounded by rich gardens and orchards. The waters of the Catarrhactes which irrigate them afterwards spill over a high cliff at the terrace edge, and a deep recess in this cliff forms Antalya's inner harbour. Behind it, the narrow streets of the old city climb steeply towards its outer fortification and pass out into purlieus more generously planned by the modern municipality. Here one notices how the new town, in common with others on the same coast, gives the peculiar impression of turning away from the sea and in upon itself, as though the attractive little port, with its historic battlements rising above the tangle of shipping, were for some reason a sight to be avoided. Yet well-stocked flower-beds and the sound of running water make a pleasant setting for the fine three-arched gateway built by the Emperor Hadrian at the entrance to the fortified area.

The Lycian country to the west of Antalya is so mountainous that until recent years there were few roads, and to visit the coastal cities one had either to travel laboriously on horseback or take a ship. There is little doubt that the approach from the sea is still the most congenial, since the rocky capes and islands of the coast, decorated everywhere with ancient castles and classical ruins, have a particular fascination when seen from beneath the sails of a caique. Two characteristic Graeco-Lycian cities which can be reached in this way may here be specially mentioned, if only because of the remarkable disparity in their size and situation. One is Myra, a city made famous by its rock-cut tombs; the other Antiphellus (Kaş), a tiny port through which the now Greek island of Megiste (Castellorosso) at one time effected its trade with the mainland.

The valley mouth in which Myra stands provides yet another example of the freakish effects of accumulating silt (Fig. 33). The ruins of some Roman warehouses marking the site of the old harbour show that the sea has not noticeably receded, and can never have been less than its present distance of about three miles from the city. Yet, with the exception of the theatre, which is built in a somewhat elevated position, the whole town is buried beneath a deep deposit of alluvium. It appears that in this case the prevailing winds must have built up a high line of sand-dunes along the shore, and eventually obstructed the outlet of the river on whose bank Myra stands. Its consequent flooding created a marsh, by which the water-borne silt was evenly deposited over the whole valley. (This must have been the port at which St Paul trans-shipped when he was being taken under arrest from Jerusalem to Rome.[10] It would seem at first incongruous that he should have had to travel so far afield from the direct route to Italy; but there were elements in the custom of navigation at that time with which we are not today familiar. It is known that Myra owed its fame as a seaport to the fact of its being a point of departure for the great grain-ships upon which the food-supply of Rome depended. This

75. Part of the restored façade of the great Celsian Library at Ephesus, built in AD 110.

76. The mountainside at
Myra is honeycombed
with rock-cut Lycian
tombs, mostly of the
fourth century BC.

would explain the granaries mentioned above, which were built by Hadrian.)
At nearby Demre the depth of the alluvium is exactly demonstrated by the
fine, fourth-century church of St Nicholas, which is now buried up to its eaves,
with only the vaulted roof projecting above the modern surface. The body of
the church, which is perfectly intact though in a ruinous state, is approached
by a steep flight of steps leading down into the paved atrium. A dark vault
contains the tomb of the saint, an ornate sarcophagus surmounted by two
headless reclining figures of different sizes, from which his bones were at some
time removed to Italy.

The theatre at Myra is built at the base of a high spur of rock, crowned by
a Byzantine castle. The seating is divided into two tiers by a *diazoma*, or
promenade, skilfully designed to break the monotony of the auditorium, and
is supported on a labyrinth of vaulted corridors and galleries. The almost
vertical face of the rock behind the theatre is completely honeycombed with
the ornate, rock-cut tombs of Myra's early inhabitants. A few stand free from
the cliff-face on little platforms, but the majority are mere façades, divided into
doubly or triply recessed panels, and, as Charles Fellows observed, curiously
resemble the rectilinear mullioned windows of Elizabethan England. The façade
is occasionally surmounted by a pediment, beneath which the projecting ends
of wooden joints are imitated in stone. One of the panels gives access to the
tomb itself, an undecorated chamber with accommodation for several members
of the family. There is an even larger group of such tombs on the eastern side
of the rock, overlooking the river, and it was this that one Victorian traveller

went so far as to consider 'finer than the celebrated acropolis at Petra'.[11]
Certainly there are more elaborate examples, having open porticoes, ornamented with sculptured friezes and free-standing columns. There is also one
tomb whose façade is turned sideways to face an open vestibule, embellished
with life-size figures in relief. Other similar figures are carved on the rock-face
between the tombs or above the pediments.[12]

In the course of a long journey among the ruins of Greek cities, to be
confronted suddenly with a series of almost undamaged portraits of the very
people who created and lived in them is a curiously moving experience.[13] One
is accordingly perhaps to be excused for finding one's interest in the stylistic
peculiarities of these sculptures supplemented by a good deal of frank, unpro-
fessional curiosity. For here are no archaic obsequies or symbols of trans-
migration. Instead, one is shown a number of intimate scenes from everday life,
where the occupants of the tombs are recognisable in the familiar postures of
normal domestic behaviour. One is struck by the elegance of their carriage,
by the vitality of their physique, and also, most abruptly, by their nakedness.
The idealised nudity which forms the subject of much Greek art has become
such a commonplace of elementary education, that, in the course of time, it
has ceased altogether to be considered objectively. For the average mind, it
has become a mere artistic convention, as unrelated to reality as the impersonal
monochrome of the stone on which it is generally depicted. In accepting the
convention, one has forgotten the reality; the implication that, here in the
Aegean, for a period of some centuries, a race of cultured individuals often

went naked by deliberate choice. At Myra an unusual aspect of the sculptures causes one's complacency in this respect to be suddenly shaken. For the figures are painted; not tinted like the sculptures of the Parthenon, but brightly painted in natural colours, which have been hardly affected by the passage of time.

Rock-cut sculptures were not the only form of tomb in use in Lycia. Another consisted of a colossal block of stone hollowed to make a burial-chamber, raised on a stone plinth and covered with a gabled roof, also carved from a single block. One such tomb stands beneath an ancient plane-tree in the little cobbled high-street of a fishing-village called Kaş, which occupies the site of Antiphellus. A panel has been broken by tomb-robbers and the carved ornament has become a little chipped, but the long inscription in Archaic Lycian is still perfectly legible and the curved gables are intact. The people of Kaş find it no more remarkable than English villagers their local war-memorial.

Antiphellus had no river. The town stood between the sea and a wooded mountainside, drawing its water in abundance from springs and wells. The passage of two millennia therefore left its setting substantially unchanged until its recent transformation into a Mediterranean resort, and there is no reason to believe that the tiny Greek city (the theatre is smaller than that at Priene)

78. A village street in Kaş (Antiphellus). Beneath the tree stands a Lycian tomb of the fourth century BC.

79. The theatre at Aspendus was built during the reign of Marcus Aurelius (AD 161–80) and is reputedly the best-preserved theatre of antiquity.

had less charm than the Turkish village clustered around the ancient harbour, where one watches pine-logs loaded onto painted caiques, and eats fish and fruit at a table standing upon the worn stonework of the original quay. The acropolis-hill, from which the buildings have vanished leaving only the more solidly constructed tombs, stands at the narrow, landward end of a five-mile-long arm of rock, reaching out into the sea towards the distant island of Meis. On the side away from the village, it looks down onto a sheltered fiord of the type so common along the Aegean coast. Here the tombs descend as far as the last fringes of rock, and are reflected in the unrippled surface of a tideless sea. Until recently the halcyon stillness was broken only by an occasional flash of kingfisher's wings or the gleam and splash of a leaping mullet.

East of Antalya, in the coastal plain of Pamphylia, three important cities, Aspendus, Sillyum and Perge, are grouped within a few miles of each other. Of these the first at least cannot be ignored, since it possesses what is generally considered to be the finest and best-preserved of all Roman theatres. In addition to the auditorium, which has forty tiers of seats to hold 7,500 spectators, the whole structure of the proscenium remains intact. The scale and severity of its gigantic external façade is relieved only by a few small windows and two identical inscriptions recording the name of a local citizen who dedicated the building to the emperors Marcus Aurelius and Lucius Verus. Inside, it was ornamented with two superimposed orders, above which one may still see the marks of a raked sounding-board, constructed no doubt to improve the acoustics. In Seljuk times, the flanking walls of the *scena* were covered in plaster and gaily painted with an elaborate chevron ornament. High above the stage, a central tympanum is adorned with the sculptured figure of what appears to be a somewhat mature woman, emerging from the calyx of a flower. It is to this figure that the site owes its modern Turkish name of Bal-kız (honey-girl) and consequently its association with Solomon's Sheban queen. More prosaically it is indentifiable as an image of Bacchus.

The main buildings of the Roman town occupy a walled area at the summit of a rocky hill behind the theatre. They comprise a fine Nymphaeum, agora, peristyle-hall and basilica, all much overgrown with trees and scrub. Until the beginning of the tourist era, the place was seldom visited except by local sportsmen in search of *chikor* partridges. The river Eurymedon passes below, and must in its time have been sufficiently navigable to bring freight vessels up from the sea, which is just visible seven miles to the south.

At the eastern extremity of the coastal plain, where the curve of the foothills returns to the sea, is the site of Side, for some reason known as Eski (Old) Manavgat. Here is a very magnificent Roman city, grown up on the site of an original Greek settlement. Its impressive and beautiful ruins occupy a low promontory projecting into the sea, with substantial remains of two separate harbours and a double fortification wall on the landward side. Such walls, when dating from classical times, are always of great interest, and these, like those at Perge, are remarkably well preserved.[14] Side was excavated from 1947 onwards by Turkish archaeologists, and a number of important buildings have been completely cleared. They are for the most part constructed of coarse local conglomerate faced with particularly fine white marble, and it is an especial pleasure to see the great column-bases and huge fragments of architectural ornament, with their detail and enrichment, protected by the earth which until recently covered them, as clean and sharp as in the days when they were first carved and polished.

There is a magnificent processional way marking the main axis of the city and terminating in an open screen of columns with the harbour and sea beyond. At the landward end, it is approached by an avenue of sarcophagi and a gateway in the inner fortification, which is very curiously designed. It has huge, round flanking towers and a kind of semicircular forecourt whose walls appear to have been ornamented with an elaborate architectural treatment in white marble and many statues. At the head of the promontory the excavators have uncovered the remains of three temples, one of them circular. An unidentified building to the east of the great agora, whose inner façades are enriched with ranges of marble niches, has yielded a great quantity of sculpture, including fragments of a number of more than life-size statues. A building whose function was more easy to guess is a cool, vaulted *çeşme* or

drinking-fountain, for the use of the crowds emerging from the theatre. It is interesting to notice that the ruins of a large three-aisled basilica, dating from the early Byzantine period and cleared during the first years of the excavation, have once more become almost entirely obscured by the rich foliage of creepers and flowering shrubs.

Since the northern frontiers of Lycia marched with those of Asia, our geographical circle is completed and the six provinces of Anatolia accounted for. We must now pause to examine the progress of a momentous popular movement for whose early stages they formed a background: the spread of Christianity and the establishment of the early Church. For it is through the New Testament that the names of provinces and cities in Asia Minor have become familiar to millions all over the world.

CHAPTER 20

St Paul
and the Early
Christian Church

At the time of Christ's birth in about 5 BC Augustus had been emperor for almost three decades and was still at the height of his power. The eastern world was temporarily at peace and showed few outward symptoms of any desire for a change in its way of living. Yet, if we consider more closely the character of philosophical thinking in Augustus' time and the current attitude towards religious beliefs, it may be possible to understand the degree to which the intellectual climate of the age had in fact already prepared the way for the advent of Christianity.

The old Greek religion had been a simple, objective affair, concerned with a familiar and well-defined pantheon of gods and goddesses; immortal and ageless, but having a reassuringly personal and proprietory interest in the communities which had gained their favour. They were 'normally beneficent to Mankind, and as man needed their help and protection in all the business of his daily life, their favour could be obtained and their help secured, if he honoured them by regular worship and by appropriate sacrifices, according to the traditional rites of his country'.[1] But in the more sophisticated and cosmopolitan atmosphere of the Hellenistic world, contacts with alien forms of thought and an increasing capacity for introspection had begun to generate individual discontent, which the easy objectivity of the old paganism was no longer adequate to appease.

In Asia Minor, this symptom of change is already reflected in the Hellenistic art of the cities during the early years of the Republic. In works, for instance, like the sculptures of the great altar at Pergamum, some critics have professed to detect an exaggerated intensity, which suggests a background of emotionalism, quite alien to Greek art of the classical period. One of them says of the famous Battle of Gods and Giants, 'The half-human, half serpentine forms of the earth-born monsters, the writhing coils of their lower extremities, their agonised and ferocious expressions, all show that the old Greek spirit, no longer self-contained and self-sufficient, had come to a sharp and painful realization of the essential discord between the actual and the ideal, between the perverse material world in which men live and the philosophical world of ideal thought and ethical speculation.'[2] It has been suggested that, probably through the influence of Hebrew thought, a sense of guilt had crept in; a feeling of personal responsibility for the moral shortcomings of a despondent age. Naturally, new grounds for such feelings were to be provided by the crisis of political and social disorientation in which the temporary disintegration of the Empire culminated during the third century AD. But in the time of Augustus, some sort of moral perturbation was already in evidence and the search for a remedy had unconsciously begun.

At first, and for the few, philosophy provided a refuge. We have already referred to the two principal schools of philosophy in Hellenistic times, the Stoic and the Epicurean. A third school, that of the Neo-Platonists, came into favour and their system later exerted a strong influence on early Christian thought. They strove 'to attain a knowledge of the Highest by assuming a capacity in man for passing beyond the limit of his empirical knowledge and acquiring an intuitive knowledge of the Absolute, the True, that which is beyond and above the fluctuations and doubts of opinion. They thus gave emphasis to spiritual factors and drew a clear moral distinction between good and evil.'[3] There can be no doubt that from the dialectics of Neo-Platonism the early Church Fathers obtained valuable material for their posthumous interpretation of the teachings of Christ.

In the sphere of personal religion, from the fourth century BC onwards, interest shifted from the old objective cults of classical times to the more promising abstractions suggested by the Mysteries, such as those celebrated at Eleusis. The mystic cult of Orpheus was another which attracted increasing interest, since implicit in it were conceptions like the remission of sin and survival after death. The symbolism of the Orpheus story also suggested a new significance for the recurring cycle of death and resurrection to be seen in nature, and this prepared the way for acceptance of the oriental fertility cults with which the Greeks were already in contact, for instance in Asia Minor.

In the east, during the first two centuries of the Christian era, the tolerant flexibility of the Roman state religion had already permitted the assimilation of several major oriental cults, such as the age-old Osiris worship of Egypt and the Persian cult of Mithras. The second of these established a considerable foothold in Asia Minor, whither it is supposed to have been introduced by the Cilician pirates suppressed by Pompey in 68 BC. With its simple ethics and suggestion of freemasonry among men, it had a special appeal both for traders and professional soldiery, so that Mithraic meeting-places, which usually took the form of natural or artificial caves decorated with relief-carvings, are most often found at busy seaports or garrison towns. All such forms of religion were officially tolerated, provided their celebrations were open and unconcealed. Even the advanced monotheism of the Jews made many converts.

Yet none of these philosophies or beliefs satisfied the requirements of a universal creed for the Roman world. The uneasy bewilderment of the ordinary man could still be summed up in the almost childish appeal of the question 'What shall I do to be saved?'.

The formula which eventually supplied the answer came from a new sect, which at first seemed no more than an eccentric foster-child of Judaism. Its founder was a convicted criminal who had suffered the extreme penalty of Roman law. Yet his followers appeared to be profiting from some supreme revelation:

> ... a revelation of God, as a loving Father to all men, a revelation given by God Himself in the person of His Son, who lived on earth as a man, had taught men 'the good news about God' and backed his teaching by wonderful works, had been executed on the suspicion of rebellion by the Roman governor, yet had wonderfully overcome death and risen again: before His departure from earth He had founded a new society of love to God and man: inspired by His spirit, expecting His return one day, the Christians were leading a life of goodwill and friendship, and carrying out their Master's wishes.[4]

Here at last was something new for the individual; something plainer and far easier to understand than the legends of the mystery cults, yet drawing their distinction between sinful humanity and the ideal of supreme goodness, with a new emphasis on humility and fellowship as the approach for all men to this ideal and the way to obtain favour and salvation.

It is interesting at this point to take a preliminary glance at the teaching of St Paul, and to observe his attitude towards the earlier religious and philosophical beliefs which the Christian faith was now to supersede. Greek philosophy, in particular, he clearly did not regard as inimical but rather as a well-intentioned rival erring on false lines. St Paul did not in fact advocate a total break with the past or maintain that all earlier forms of belief had been heresy, an attitude which, as Ramsay points out,[5] he made perfectly clear in his Epistle to the Romans. He believed that

> ... there existed originally in the world a certain degree of knowledge about God and His character and His relation to mankind; but the deliberate action of man had vitiated this fair beginning; and the reason lay in idolatry. This cause obscures the first good ideas as to the nature of God; and thus the Divine Being is assimilated to and represented by images in the shape of man who is mortal, and birds and quadrupeds and reptiles. In idolatrous worship a necessary and invariable accompaniment was immorality, which goes on increasing from bad to worse in physical passions, and thus corrupts the whole nature and character of man.[6]

This suggestion of continuity must have made the new teaching more acceptable to those whom St Paul addressed, overcoming their inclination to regard his creed merely as a new Graeco-Oriental philosophy of the sort whose developments they were used to following with detached interest. For one must remember that his propagation of the gospel took place in an urban setting, amidst the ferment of new ideas and rival doctrines which characterised the world of Romanised Greeks and orientals in the eastern provinces. This fact is even reflected in the word 'pagans' (*pagani*), which the early Christians contemptuously applied to the devotees of older cults, meaning yokels or country bumpkins.

This situation, however, changed rapidly during the first century after Christ's death. The new religion spread at an amazing speed through Syria and Asia Minor, and by AD 60 had already reached the capital. It was now no longer restricted to populous centres, but had reached the agricultural communities. By AD 112, when Pliny was governor of Bithynia, he could report in some consternation that even the religious conservatism of the villages was overcome and their old pagan shrines neglected.

Asia Minor was, in fact, so early affected by this movement, and the country itself made a background for so much early Christian history, that we should here perhaps return to St Paul and recollect in some detail the story of his successive missions.

The Acts of the Apostles must be regarded as a remarkable document, if only in its capacity as one of the most striking travel accounts of antiquity. The attempts made during the nineteenth century to discredit it have been largely countered by the untiring work of Sir William Ramsay, both in the field of pure scholarship and in practical research. The sheer magnitude of Ramsay's output as a writer is impressive in itself, and its orientation can be

81. The travels of St Paul. From S. Lloyd, 'St Paul in Asia Minor', *Asian Affairs* 59 (June 1972), pp. 182–90.

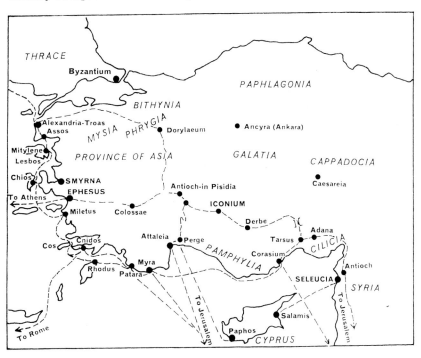

judged by the titles, *Saint Paul the Traveller and Roman Citizen, The Cities of Saint Paul, Luke the Physician, Pauline and Other Studies,* etc. These books (often first delivered in the form of lectures or papers read before learned societies) brought to the world of New Testament studies the superior authority of a mind impregnated with the atmosphere in which St Paul worked, familiar in every detail with the history and geographical physiognomy of the countries which had been the setting of his ministry. The impact of Ramsay's remarkable mind on the subject of St Paul's personality and accomplishments, tempered by his liberal understanding of contemporary metaphysics and anthropology, raised it from the toils of theological pedantry to the status of an inspiring historical reality. Much of what follows has been taken from his writings.

The theme of The Acts, then, is the spread of Christianity from Jerusalem to Rome and the travels of those to whom its dissemination was entrusted. But the story serves a secondary purpose in that it provides us with a portrait of the second greatest personality in the New Testament: St Paul, the first Christian missionary. Yet his work as a missionary was by no means limited to proselytising and conversion. In the twenty or so years of his ministry, he founded a chain of 'churches' across the breadth of Syria, Asia Minor and Greece, and the welfare of each one of these was from then onwards his personal concern and responsibility. His care of the churches and anxious preoccupation with their morale is in fact one of the most significant and endearing tokens of his character, and it is for this reason that we are so fortunate in having the actual letters of encouragement or admonition addressed by him to this first generation of Christians, to amplify the picture of his personality which is presented by The Acts.

St Paul was, we know, born in Tarsus, a tent-maker by trade though not necessarily a humble craftsman, for his family were sufficiently high-born to have acquired Roman citizenship. They may in fact have been proprietors of some fairly large manufacturing concern, in which, in the manner of the times, their son would have served an apprenticeship. They were Jews; and among them the boy would have been called Saul until his entry into public life made the Latinised form of his name, Paul, more convenient. When his conversion took place (probably between the years AD 32 and 37), the early Christians were no more than an 'infant sect in the arms of Jewry', and afterwards it was through Jewish channels that he set about organising the propagation of the new faith: his first missionary posts were established in centres where Jewish communities already existed. For these were the Jews of the diaspora: a people scattered throughout the Roman cities in small, well-organised colonies. Commercially adroit and religiously aloof, their presence was something of an irritation to the administration, though on the whole they were tolerated and in some places even afforded certain privileges and exemptions. Their ranks, as we have said, had been strengthened by the accession of a certain number of converts, fugitives from the bewilderment of a restless age who sought consolation in the exalted monotheism of the Jewish synagogue. Their number has been estimated at approximately seven per cent of the whole population of the Empire.

Paul's missionary work did not begin directly after his conversion. From Damascus he travelled to Jerusalem, with the intention of joining the Christian community and testifying to his own new faith. But the brethren there, remembering his previous record, could not be easily convinced of his sincerity, and his defection from the anti-Christian party left him exposed to some danger of violence at their hands. He accordingly returned to his home at Tarsus, and thereafter there is a period of about ten years unaccounted for in the story of his life, during which he is believed to have moved quietly from place to place, preparing himself in spirit and understanding for the summons which he knew must eventually come to him. Meanwhile, from its centre in Jerusalem, the great evangelical movement had begun, under the direction of St Peter and the other apostles who had made it their headquarters after the Crucifixion. One imagines that they must have been greatly aided in these early stages by the fact that for all Jewry, Jerusalem was already at this time a centre of pilgrimage. From the remotest outposts of the diaspora, Jews returned at intervals, like Muslims to Mecca, to worship at Herod's temple. And there would have been time, during their stay in the Holy City, for many of them to become converted to the new faith. They could carry back with them the gospel of the apostles' teaching, and new embryo centres of Christianity would thus be created within the Jewish communities of the cities whence they came.

One of the earliest centres of this sort, at Antioch-in-Syria (now Antakya), soon increased so rapidly that a sister church to the one at Jerusalem could be founded; and it was here, in about AD 43, that some members of the church took the important step of converting Gentiles. Their action created some doubts among the Jewish Christians in Jerusalem, and raised major problems of conduct, on which it was necessary to obtain authoritative rulings. For this purpose, Barnabas soon afterwards travelled to Antioch, and finding that the conversions were genuine, he stayed on to help with the work. It appears to have been at this juncture that he suddenly remembered Paul, and realised the unique qualifications which he might have for such a mission. So he probably travelled down to Seleucia at the mouth of the Orontes, which was the port of Antioch,[7] and found a ship which would carry him across the Bay of Alexandretta to the anchorage in the marshes below Tarsus. There is a suggestion that, after so long a time, he had some difficulty in finding where Paul was living; but they did eventually meet, and Barnabas persuaded him, first, to return with him to Antioch, where 'for a whole year [they] met with the church and taught' before going to Jerusalem, where there was a famine and much relief work to be done. When Paul and Barnabas finally set out on their first missionary journey, they were accompanied by Mark, who was later to become Peter's secretary and companion. Once more the point of departure was Seleucia, whence the three friends sailed to Cyprus. Paul's life-work had begun.

From Cyprus, the apostles took ship again and came to Perge in Pamphylia, sailing probably up the river Cestrus (Ak Çayı), which may in those days have been navigable almost as far as the city. Here Mark separated himself from the party, after a difference of opinion with Paul, who from now onwards made all decisions for the conduct of the mission. Its immediate destination was Pisidian Antioch (Yalvaç, sixty miles west of Konya), to reach which, unless he was prepared for a long detour, Paul must have taken a direct northerly route across the mountains, on the line of the present road northward from Antalya.

With this picture of the earliest Christian missionaries taking the road for their first major journey into the interior of Asia Minor, one's mind turns to the actual method of travel at that time. Though Paul, with his taste for austerity, would no doubt have been satisfied with the humblest form of transport, it is interesting to remember that travel for Romans, at least on the main lines of imperial communications, was at that time sufficiently well organised to involve little hardship. H. V. Morton gives a good picture of traffic on the Roman roads:

> Along the roads caravans crossed the world heavy with riches. The Imperial Post, instituted by Augustus, speeded from point to point, changing its horses at post-stations set at intervals on all the great highways of the Empire. Dispatches from generals in the field, instructions to colonial governors, imperial edicts and other official information, crossed mountain and plain at a steady five miles an hour, the average speed of the Imperial messengers.
>
> Ordinary travellers in hired carriages were content to travel from forty to fifty miles a day. Many and varied were the types of carriages that could be hired in Roman times. The huge, luxurious Rolls Royce of antiquity was the *carruca* which was sometimes fitted as a *carruca dormitoria*, complete with soft beds and so beautifully painted and decorated that one of them could cost as much as a farm. The *basterna* was a comfortable litter, slung on shafts between two mules, one fore and the other aft. The *carpentum* was a smart two-wheeled carriage popular with ladies, and sometimes hooded with silk curtains. The *cisium* was a swift cabriolet and the *reda* was an ambling four-horse coach. In cities, or for short distances, the old-fashioned litter was used, often carried on the shoulders of eight trained bearers.

He also quotes Cicero's account of how he met Vedius in the depths of Asia, 'with two chariots, a carriage, a litter, numerous slaves, and, besides, a monkey on a little car and a number of wild asses'.[8] Anyone who has observed the good surface on the many surviving sections of Roman roads in Anatolia will imagine that even the monkey travelled in comparative comfort.

Paul seems often to have preferred to take a ship from one coastal town to another, rather than go by road, though we know that on one occasion, when his companions did so, he decided that a long walk would do him good, and so travelled twenty miles on foot across the Troadic peninsula. In the normal way, he would probably have been found riding, among a fairly large group

82. The stadium at Perge was probably erected in the second century AD. It could seat 12,000.

of fellow-travellers who clung together for companionship and safety. Thus he arrived in Pisidian Antioch, and made contact with the Jews in the local synagogue to whom he was intending to preach, before going on to Iconium, Lystra and Derbe.

The churches which Paul founded among these cities of Galatia were afterwards to become the subject of his most affectionate preoccupation, but also of his greatest anxieties. Even on this first visit he must have received some premonition of future difficulties, for though he was received by the local synagogues, there was a good deal of opposition from the orthodox Jews, and it was in protest against this opposition that he made the most important decision of his mission. 'It was necessary', he told them, 'that the word of God should first be spoken to you: seeing ye thrust it from you, and judge yourselves unworthy of eternal life, lo, we turn to the Gentiles.'[9] Christiantity (he implied) should no longer be a mere sub-sect of Jewry, nor its benefits restricted to the Jewish people. Paul was henceforth to become the Apostle of the Gentiles. He continued indeed, in the cities which he visited, to teach first in the Jewish synagogues; but as each church was created, 'elders' were appointed to administer its affairs, and it was thus emancipated from synagogue control.

The occasion of Paul's first arrival at Iconium (Konya) provides us with the only surviving description of his personal appearance. The source is the legend

83. The surviving apse of the fifth-century church of St Thekla, near Silifke, built above the cave to which she retired, devoting herself to Christian teaching.

of Paul and Thekla, which derives from a second-century recopying of a first-century manuscript.[10] In this story, a resident of Iconium, called Onesiphorus, had heard of Paul's teaching and of his prospective arrival in the city, and had walked out some distance on the Lystra road to meet him. Not being previously acquainted with him, he was told to look out for a man 'small in size, with meeting eyebrows, with a rather large nose, bald headed, bow legged, strongly built, full of grace, for at times he looked like a man, and at times he had the face of an angel'. This curious description would to some extent agree with Sir John Myres' imaginary picture of a Cilician Jew, 'with the low forehead, bushy eyebrows and high beard of Socrates and the backwoodsmen of old times'.[11] In any case, as it has often been pointed out, the legendary description, which derives from a devout Christian source, would be pointlessly unflattering if it had not depended upon some lingering verity of actual human memory. The only other physical fact which we know about Paul is that he was afflicted with some recurring ailment which resulted in periodic pain and debility. Ramsay has suggested that it might have been malaria, contracted during his travels or even at his home in the unhealthy climate of Cilicia.

Once they had satisfied themselves that the Galatian communities could take care of themselves, Paul and Barnabas set out on their return journey to Syrian Antioch. Again they came down from the mountains into Pamphylia, but this time travelled as far as Attalia (Antalya), from whose busy harbour ships probably sailed regularly to the Cilician ports and north Syria. This must have been in AD 48, and it was not until the following year that a second mission to Galatia was proposed. Barnabas now made it a condition for accompanying Paul that Mark should again be included in the party, and when Paul could not agree to this, the two apostles decided to go their separate ways. Barnabas went with Mark to Cyprus, and Paul returned to Galatia, where his Gentile converts had been in trouble. From the first, they were unpopular with the orthodox Jews, and in the agitation against them there had even been an attempt by some of the Jewish elders to undermine Paul's teaching and question his apostolic authority. In the Epistle to the Galatians (the letter which he perhaps wrote in the interval between his two visits), one becomes aware of this situation and of the emotion which it aroused in him. On this occasion, as on many others, when his pastoral responsibilities became a strain on his patience, one realises that tears of tenderness and anger are not far apart. In the end, it needed the tremendous compulsion of his physical presence to restore a proper atmosphere of harmony, and until this was done he could not extend his mission.

During a return visit to Lystra, Paul enlisted the help of a part-Jewish youth called Timothy, who was to become his faithful squire for many years. It is also considered probable that on this second mission he was joined by Luke, the 'Beloved Physician' to whom the authorship of The Acts is ascribed. For, from this point in the narrative onwards, the famous 'we passages' occasionally occur: passages in which the writer, having himself been eye-witness of an event, cannot resist breaking into the first person plural. So it was in the end perhaps the three of them who finally left Galatia in the autumn of AD 50 to continue their mission. Paul at first had the idea of travelling westwards into the province of Asia or alternatively of striking north for Bithynia; but some higher form of intuition seems to have persuaded him that neither plan was for the moment acceptable, and we next find the party at Alexandria Troas, near the entrance to the Dardanelles. It was here that he received in a dream the summons to cross over to Europe. In Luke's words: 'Straightway we sought to go forth into Macedonia, concluding that God had called us to preach the Gospel unto them.' They preached in Philippi, Thessalonica, Beroea and Athens; and afterwards Paul spent nearly two years at Corinth lodging in the house of his friends Aquila and Priscilla.

Paul's decision to postpone for the time being his first visit to Asia has been the subject of considerable speculation. One explanation which has been offered by some commentators is that St John was at this time residing in Ephesus, and that the Christian communities in the Ionian cities may have been his particular sphere of activity. It is also believed by many that when St John came from Jerusalem to live in Ephesus, he brought with him the Blessed Virgin, who had been committed to his special charge; and the subject of her possible residence there is of sufficient interest to warrant at this point a considerable digression.

Concerning the later life of the Blessed Virgin, tradition provides two alter-native theories, neither of which is unequivocally supported by any recorded authority; and it would probably be fair to say that, throughout the various Christian churches today, belief in the two is about equally divided. According to one, she remained in Jerusalem, living with St John until her death; according to the other, she travelled with him from Jerusalem to Ephesus, and lived there, latterly under the protection of the church founded by St John or St Paul. The evidence in support of each theory, both in the form of tradition and of references made by Church historians of later times, has frequently been reviewed in some detail and need not be elaborated here. Two points only will suffice to illustrate the kind of argument on which the Ephesian theory is based.

The first is a piece of purely negative evidence and derives from a remark made by the early Christian writer Epiphanius in about AD 375. He pointed out that 'the Scriptures say nothing about the death of the Virgin, whether she died or not, whether she was buried or not, and that in the Scriptures there is no authority for the opinion that when John went away into [the province of] Asia, he took her with him'.[12] This has been taken to imply that in the late fourth century the elders of the Church were already aware of an Ephesian tradition, sufficiently strong to warrant this cautionary reminder. The second point is in connection with the Council of Ephesus, which met a little later, in AD 431.

The main purpose of this council appears to have been to protest against the depreciation by Nestorius and his followers of the worship of the Virgin Mother of God, and incorporated in its records is the text of a sermon preached by Proclus, Bishop of Cyzicus, in AD 429. Proclus' subject is 'the glorification of the race of women', and in particular of 'her who was in due time mother and Virgin', for, as he says to his congregation, 'The Sacred Mother of God, Mary has brought us here together.'[13] But the most interesting part of the story is that the scene of the Council was a building known as 'the most Holy Church which is called Maria', and that, in the belief of the Austrian excavators of the Roman city at Ephesus, this is to be identified with the great Double

Basilica, whose ruins are familiar to all visitors. This building really consists of two churches, the easternmost of which dates from the time of Justinian, but the western part of it would almost certainly have been already in existence in AD 431.[14]

As has already been said, these and other arguments in favour of the Blessed Virgin's residence at Ephesus have recently received new attention, in connection with what one can only describe as the rediscovery of the alleged House of the Virgin. This beautiful little shrine on the slopes of Mount Solimissus (Ala Dağ) to the south of the city owes its fame more correctly to a supernatural event at the beginning of the last century, whose authenticity only the most captious materialists have ever doubted. Ramsay (who was not among them) summarises it as follows:

> Briefly put, the story is that an uneducated woman in a German convent saw in a vision the place in the hills south of Ephesus where the Virgin Mary had lived, and described it in detail, immediately after she had the vision; that her vision was printed and published in Germany; that after the lapse of fifty years the book came in 1890 into the hands of some Roman Catholics in Smyrna, by whom the trustworthiness of the vision was keenly discussed; that a priest[15] in Smyrna, who took a leading part in controverting the authority of the vision, made a journey into the mountains in order to prove by actual exploration that no such House existed; that on the third day of continuous search in the rugged unknown mountains, on Wednesday 29th July, 1891 (the Feast of St. Martha), he found the house exactly as it was described in the published account of the vision, some miles south of Ephesus, among surroundings which were also accurately described therein; and that he returned to Smyrna convinced of the truth against his previous judgement. A Roman Catholic festival has since the discovery been arranged and celebrated annually at the holy spot.

Anne Catherine Emmerich's personal account of her vision was dictated in 1818 to the poet Brentano, who did not publish it till 1841, and then only in a form which had a very limited circulation. This would help to explain the immensely long time which elapsed between her death in 1824 and the discovery by the Smyrna Catholics which would so much have interested her. The ruined building which so uncannily resembled the one seen in her vision, a small chapel-like affair with an apse, was already familiar to the Greek community in a neighbouring village as a holy place, and religious rites were occasionally performed there. It was also traditionally known by the Graeco-Turkish name Panaya Kapulu, literally meaning 'the All-holy [Virgin] with the door'. The building has now been partly restored, and it is reached by road from Ayasoluk, which is the modern name of Ephesus. Quite apart from the fact that some readers may have visited the place or even taken part in the regular pilgrimages which are now organised, the whole Emmerich story is of such interest that, before leaving the subject, it seems worth quoting in part Ramsay's translation from the French version of her vision:[16]

After the Ascension of our Lord Jesus Christ, Mary lived three years on Sion, three years at Bethany and nine years at Ephesus, to which place John had conducted her soon after the Jews had exposed Lazarus and his sisters on the sea.

Mary did not live exactly at Ephesus, but in the environs, where were settled many women who were her friends. Her dwelling was situated three leagues from Ephesus, on a mountain which was seen to the left in coming from Jerusalem, and which probably descended towards Ephesus – coming from the southeast the city was seen as if altogether at the foot of the mountain, but it is seen to extend all round as you continue to advance. Near Ephesus there are grand avenues of trees, under which the yellow fruits are lying on the ground. A little to the south, narrow paths lead to an eminence covered with wild plants. There is seen an undulating plain covered with vegetation, which has a circuit of half a league; it is there that this settlement was made. It is a solitary country, with many small, agreeable and fertile elevations, and some grottoes hollowed in the rock, in the midst of little sandy places. The country is rough without being barren; there are here and there a number of trees of pyramidal form with smooth trunks, whose branches overshadow a large space.

When St John conducted to this spot the Blessed Virgin, for whom he had already erected a house, some Christian families and many holy women were already residing in this country. They were living, some under tents, others in caves, which they had rendered habitable by the aid of carpentry and wainscoting. They had come here before the persecution had burst forth with full force. As they took advantage of the caves which they found there, and of the facilities which the nature of the places offered, their dwellings were real hermitages, often separated a quarter of a league from each other; and this kind of colony presented the appearance of a village with its houses scattered at a considerable distance from each other. Mary's house stood by itself and was constructed of stone. At some distance behind the house the land rises and proceeds across the rocks to the highest point of the mountain, from the top of which, over the small elevations and trees, the city of Ephesus is visible (and the sea) with its numerous islands. The place is nearer the sea than Ephesus itself, which lies at some distance. The country is solitary and little frequented. . . . Between this dwelling of the Blessed Virgin and Ephesus, a river flowed, winding in and out with innumerable turnings.

It is easy, and for some reason tempting to pick out the discrepancies between this description and the actual circumstances: historical discrepancies like the improbability of there already being a Christian community in Ephesus in the sixth year after the Crucifixion, or geographical mistakes like the reference to the Cayster river which flows to the north of Ephesus. But if, after looking at this curious little building with its sacred spring and admiring the view of Ephesus from the hilltop above, one reads the nun's description again, one cannot help being amazed to observe how much of it is accurate. Ramsay himself, of course, tempers his conviction about the authenticity of the legend with the reflection that the place could always have been a pagan shrine, and he writes a great many pages about the 'Anatolian preference for a female personification of divine power'. Yet one supposes that the general belief, at least in the verity of the Ephesian theory, must have been encouraged by the visit of Pope Paul VI to Ephesus in 1967 and the celebration a year later of High Mass, before a congregation of some thousands, in the actual ruins of the Double Basilica.

Paul came eventually to Ephesus during his third mission. When he left Corinth, after his long stay of more than eighteen months, he had first to visit Syrian Antioch; but since his ship was to call at Ephesus he took with him Aquila and Priscilla and left them there, pending his return. Then, after discharging his business in Antioch and visiting Jerusalem, he set out once more across Asia Minor, for his usual passing inspection of his beloved Galatian communities. Having finally rejoined his friends in Ephesus, he remained there the greater part of three years.

It was not the happiest part of his ministry. He was not only faced with every imaginable practical difficulty, including perhaps an actual shortage of money for his daily needs, but suffered from a continual state of mental anxiety, particularly in regard to the news which he received from Corinth. There, as previously in Galatia, his authority was in question and his relations with the elders had become strained, a situation apparent in his first Epistle to the Corinthians and in the so-called 'sorrowful' letter, both of which were written during this time. Finally and ironically, when his preaching to the Ephesians was beginning to have its effect and the number of his followers increasing, the silversmiths and merchants of pagan idols became actively opposed to his activities, and started the agitation against him which finally led to his departure from the city. H. V. Morton has reconstructed in a charming passage[17] the scene in the theatre and afterwards, when the supporters of the silversmiths demonstrated against him; and indeed it is not difficult to imagine, since much still remains of the building itself. It is from near the theatre too, that a broad paved road leads down towards what remains of the Coressian harbour, and here again a picture arises of the little apostle's final departure: the limping figure among the brethren on his last walk through the shadowed colonnades towards the tangle of masts in the distant harbour; the pause to remember the forgotten cloak, and the assurance that, since there was no time to go back, it should be sent on to him by the next friend travelling to Macedonia. He was never to return to Ephesus.

After a final journey in Macedonia and Greece, Paul made his last appearance in Asia Minor. He came across the Aegean by boat to Troas, and spent a few days there waiting for a ship to take him down the coast. (It was while he was preaching in an upper room in Troas on this occasion that a young man called Eutychus dropped asleep and fell from the window.) He sailed in the end from Assus, and the boat touched at the islands of Mytilene, Chios and Samos before landing him at Miletus. Thither he had summoned the elders from Ephesus,

84. St Paul would have walked along this columned street leading from the theatre (in the foreground) to the harbour, now silted up, at Ephesus.

because he was already conscious of the approaching end of his ministry. On a beach outside the town, he made his farewell address, ending 'And now, behold, I go bound in the spirit unto Jerusalem.' The ship carried him by way of Cos and Rhodes to Patara in Lycia, where he changed into another, bound for Tyre and the Syrian ports. This was in AD 56, and before the end of the year he found himself under arrest in Jerusalem, and committed, by his appeal to Caesar, for trial in Rome.

Paul had gone; but the churches which he had founded in Asia Minor continued to increase and flourish. The stamina which they had acquired through Paul's personal teaching and the exhortation of his periodic letters and encyclicals, enabled them to suffer with equanimity the major trials to which their faith was to be submitted. To the Romans they were now a suspect and probably undesirable sect. In AD 64, soon after Paul's departure, their punishment by Nero on the pretext of incendiarism afforded a precedent for intermittent persecution. Pliny, after making his report to Trajan on the alarming spread of Christianity in Bithynia, set about executing all those professing the new faith who would not publicly recant; and the emperor approved his action, with the minor reservation that the testimony of public informers should not be considered, since, as he said, 'they are alien to the spirit of our age'. Nevertheless, despite the certain knowledge that their adherence to the Christian belief might mean death, new converts flocked to receive the solace of its adoption. There was for the present no organised or nationwide persecution, but at any moment, anywhere in the provinces, the Christian community might become the scapegoat for some public misfortune such as a failure of crops, and such a diversion would not be discouraged by an unpopular Roman governor. The same thing was happening throughout

85. The triple-arched gateway at Patara, built about AD 100, some time after St Paul had passed through this Lycian harbour town.

86. The highest of the 'Thousand-and-one Churches' of the tenth century, near Karaman. A Hittite inscription found near the church shows that the site was venerated for over 2,000 years.

the whole Roman world. Rather than abjure Christ, the accused, whatever their sex or social position, were tortured and executed, often publicly in the amphitheatre. The word 'martyr' means 'witness', and these martyrs bore witness to their faith. 'Eighty and six years have I served my master', cried Polycarp, 'and he has never wronged me; how then can I curse my King, who saved me?'[18] The brief outburst of the people of Scili in Africa, who met their sentence with the words 'Thanks be to God!', is equally moving.

And gradually, as time went on, among the pagans and the very agents of persecution, there became noticeable a reluctant admiration of such remarkable fortitude, and an increasing curiosity about the creed by which it was generated. Attempts were made, meanwhile, at a reasoned refutation of its tenets, and in about AD 170 Celsus published his *True Tradition*. This in turn brought replies from the new leaders of Christian thought like Tertullian, Clement and Origen, whose trained minds could demonstrate the reasonableness if not the simple truth of the new doctrine. During the third century the whole subject of the Christian religion emerged from the furtive obscurity of a prohibited cult into the more healthy atmosphere of public debate.

In AD 324 Constantine the Great became emperor. This most gifted statesman is known to posterity for two major acts of policy which together revolutionised the life of the Empire and set it on new paths. One was the foundation of Constantinople and the other the establishment of Christianity as the state religion. It in fact took three centuries for the full effect of the revolution to be felt, for it amounted to no less than the creation of a new East Roman or Byzantine state.

Epilogue

Woven prominently into the tapestry of peoples and events presented in this book are the names of great leaders in all periods: hereditary rulers, soldiers, statesmen and political adventurers, whose triumphs and treacheries have assured them a place in the historical record. But behind them, and less clearly depicted, are the anonymous masses of the common people upon whom their activities depended. By whatever names they are distinguished in these pages – Hittites or Hurrians, Phrygians or Lydians, Greeks or Romans – they have all contributed their quota to the shaping of Anatolian civilisation. Meanwhile, we have seen their lives profoundly and continuously affected by developments beyond their control. Yet few will have failed to observe the ultimate imper-manence of historical situations in which, willingly or unwillingly, they par-ticipated. Tribal migrations, the sweep of conquering armies, earthquakes, floods or famines have been transient misfortunes whose memory has eventu-ally faded, leaving unchanged the traditional pattern of domestic behaviour and the timeless image of Anatolian man.

If a simple parable on this theme be required, it can be found in the attractive story of the 'Seven Sleepers of Ephesus'. Fugitives from the religious persecution of the Emperor Decius, these Christian youths took refuge in a cave behind Mount Prion, where they presently slept. Awaking two centuries later, in the reign of Theodosius II, 'they went down to the town to buy bread', and learnt, with no more than mild surprise, that Christianity was now the state religion. In the same vein is the polite enquiry which St Jerome attributes to one of the Desert Fathers: 'Tell me, I pray thee, how fares the human race? If new roofs be risen in the ancient cities, whose empire is it that now sways the world?'

87. Changing civilisations at Urfa: Byzantine capitals in the foreground and Ottoman gravestones behind.

Notes

Abbreviations

CAH 1973 = *Cambridge Ancient History*, 3rd ed., Vol. II, Part 1, *The Middle East and the Aegean region c. 1800–1380 B.C.*, Cambridge 1973.

CAH 1975 = *Cambridge Ancient History*, 3rd ed., Vol. II, Part 2, *The Middle East and the Aegean region c. 1380–1000 B.C.*, Cambridge 1975.

CAH 1982 = *Cambridge Ancient History*, 3rd ed., Vol. III, Part 1, *The Prehistory of the Balkans; the Middle East and the Aegean world, tenth to eighth centuries B.C.*, Cambridge 1982.

Chapter 1

1. M. Cary, *The Geographical Background of Greek and Roman History*, Oxford 1949, p. 151.
2. W. R. Ramsay and G. Bell, *The Thousand-and-one Churches*, London 1909, p. 297.
3. Ibid.

Chapter 2

1. S. Lloyd, *Early Highland Peoples of Anatolia*, London 1967, pp. 42–56.
2. Ibid., pp. 20–24.
3. J. Garstang, *Prehistoric Mersin*, Oxford 1953.
4. J. Mellaart, *Çatal Hüyük*, London 1967.

Chapter 3

1. Genesis 15:19–21; 26:34; 36:1–3; Numbers 13:29.
2. 2 Chronicles 1:17; 2 Kings 7:6–7.
3. O. R. Gurney, *The Hittites*, Harmondsworth 1952, p. 180.
4. M. J. Mellink, 'Archaeology in Asia Minor', *American Journal of Archaeology* 73 (1969), pp. 207–8.
5. Id., 'Archaeology in Asia Minor', *American Journal of Archaeology* 80 (1976), p. 266.
6. O. R. Gurney in *CAH* 1973, p. 669.
7. Ibid., p. 235.
8. E. Akurgal, *The Art of the Hittites*, London 1962, p. 52.
9. Ibid., pp. 53–4.
10. Gurney, *The Hittites*, op. cit., pp. 67–8.

Chapter 4

1. O. R. Gurney in *CAH* 1973, p. 669.
2. Discussed by Gurney, op. cit., p. 681.
3. See H. G. Güterbock, 'The deeds of Suppiluliuma, as told by his son Mursili II', *Journal of Cuneiform Studies* 10 (1956), pp. 41 ff and 75 ff. Gurney, op. cit., p. 682, explains that 'since this is not a history but a biography, it opens at the moment when young Suppiluliumas was first entrusted by his father with command of troops in the field'.
4. A. Goetze in *CAH* 1975, p. 18.
5. O. R. Gurney, *The Hittites*, Harmondsworth 1952, p. 31.
6. Goetze, op. cit., p. 19.
7. *CAH*, Vol. II, 1926 ed., pp. 142 ff.
8. Gurney, *The Hittites*, op. cit., p. 109.
9. Goetze, op. cit., p. 256.
10. Gurney's *The Hittites*, first published in 1952 and revised in 1981, was subtitled *A summary of the art, achievements and social organisation of a great people of Asia Minor during the 2nd millennium B.C., as discovered by modern excavations*. For more recent treatments of the subject, see J. G. Macqueen, *The Hittites*, London 1975 (rev. 1986) and K. Bittel, *Die Hethiter*, Munich 1976.
11. Goetze, op. cit., p. 268.
12. See K. Bittel, *Hattusha: The Capital of the Hittites*, New York 1970, for a useful discussion of the site and its history.
13. J. Mellaart, *The Archaeology of Ancient Turkey*, Oxford 1978, pp. 60–77.

Chapter 5

1. N. K. Sandars, *The Sea Peoples: Warriors of the Ancient Mediterranean*, London 1978, p. 29. (A revised edition was published in 1985.)
2. F. H. Stubbings in *CAH* 1975, p. 186.
3. A. Goetze in *CAH* 1975, p. 261.
4. O. R. Gurney in *CAH* 1973, pp. 678 and 812.
5. I. Singer, 'Western Anatolia in the thirteenth century B.C. according to the Hittite sources', *Anatolian Studies* 33 (1983), pp. 205–17.
6. Cf. for instance Sandars, op. cit., pp. 14–15, and J. Mellaart, *The Archaeology of Ancient Turkey*, Oxford 1978, p. 72.
7. Quoted in Sandars, op. cit., p. 119.
8. Ibid.
9. Mellaart, op. cit., p. 72.
10. The whole story of the search for and identification of Troy is told and discussed by J. M. Cook in *The Troad: An Archaeological and Topographical Study*, London 1973.
11. C. W. Blegen, *Troy and the Trojans*, London 1963, p. 13.
12. J. G. Macqueen, *The Hittites*, London 1975, p. 38, fig. 16.
13. G. A. Wainwright, 'The Teresh, the Etruscans and Asia Minor', *Anatolian Studies* 9 (1959), p. 206.

Chapter 6

1. E.g. Herodotus, *Histories*, Book 1, Ch. 14; see G. Rawlinson's translation, 3rd ed., London 1875, p. 154, footnote.

2. R. S. Young *et al.*, *Three Great Early Tumuli*, Philadelphia 1981.
3. C. H. E. Haspels, *The Highlands of Phrygia*, Princeton 1971.
4. See R. D. Barnett, 'The Phrygian rock façades and the Hittite monuments', *Bibliotheca Orientalis* 10 (1953), pp. 77 ff.
5. Id. in *CAH* 1975, pp. 433–4.

Chapter 7

1. J. D. Hawkins in *Reallexikon der Assyriologie*, s.v. 'Hatti'; id., 'Assyrians and Hittites', *Iraq* 36 (1974), pp. 67–83, especially p. 70; id. in *CAH* 1982, pp. 372–441.
2. D. G. Hogarth, *Carchemish*, Vol. I, London 1914; C. L. Woolley, *Carchemish*, Vol. II, London 1921; C. L. Woolley and R. D. Barnett, *Carchemish*, Vol. III, London 1952; C. L. Woolley, *Dead Towns and Living Men*, Oxford 1920.
3. M. E. L. Mallowan, 'Carchemish', and J. D. Hawkins, 'Building inscriptions of Carchemish', both in *Anatolian Studies* 22 (1972), pp. 63–85 and 87–114; J. D. Hawkins in *Reallexikon der Assyriologie*, s.v. 'Karkamiš'.
4. E. Akurgal, *The Art of the Hittites*, London 1962, pl. 131.
5. Mallowan, op. cit., p. 85.
6. Akurgal, op. cit., p. 130 and pls 104, 107; J. D. Hawkins, 'Kuzi-Tešub and the "Great Kings" of Karkamiš', *Anatolian Studies* 38 (1988).
7. R. D. Barnett in *CAH* 1975, p. 424.
8. J. D. Hawkins, 'Some historical problems of the hieroglyphic Luwian inscriptions', *Anatolian Studies* (1979), pp. 153–67, especially pp. 153–7.

Chapter 8

1. Strabo, *Geography*; trans. H. L. Jones, London and New York 1917, XIV, 1, 21.
2. J. M. Cook, *The Greeks in Ionia and the East*, London 1962.
3. Ibid., p. 27.

Chapter 9

1. Herodotus' *Histories*, trans. G. Rawlinson, 3rd ed., London 1875, Vol. I, p. 344.
2. E. Akurgal, *Ancient Civilisations and Ruins of Turkey*, Istanbul 1969, p. 132; G. Bean, *Aegean Turkey*, London 1972, pp. 271–2. George Bean's other books, *Turkey beyond the Maeander* (1971) and *Turkey's Southern Shore* (1968), are also recommended (all three books were reissued in 1979), as is his *Lycian Turkey* (London 1978).
3. W. J. Hamilton, *Researches in Asia Minor*, I, London 1842.
4. Rawlinson, op. cit., Vol. 1, p. 219.
5. G. M. A. Hanfmann (ed.), *Sardis from Prehistoric to Roman Times: Results of the archaeological exploration of Sardis 1958–1975*, Cambridge (Mass.) and London 1983, especially pp. 53–9.
6. *CAH*, Vol. III, 1925 ed., p. 519.
7. D. G. Hogarth, *The Wandering Scholar*, Oxford 1925.
8. *Türk Arkeoloji Dergisi* 18/1 (1969), pp. 61 ff.
9. Strabo, *Geography*, XIII, 4, 5.
10. Rawlinson, op. cit., Vol. 1, p. 367.
11. *CAH*, Vol. III, 1925 ed., p. 520.
12. Rawlinson, op. cit., Vol. 1, p. 166.

Chapter 10

1. H. F. B. Lynch, *Armenia*, London 1901.

2. C. A. Burney and D. M. Lang, *The Peoples of the Hills: Ancient Ararat*, London 1971, p. 130.
3. C. A. Burney, 'Urartian fortresses and towns in the Van region', *Anatolian Studies* 7 (1957), pp. 37–53; id. and G. R. Lawson, 'Measured plans of Urartian fortresses', *Anatolian Studies* 10 (1960), pp. 177–96.
4. B. Piotrovski, *The Ancient Civilization of Urartu*, London 1969.
5. Burney and Lang, op. cit., p. 140.
6. Ibid., p. 142.
7. Piotrovski, op. cit., pp. 69 ff.
8. N. Y. Orr and I. A. Orbeli, *The 1916 Expedition to Van*, Petrograd 1922, p. 86.
9. Piotrovski, op. cit., p. 86.
10. F. Thureau-Dangin, *La huitième campagne de Sargon II*, Paris 1912.
11. Piotrovski, op. cit., pp. 111 ff, gives an intriguing summary of the catalogue.

Chapter 11

1. Herodotus, *Histories*, Book III, Ch. 90, trans. G. Rawlinson, 3rd ed., London 1875, Vol. 2, Essay 3.
2. R. Ghirshman, *Iran*, Harmondsworth 1954, p. 114. This curious institution is discussed by R. N. Frye, *Heritage of Persia*, London 1965, p. 102.
3. J. Boardman, *The Greeks Overseas*, London 1964, p. 119. (A new and enlarged edition was published in 1980.)
4. W. C. Brice, *South-West Asia: A Systematic Regional Geography*, London 1966, p. 89.
5. R. S. Young, 'Gordion 1956', *American Journal of Archaeology* 61 (1957).
6. Herodotus, Book IV, Ch. 87; Rawlinson, op. cit., Vol. 3, p. 79.
7. Rawlinson, op. cit., Vol. 4, p. 25, n. 5, with a map showing the position of the canal.
8. Ibid., p. 33, n. 1, 'The site of the bridge is supposed to have been from Nagara Point to the low spot eastward of Sestos, where the level shore on either side is convenient for the march of troops. The channel is more than 7 stadia broad, being about $1\frac{1}{2}$ miles English.' Rawlinson illustrates this with three small engravings of the site in his time.
9. Ibid., p. 36, n. 7, clarifies this rather complicated description.
10. J. B. Bury, *History of Greece*, London 1929, pp. 157–8.
11. J. M. Cook, *The Greeks in Ionia and the East*, London 1962, p. 121. See also *The Persian Empire* by the same author (London 1983).

Chapter 12

1. W. F. Ainsworth, *A Personal Narrative of the Euphrates Expedition*, London 1868; A. H. Layard, *Nineveh and Babylon*, London 1853; Xenophon, *Anabasis*, trans. J. S. Watson, London 1875.
2. S. Der Nersessian, *The Armenians*, London 1969, p. 22.
3. Layard, op. cit., Vol. 1, pp. 63 ff.
4. Ainsworth, op. cit., pp. 317 ff.
5. Xenophon, op. cit., Book IV, Ch. 5, 24.
6. For references see Ainsworth, op. cit., p. 142, n. 1.

Chapter 13

1. M. Andronikos, *Vergina: The Royal Tombs and the Ancient City*, Athens 1984.
2. Plutarch, *Life of Phocion*, trans. John Dryden, rev. A. H. Clough, New York 1910, repr. 1957.

Chapter 14

1. A. Weigall, *Alexander the Great*, London 1935.
2. F. Stark, *Alexander's Path*, London, 1958.
3. The location of these tombs and the whole subject of Homeric topography has been studied in great detail by J. M. Cook. *The Troad: An Archaeological and Topographical Study*, Oxford 1973; see especially Ch. 4, and the map p. 105, fig. 5.
4. Plutarch, *Life of Alexander*, trans. J. Dryden, rev. A. H. Clough, New York 1910, repr. 1957.
5. Weigall, op. cit., p. 147.
6. Pliny, *Natural History*, xxxv, 10, 85.
7. One remembers the formidable figure of an earlier Carian queen at the battle of Salamis, see Chapter 11.
8. Stark, op. cit., p. 235, quoting Plutarch, *Sayings of Kings*.
9. Plutarch, *Moralia*, 180a (Alexander no. 9).
10. Stark, op. cit., Appendix 1 and maps.
11. Arrian calls it Telmissus, confusing it with a town of that name between Halicarnassus and Myndus. See Stark, op. cit., p. 254, n. 29.
12. Arrian, *Campaigns of Alexander the Great*, trans. A. de Selincourt, Harmondsworth 1971, p. 115.

Chapter 15

1. M. I. Rostovtzeff, *The Social and Economic History of the Hellenistic World*, Oxford 1941.
2. W. W. Tarn, *Hellenistic Civilization*, London 1927.
3. Ibid., pp. 6–42.
4. Ibid., p. 136, quotes one of these inscriptions as an instance of mixed Hellenism: 'It is written in very florid Greek like Babu English, by one who did not understand the use of the Greek article.' See also E. Akurgal, *Ancient Civilisations and Ruins of Turkey*, Istanbul 1969, pp. 292–5.
5. E. V. Hansen, *The Attalids of Pergamum*, 2nd ed., New York 1971.

Chapter 16

1. Cf. Herodotus, *Histories*, Book I, Ch. 142, trans. G. Rawlinson, 3rd ed., London 1875, Vol. 1, p. 267.
2. W. M. Ramsay, *The Historical Geography of Asia Minor*, London 1890, p. 24.
3. C. J. Cadoux, *Ancient Smyrna*, Oxford 1938, p. 3.
4. George Bean, *Aegean Turkey*, London 1972, p. 161.
5. Plutarch, *Life of Alexander*.
6. Strabo, *Geography*, XIV, 1, 21.
7. J. T. Wood, *Discoveries at Ephesus*, London 1877.
8. D. G. Hogarth, *The Wandering Scholar*, Oxford 1925.
9. H. V. Morton, *In the Steps of Saint Paul*, London 1936, p. 336.
10. Bean, op. cit., p. 160.
11. Austrian Archaeological Institute Publications, *Forschungen in Ephesos*, 1906 onwards.
12. C. Texier and R. P. Pullan, *Principal Ruins of Asia Minor*, London 1865.
13. Plutarch, *Life of Antony*, 58.
14. Revelation 2:13.
15. Strabo, *Geography*, trans. H. L. Jones, London and New York 1917.
16. R. E. Wycherley, *How the Greeks Built Cities*, 2nd ed., London 1962.
17. Ibid., pl. IIa (model by H. Schleif).
18. Ibid., fig. 37.
19. Th. Wiegand *et al.*, *Vorläufige Berichte über die Ausgrabungen in Milet* (Sitzungsberichte of the Berlin Academy), 1900 onwards.

20. Murray's *Handbook for Travellers in Asia Minor, Transcaucasia and Persia*, London 1895.
21. Herodotus, Book VI, Ch. 19.
22. Th. Wiegand, *Didyma* (2 vols), Berlin 1941–58; E. Pontremoli and B. Haussoullier, *Didymes*, Paris 1904.
23. Herodotus, Book I, Ch. 157–9.
24. She was a namesake of the Artemesia who fought the Persians in the battle of Salamis (see Chapter 11).
25. C. T. Newton, *Travels and Discoveries in the Levant*, London 1865.

Chapter 17

1. H. F. B. Lynch, *Armenia*, London 1901.
2. D. Magie, *Roman Rule in Asia Minor*, Oxford 1951.
3. Called Pontica to distinguish it from Comana-in-Cappadocia, where there was also a famous temple of Ma.
4. J. G. C. Anderson, *Studia Pontica*, Brussels 1903.
5. Magie, op. cit., p. 199.
6. Cicero, *In Verrem*.
7. Lynch, op. cit., Vol. 1, Ch. 12 and 13.
8. Ibid., p. 128.
9. Ibid., p. 197.
10. Strabo, XI, 14–18.
11. Plutarch, *Life of Lucullus*, trans. John Dryden, rev. A. Clough, New York 1910, repr. 1957.

Chapter 18

1. W. H. Buckler, *Monumenta Asiae Minoris Antiquae*, Vol. III, Manchester 1931, Ch. x.
2. Ibid., Ch. VIII.
3. Ibid., Ch. IX.
4. Ibid., Ch. IV–V.
5. M. Gough, 'Anazarbus', *Anatolian Studies* 2 (1952), pp. 85–150.
6. D. Magie, *Roman Rule in Asia Minor*, Oxford 1951, p. 412.
7. *Sic*; he was born in 100 BC and must have been 53.

Chapter 19

1. It was a peripteral temple, but the peristyle has fallen, leaving the Greek inscription exposed.
2. A. H. M. Jones, *Cities of the Eastern Roman Provinces*, Oxford 1937; W. M. Calder and G. E. Bean, *A Classical Map of Asia Minor*, supplement to *Anatolian Studies* 7 (1957).
3. Now called Çavdarhisar; well described by E. Akurgal, *Ancient Civilisations and Ruins of Turkey*, Istanbul 1969, pp. 235–6.
4. Ibid., pp. 171–4.
5. W. M. Ramsay, 'Historical commentary on St Paul's Epistle to the Galatians', in *Anatolian Studies Presented to W. H. Buckler*, Manchester 1939.
6. Ibid.
7. Id., *The Church in the Roman Empire*, London, 1904.
8. D. Magie, *Roman Rule in Asia Minor*, Oxford 1951, pp. 491 ff.
9. Jones, op. cit., p. 208.
10. H. V. Morton, *In the Steps of Saint Paul*, London 1936, p. 373.
11. Murray's *Handbook for Travellers in Asia Minor, Transcaucasia and Persia*, London 1895.
12. C. Fellows, *Discoveries in Lycia*, London 1841.
13. This applies equally to the Graeco-Lycian painted tombs discovered by American archaeologists near Elmalı in Lycia; see reports by M. Mellink in *American Journal of Archaeology*, 1971 onwards.
14. F. C. Beaufort, *Karamania*, London 1841.

Chapter 20

1. M. P. Charlesworth, *The Roman Empire*, Oxford 1951, p. 135.
2. E. Swift, *Roman Sources of Christian Art*, New York 1951.
3. Ibid., p. 51.
4. Charlesworth, op. cit., p. 148.
5. W. M. Ramsay, *Pauline and Other Studies*, London 1908.
6. Id., *Cities of St Paul*, London 1907.
7. C. L. Woolley, *A Forgotten Kingdom*, Harmondsworth 1953.
8. H. V. Morton, *In the Steps of Saint Paul*, London, 1936, p. 150.
9. Acts 13:46.
10. S. Lloyd, 'Paul and Thekla', *History Today* II/8 (August 1952), pp. 527–31.
11. J. L. Myres, *Who were the Greeks?*, Berkeley 1930, p. 78.
12. Ramsay, *Pauline and Other Studies*, p. 144, where the Greek text is also quoted.
13. Extracts from this sermon, quoted by Ramsay in English translation (ibid., p. 134), have the authentic poetry of a still almost pagan imagery, and something of the quality of the apostle's own writings. Mary is the 'fleece very pure, moist from the rain of heaven, through whose agency the Shepherd put on Him [the form and nature of] the sheep, she who is slave and mother, virgin and heaven, sole bridge by which God passes to me'.
14. The history of this building is explained with a plan in G. Bean, *Aegean Turkey*, London 1972, pp. 173–4, fig. 34.
15. Ibid., pp. 179–82, especially p. 181, for an account of this episode in which the priest is named as 'M. Poulin, Superior of the Lazarists'.
16. *Pauline Studies*; see also M. Palairet, *Life of the Blessed Virgin Mary, from the Visions of Catherine Emmerich*, London 1954.
17. Morton, op. cit., p. 334.
18. C. Williams, *The Descent of the Dove*, London 1939.

Index

References to illustrations are in **bold type**

INDEX